THIRD EDIT

SPORTS
JOURNALISM

AN INTRODUCTION TO REPORTING
AND WRITING

JAMES R. SCHAFFER

STEVE SCHAFFER

AMIE JUST

KATHRYN T. STOFER

ROWMAN & LITTLEFIELD
Lanham • Boulder • New York • London

Executive Acquisitions Editor: Natalie Mandziuk
Assistant Acquisitions Editor: Yu Ozaki
Sales and Marketing Inquiries: textbooks@rowman.com

Credits and acknowledgments for material borrowed from other sources, and reproduced with permission, appear on the appropriate pages within the text.

Published by Rowman & Littlefield
An imprint of The Rowman & Littlefield Publishing Group, Inc.
4501 Forbes Boulevard, Suite 200, Lanham, Maryland 20706
www.rowman.com

86-90 Paul Street, London EC2A 4NE

British Library Cataloguing in Publication Information available

Library of Congress Cataloging-in-Publication Data
Names: Schaffer, James, 1949– author. | Schaffer, Steve, 1988– author. | Just, Amie, 1994– author. | Stofer, Kathryn T., author.
Title: Sports journalism : an introduction to reporting and writing / James R. Schaffer, Steve Schaffer, Amie Just, Kathryn T. Stofer.
Description: Third edition. | Lanham : Rowman & Littlefield, 2024. | Includes bibliographical references and index.
Identifiers: LCCN 2024033027 (print) | LCCN 2024033028 (ebook) | ISBN 9781538196298 (cloth) | ISBN 9781538196304 (paperback) | ISBN 9781538196311 (epub)
Subjects: LCSH: Sports journalism.
Classification: LCC PN4784.S6 S88 2024 (print) | LCC PN4784.S6 (ebook) | DDC 070.4/49796--dc23/eng/20240722
LC record available at https://lccn.loc.gov/2024033027
LC ebook record available at https://lccn.loc.gov/2024033028

∞™ The paper used in this publication meets the minimum requirements of American National Standard for Information Sciences—Permanence of Paper for Printed Library Materials, ANSI/NISO Z39.48-1992.

Contents

Preface

On crisp fall Saturdays in Princeton, New Jersey, 10-year-old John McPhee would run onto the field with the Tiger football team and stand on the sidelines with them. McPhee's job was to station himself behind the goalpost after each score and catch the extra point. That seemingly insignificant job, however, led to a life-changing insight: "One miserable November afternoon, soaked in a freezing rain, I turned around and looked up at the press box. I saw people up there with typewriters, sitting dry under a roof in what I knew to be heated space. In that precise moment, I decided to become a writer."[1] You may not have had a flash of inspiration quite like that, but if you're smart enough to come in out of the rain, you're ready to be a sportswriter.

Enter the third edition of "Sports Journalism: An Introduction to Reporting and Writing." This book has passed the test of time, been used in classrooms internationally, received approval and praise from professors and students, and now it, too, has moved into a new era of sports media with new information, examples and references to current technology. Whether you choose to read from a tablet, a smartphone, a Chromebook or old-fashioned paper wrapped in a cardboard cover, this book will be your guide to the evolving sports landscape.

Sports reporters are journalists who write about sports. Fans and editors expect them to know the rules of the game and the rules of journalism and be able to meld the two into colorful, action-packed game stories, picturesque profiles, informative features and thoughtful analysis in as few as 280 characters.

Inside this edition you'll find

- Several new chapters, including one on social media and another on building relationships with sources, colleagues and media contacts.
- Freshly revised chapters that take into account changes in the rapidly evolving sports world.

- Interviews with journalists whose circulation is measured by their many, many followers.
- New discussions throughout the book on issues affecting today's sports scene: How much should college athletes be paid? Can play be too violent? Is there a level playing field for men and women?
- An expanded glossary that includes terms such as 'hot take,' 'scrum' and 'trolls.'

The introductory chapters of "Sports Journalism" will acquaint students with the challenges a sports media reporter faces today, including the erratic hours of a deadline-dictated lifestyle, rapidly changing technology, the participation of citizen journalists and bloggers via social media, and the need to balance coverage of men's and women's sports.

The writing skills chapters in "Sports Journalism" elaborate on news values and the conventions of the journalistic genre as they apply to sports writing while providing guidelines for novice sports writers. Other chapters of the book focus on interviewing techniques, using numbers and statistics accurately and effectively, practicing AP style, understanding legal terms as they apply to published work and promoting ethical standards.

Sports writers do much more than write about sports. The job description now includes words like blogger, videographer, commentator, talk show anchor and webmaster. Filled with examples from newspapers, websites, sports books and personal experience, "Sports Journalism" is an easy-to-read textbook that can also serve as a handbook to help beginners get started in sports media and media relations careers. At the end of each chapter a feature called Upon Further Review provides exercises for practicing concepts and skills, stimulates discussion of contemporary issues in sports and suggests activities to accompany chapter content.

In today's rapidly changing sports environment, the authors recognize that parts of this book are already technologically dated. We also recognize that the fundamentals of writing well and acting honorably and ethically will remain at the heart of the profession, no matter what the medium. For that reason, "Sports Journalism" is dedicated to encouraging those values in journalists who choose to spend their time with the people who play the games.

NOTE

1. The story of John McPhee's appearance at a Princeton football game is recounted in his article "Rip Van Golfer," *New Yorker*, Aug. 6, 2007.

1

Living the Life

What's it like to cover sports for a living? Amie Just, a sports columnist for the Lincoln Journal Star, reflects on a working life full of crazy deadlines, long weekends and plenty of unplanned moments. But what fun!

There are seven wedding invitations plastered on my refrigerator door. Normal decor for a twentysomething. But on closer inspection, there's a trend that pops out. All of these invitations, they're from months prior, years even. I went to three of them, maybe, but I keep them there as a reminder.

As a sports writer, you miss things. Small things, happy hour drinks or game night with friends. Big things, holidays and, yes, so many weddings — especially ones that occur during football season. It comes with the territory. If you want a nine-to-five job with nights and weekends off, this isn't the line of work for you. But if you're interested in a career that keeps you on your toes and is full of unpredictability (both positive and negative), you've come to the right place.

ORGANIZED CHAOS

Being a sports reporter is the perfect blend of organization and chaos. Schedules get released months ahead of time, but there's no telling what's going to happen until the final whistle. You know what your deadline is in advance, but crafting the words on the page, that's wholly dependent on what unfolds in front of you and wherever your creative brain takes you.

Breaking news is a whole other animal. Always adrenaline producing, but not always a happy story. With sports journalism these days, you're always on call. When you're at the gym, on a run, in the pool, at a movie, on a date — you're on call. (Thank you, Trevor Siemian [Chicago Bears quarterback], for unwittingly giving me a convenient excuse to leave an awkward first date.) If stories had hyperspecific datelines attached to them, some of mine would read

Organized chaos. Nebraska volleyball coach dives for cover as the action spills off the court.
© Lincoln Journal Star.

- WAFFLE HOUSE PARKING LOT DURING MARDI GRAS, LaPLACE, La.
- ON TOP OF JEEP, FLATHEAD RESERVATION, ARLEE, Mont.
- UNDERNEATH TABLE WITH MIGRAINE, SUPERDOME, NEW ORLEANS, La.
- O'BRIEN STRAATMAN REDINGER FUNERAL HOME, KEARNEY, Neb.
- DURING HAIR CUT, HAIR NERDS SALON, NEW ORLEANS, La.
- BACK SEAT OF RENTAL CAR, TURTLE BEACH, KAHUKU, Hawaii

Is it frustrating? It can be in the moment — never knowing when you're going to get to go to the grocery store in peace. But it can make for hilarious stories later. The Siemian story, for example, is a personal favorite. Or how I showed up to Sean Payton's "retirement" press conference with my hair perfectly blown out because I had been at the salon right before the news broke that he was stepping away from the Saints.

POLL RESULTS STIR DISCUSSION

It's not quite the same as being named the most popular kid in high school, but landing a spot in one of the football, basketball or volleyball polls might be the next best thing.

The Associated Press Top 25 men's college basketball poll was first published in January 1949, and in all the years since, it has done exactly what was intended: spark debate. "Sports was living off controversy, opinion, whatever," Alan Gould, then sports editor for the Associated Press, explained. "This was just another exercise in hoopla."

Basketball wasn't the only poll. Gould had dreamed up an AP college football poll back in 1936 when he asked newspaper editors across the country to rank teams each week. The basketball poll followed 13 years later, and finally, in 1967, the AP established a women's basketball poll. For each season today, the AP selects an expert panel of sports writers and broadcasters from across the country to vote. Four are considered "national writers" while the rest are chosen to represent geographic diversity—at least one from each state.

It's a thankless job in some ways—no financial compensation, and as Amie Just, Nebraska's rep, puts it, "Lots of jerks in my inbox. I always have football on my TV during football season," she said, "but it was usually background noise while I was doing other things. Now that I'm a voter, I pay closer attention to as many games as I can."

Voters know that their individual ballots will be made public each week, so they also know their opinions may come under intense scrutiny. Social media, for better or worse, has made it easier for fans to interact with AP voters, taking spirited conversations from water coolers to the internet. But the poll still drives discussion, just like it was intended to do 75 years ago.

To commemorate the 75th basketball anniversary, the AP determined that Kentucky, the winningest program in college basketball, had also placed number one most often in the polls, edging out North Carolina. Rounding out the top five were Duke, Kansas and UCLA. "When I got here," Kentucky coach John Calipari recalled, "it was just knowing that it matters in this state. The fans are incredibly engaged. There were people who knew more about our recruiting than I did. That's when you realize this is different."

In all, 206 teams have appeared in the poll, including 13 that made only a single appearance. Some, such as Wayne State and West Texas A&M, dropped to Division II; a few others, including Beloit, New York and Hamline, now compete in Division III.[1]

Basketball fans turn to the results of opinion polls each week to see how their team is doing.
© Nebraska Wesleyan Sports Information.

MY BACKSTORY

There are so many stories. Partially because I've covered a truly amazing amount of insanity, and — at the time of this book's publishing — I haven't even yet turned 30. After graduating from high school in 2013, I spent the next four years at the University of Kansas studying journalism, English, and women and gender studies. While there, I interned at the Washington Post, the Associated Press, and the Topeka Capital-Journal. That doesn't count the countless hours working at the university's Daily Kansan in various roles, too.

Straight out of college, to the Missoulian in Missoula, Montana, for 18 months. Then NOLA.com/the Times-Picayune for eight months before the paper's demise resulted in a mass layoff. I was lucky enough to latch on with the new iteration of the Times-Picayune and spent three years in New Orleans before I moved home to Nebraska in July 2022 to be the Lincoln Journal Star's sports columnist.

No lie, 2022 was the wildest year of my professional life, in the best and worst ways. A quick synopsis: Cover two NFL games (vs. Carolina, at Atlanta) before the Saints fail to make the playoffs. Sean Payton "retires." Cover the Super Bowl in Los Angeles. Cover NFL Combine in Indianapolis. Break news that LSU's Will Wade gets fired. Interview for months for a job I don't get. Cover men's basketball Final Four in New Orleans. Take a monthlong vacation. Move from New Orleans to Lincoln. Officiate my sister's wedding right before I go to Ireland for a college football game. Cover two more games before Scott Frost gets fired (at Nebraska). Cover basketball media days in Minneapolis. Juggle football, volleyball, men's basketball and women's basketball coverage. Report that Nebraska has named Matt Rhule as coach while I have the flu. Cover the NCAA volleyball tournament, including the Final Four in Omaha.

I was in 11 different states — Louisiana, Georgia, Alabama, California, Indiana, Nebraska, New Jersey, Minnesota, Michigan, Iowa and Kentucky — plus Ireland, for work. And took a quick detour to New York for dinner while in Jersey. That's the dream. Even if there's a wedding or two missed along the way.

A DAY LIKE NO OTHER

Conversations with my mother often revolve around one question in particular: "What are you doing today?" Emphasis on "today." I've been in the business long enough to where she knows how often things change. I don't have set days off and instead take a day when I can. And things often crop up when you least expect it.

There was no day, though, quite as chaotic as the day Sean Payton stepped down as the Saints' head coach: Jan. 25, 2022.

Morning

9:30 a.m.: Walk to my local coffee shop, Old Road, order a large iced caramel latte with oat milk and make small talk with the baristas. 10 a.m.: Complete the Wordle in four tries. The answer, "sugar," which, in hindsight, was something I'd need plenty of to get through the day. 10:30–10:45 a.m.: Tweet out the news that New Orleans' premiere road race, the Crescent City Classic, is going to be sponsored by Saints owner Gayle Benson and Caesars. 10:45 a.m.: Drive five miles to my hair salon for my 11 a.m. appointment.

Afternoon

12:40 p.m.: Leave the salon. 12:47 p.m.: News breaks that Sean Payton is stepping away as I am, poetically, driving over the bridge right next to the Caesars Superdome. 12:48 p.m.: My phone floods with texts from friends, full of four-letter expletives. 1 p.m.: Spend an hour in therapy, talking about who knows what, since I'm distracted. 1:08 p.m.: Tweet how the Saints are having a press conference at 3 p.m. 2 p.m.: Change outfits into something presentable: a green sweater, nice jeans and a peacoat. 2:15 p.m.: Jump on a radio hit. 2:35 p.m.: Drive to the Saints facility. 2:45 p.m.: Order a large iced cinnamon roll latte with oat milk at French Press, the coffee shop close to the Saints facility. 2:53 p.m.: Arrive at Saints facility. 2:58 p.m.: Sean Payton's press conference begins, lasting 90 minutes and 20 seconds. His opening statement alone lasted 31 minutes. 4:31 p.m.: Payton ends his press conference by giving Gayle Benson a hug and walking out the door. 4:40 p.m. Interview Benson, who gives brief comments for five minutes. 5:00ish p.m.: Huddle up with my coworkers and figure out a plan for stories. I write the "why" story, which serves as our first sidebar. 5:15 p.m.: Leave the

Saints facility to go write. I believe I wrote at a bar, but that part's hazy, and schedule interviews for the next week with several current/former Saints.

Evening

7:00 p.m.: Get a little frustrated that my friends are starting our crew run without me. 8:43 p.m.: Post my 900-word story: Here's how Sean Payton came to realize "it was time" for him to leave the Saints and why "it feels good." 9:21 p.m.: Take advantage of the perfect, 51-degree night and go for a 3-mile run. Average 9:02-minute miles. 10:40 p.m.: Post several of our stories on Instagram. 11 p.m.: Wind down by watching Netflix. Sometime after midnight: Go to sleep.

This is far from the norm. Future Hall of Fame head coaches don't usually step away with little-to-no notice. But you have to be prepared for everything.

NOTE

1. Information drawn from two online articles by Dave Skretta: "In Its 75th Year, the AP Top 25 Men's Basketball Poll Is Still Driving Discussion," Associated Press, Dec. 7, 2023, and "Kentucky Is the All-Time No. 1 Team through 75 Storied Years of AP Top 25 College Basketball Polls," Associated Press, Jan. 10, 2024.

Working With Sources

Watch a football practice. Long before the team huddles up and has its full-speed 11-on-11 drill, there are several other activities for players to complete. There's stretching, individual and positional drills, one-on-ones, walkthroughs and more. The premise behind the little things is simple: perfecting the small stuff helps you find success on game day. Fans usually don't pay attention to an offensive lineman's footwork or realize how many tip drills a receiver went through to catch that Hail Mary pass, but that behind-the-scenes work is integral to the team's success. Without that meticulous preparation, the team may look lackluster on game day — and fans will raise their eyebrows.

The same thing is true for sports reporters. There's more to the job than showing up on game day and writing a gamer. Audiences expect near perfection but aren't so concerned about how the sausage is made. Sports reporters must know their sausage. They have plenty of work to do before that first game. They need to forge relationships with sources, keep up-to-date on everything, develop story ideas and work with the media relations departments of the teams they cover.

That's why a beat reporter's job exists.

BEAT REPORTING

A beat writer (or beat reporter) is someone who covers the same team, sport or league on a full-time basis. Beat reporters are common at most media outlets, including newspapers, broadcast stations and websites. The news section has education reporters, police and courts reporters, business reporters. The same concept applies to sports.

Having the same reporter in charge of covering one thing makes sense across the board. There's less confusion about who is covering what event or story, and having a dedicated beat reporter makes for a more streamlined process when breaking news occurs. Some beat writers are assigned to the same team for years.

Nebraska basketball coach Amy Williams and two players take postgame questions from the media.
© Lincoln Journal Star.

A beat writer might also cover more than one team or sport, for example, with high school athletics, where the reporter is typically in charge of covering numerous high schools (think 20 or more, depending on newspaper staffing and geographic area) and all the sports offered at those schools. A college beat reporter might follow just one university but might be tasked with covering multiple sports. Professional beat writers are often responsible for one pro team and will write about that topic year-round.

Beat Responsibilities

Beat reporters help peel back the curtain for fans to get to know the people on their favorite teams and provide as much information as possible. Who will be in the starting lineup? Which players stand out in practice? How are the transfers acclimating? Who is dealing with an injury? Where are the assistants concentrating their recruiting efforts?

The best beat reporters know everything about the team they cover. They know what public appearances the head coach has made recently and which players are considering entering the transfer portal. There are always surprises, like a homegrown kid forgoing his final year of eligibility to enter the NFL draft, but beat reporters shouldn't be too surprised by most breaking news.

A beat reporter is typically busiest in season. College football reporters, for example, are working nonstop from July to December. College basketball beat reporters are on the clock from October to April. High school sports reporters are busy from mid-August to May (or June). NFL reporters have full calendars from late July to early February.

But the offseason isn't truly an offseason — especially for college and professional beat reporters. NFL writers are busy covering the NFL Combine in February, free agency in March and then the draft in April. There are organized team activities and minicamps in the summer. The only true dead period is from late June before training camp begins to late July. But even then, news inevitably crops up. For college reporters, there are coaching changes, transfer portal news, recruiting and then more recruiting. Camps are going on all summer, and high school seniors begin committing in waves during that time, too.

With limited access in the offseason, though, finding unique story ideas and keeping up with the day-to-day is more of a challenge. That's part of why cultivating relationships with sources is crucial. Developing relationships with sources can take weeks, months or even years for a new beat reporter. The process is constant. Beat reporters are always adding folks to their address book and their phone contact list. It's impossible for beat reporters to be on top of everything without the help of sources.

PRIMARY SOURCES

Primary sources are just that, primary. They're the most important. These people are the gatekeepers of the information that is vital to your reporting. Coaches, players, athletic directors and other administrators are all considered primary sources. Game stories will always contain information gleaned from interviews with coaches and players. The following story shows the importance of relationships with individual players:

> With smiles beaming from ear to ear, Sam Griesel and C.J. Wilcher hid behind the Pepsi vending machine in their locker room.
>
> As each of them gripped an orange handle on the five-gallon Gatorade jug that had been filled to the brim with freezing cold water, they patiently waited for Nebraska coach Fred Hoiberg to return. As Hoiberg turned the corner? Celebratory yelling and a locker room baptism of extraordinary proportions.
>
> Nebraska did the unthinkable Sunday: upsetting No. 7 Creighton at the CHI Health Center, 63-53.
>
> "It's hard to put into words," said Griesel, a Lincoln native who posted an 18-point, 12-rebound double-double Sunday. "I get a little bit emotional thinking about it because it means so much to me, and so much to this group and so much to this state."

Griesel, Nebraska's leading rebounder, is the obvious primary source.

A story about a player being named the starting quarterback will require vital information from the coach — why he was named the starter over the competition, what the coach saw from the player during the QB competition, how the coach believes he will fit the offense. Coaches make those decisions; therefore, they are the primary sources.

When players rewrite the record books, win awards or reach benchmarks, they become primary sources. Even though a player's thoughts on the matter might be predictable—"I just do what I can to help the team"—fans want to know their thoughts. Can you imagine a story about the Naismith Award without any reaction from the winner?

The best stories often include multiple primary sources. Single-source stories should be avoided unless they're a Q&A or breaking news where only one person is made available or has posted news on social media. A story about a coach's contract extension needs details from the athletic director, not just the coach. The coach, while considered a primary source in this instance, may not want to discuss those details.

For hirings, firings and extensions, reporters need to reach out to athletic directors (or the person who oversees the AD if the story is about the AD) to ask questions about contract information. A "no comment" response is sometimes inevitable but can be informative anyway. A coach's agent could be a primary source in these situations. Agents often serve as spokespeople for their clients and can provide more details. Many coaches are hands-off with their contracts.

In feature, enterprise or other sports stories, primary sources will depend on the topic. A story about the troubles and travails of taking a football team on the road, for example, might involve the equipment manager or operations director as primary sources. A story about a new professional volleyball league taking root in the city will have investors and local businesspeople as primary sources.

Athletes are taking agency of their own stories as well. It's quite common for high school students to break the news of their recruiting visits and commitments on their social media accounts. The same goes for college athletes who have a new NIL deal or have entered the transfer portal. Some professional athletes have broken news of their own contract extension through platforms such as X and Instagram.

SECONDARY SOURCES

Secondary sources are like the multitude of fresh ingredients at a salad bar. It's totally fine to eat lettuce and spinach by themselves, but the dressing, croutons, onions, carrots, and tomatoes make the dish much more enjoyable. Secondary sources aren't essential to the story, but they certainly make stories more interesting.

Use secondary sources as often as possible. When breaking news is concerned, it's OK to write and post a single-source story, but try to update it with more secondary sources as they become available. The story about the Naismith Award winner? The winner's mom might tell you a cute story about how the winner first learned to play.

TRAVIS KELCE WAS A STAR. TAYLOR SWIFT PUT HIM IN ANOTHER ORBIT.

Physicists say that when two stars collide, in what they call a kilonova or "cosmic car crash," they produce a fireball of blue and red. That's approximately what happened on Sept. 26, 2023, in Kansas City's Arrowhead Stadium when Travis Kelce, a tight end for the Chiefs, invited 12-time Grammy-winner Taylor Swift to watch his game.

Kelce was no slouch in celebrity terms. He had already won two Super Bowls and hosted "Saturday Night Live." But nothing pushed him into the cosmos like his brush with the Taylor Swift constellation. Swift, whose Eras Tour in 2023 broke concert records, can make the ground tremble, literally. Her concert in downtown Seattle shook the ground so hard that it registered on a nearby seismometer roughly equivalent to a 2.3 magnitude earthquake. "We're talking about 70,000 people and all the music and paraphernalia associated with the concert," said Mouse Reusch, a seismologist at the Pacific Northwest Seismic Network.

The meeting of these two megastars came about in July when Kelce said on his podcast that he wanted to give Swift a friendship bracelet during her concert tour stop in Kansas City, but that she had declined to meet him in order to save her voice. Later he invited Swift to a game.

"I told her that, 'I've seen you rock the stage in Arrowhead. You might come see me rock the stage in Arrowhead, and see which one's a little more lit,'" Kelce said.

Kelce and Swift, both 33, have remained quiet about whether they are friends or a couple, or just two celebrities trying to leverage each other's fame. Despite Kelce's relative fame in the sports world, becoming part of the frenzied conversation around Swift's every move is another ball game. Kelce now has 3.2 million followers on Instagram. Swift has 273 million. "This is celebrity on steroids, and it has a powerful impact," said Daniel Durbin, a professor of communication at the University of Southern California.

Asked at a team news conference about his new paramour, Travis replied with a sexy smile, "I was on top of the world after the Super Bowl, and right now even more on top of the world, so it's fun, man."[1]

Taylor Swift and Travis Kelce mingle in the crowd after the Chiefs' Super Bowl victory over the 49ers.

© UPI / Alamy

Roommates might be able to share a story about how competitive the winner was while doing other things not related to basketball.

Secondary sources are also integral for feature stories. A story on a senior football player could easily be told by just talking to him, but who wants to read that? Anecdotes from secondary sources—teammates, parents, roommates, friends, a romantic partner—will give your story much more oomph.

MATERIAL SOURCES

Sources don't have to be people. Oftentimes, reporters obtain information from media guides, record books and stat sheets. Those are called material sources.

When covering a game, a beat reporter will certainly want information from the postgame box score—the final score, key statistics, records that might have been broken. If the reporter is writing a feature story on an incoming transfer, for example, they will likely turn to the media guide of the player's previous school to examine their old player bio.

A feature story on the 100-year anniversary of a college football stadium will probably have multiple quotes from those who've been around for at least half of its history.

But what if the reporter wants to include historical perspective from the stadium's builders? No need for a seance. A material source here could be the archives — either through Newspapers.com, where so many newspapers have their digitized archives, or through the microfilm located at the local library.

Tread carefully, though. Material sources might not be 100 percent correct or could be biased. Archived material should be verified, like checking for a potential correction in another issue. Additionally, information from older sources might be phrased in ways that are offensive by today's standards.

BEHIND-THE-SCENES SOURCES

Not all sources will be easy to spot in your story. Behind-the-scenes sources are people who provide important information or ideas for stories but aren't used as primary or secondary sources. For beat reporters, forging relationships with behind-the-scenes sources is a vital part of keeping up with what's going on. You rarely find quotes from the equipment manager, the facilities manager or the security guard stationed outside the team locker room, for example, but those people can still be key figures to know for sports reporters. They're generally more involved with a team than reporters are, and likely know more information than you do.

Behind-the-scenes sources are also boosters, friends of the program, former players, people in the ticketing office — anyone who is around the team with information you might not know. Most of the time, behind-the-scenes sources are trustworthy, reliable and, most important, accurate. They could provide you with information that leads to a breaking news story.

This is vitally important, though: any information you learn from a conversation with a behind-the-scenes source must be verified with a primary source before you run with the story.

ON THE RECORD, OFF THE RECORD AND ON BACKGROUND

As a reporter, you assume that you're on the record when speaking to a source. A source who has plenty of experience with reporters will also be under that presumption. That means that you are free to report anything they say in that conversation. Some sources, though, don't have much experience working with reporters, so it's never a bad thing to be extra careful and confirm with them that conversations are on the record. In an age of poor media literacy, there are teaching moments everywhere.

If a reporter or a source wants to speak off the record—meaning that information learned in the conversation won't be repeated in a story or attributed to anyone—both parties must agree and confirm that they're speaking off the record. That means off limits. There are plenty of reasons for sources to want to speak off the record. For instance, they want to keep their job. Primary sources, like coaches, may want to give you context about their recruiting or free agent strategy, but college coaches aren't allowed to talk about recruits by name, and NFL coaches have strict rules about speaking about players on other teams.

This is where developing trust is of the utmost importance. If a reporter burns a source by using off-the-record information in a story or on social media, that bridge is most likely gone. That source will probably never speak with you again and could inform other potential sources of your misconduct.

Why even have off-the-record conversations then? Just because you learn something off the record doesn't mean you can't ask about it on the record. Let's say there's a former player watching a closed practice that you're not allowed to attend. While you're grabbing coffee later, he tells you that the starting quarterback limped off the field during 11-on-11s. Now aware of this, you ask the coach during their weekly availability what the QB's status is. Since it's an on-the-record interview setting, anything the coach says is news. (Some coaches refuse to speak on injuries out of principle, but others give detailed injury reports. Depends on the coach.)

The coach becomes the primary source in this instance since they're speaking on the record. But the information from your behind-the-scenes source helped lead to the story, even though his name is nowhere to be found. This is called a "tip" or a "lead."

There's a third type of information gathering, too: on background, also called "not for attribution." In this case the information can be reported but cannot be linked to a specific person. So, for example, a reporter might write "according to a university spokesperson."

ANONYMOUS SOURCES

While not ideal, there are plenty of situations that arise where you might have to use an anonymous source. These people are not named in the story and can't be identified either by pseudonym or a descriptor. This is becoming increasingly more common in sports reporting.

A reporter usually doesn't offer a source anonymity without a conversation first with other staff members about whether the offer is warranted. Those conversations will include questions pertaining to several of the five Ws.

- Who is the anonymous source? Just because they're anonymous to the public doesn't mean they're anonymous to the paper. Are they reputable? Are they dependable? Is there anyone who will speak on the record?
- What is the news value of the story? How earth shattering is the news?
- Why don't they want to speak on the record? Could they get fired? Could they get sued? Will they be arrested?

There is an immense risk of running stories with unnamed sources. They could be wrong, for starters. But what if there's a major story there? Breaking a big story about how an institution covered up sexual assault could create a major ripple effect, like policy change. Speaking truth to power is important.

One of the founding members of the Big Ten Conference was rocked by charges of hazing and sexual harassment during the summer of 2023. The Northwestern football program found itself in the middle of a scandal involving not only the coaching staff but the entire athletic department. And the story broke because of anonymous reporting. On July 8 the university's student newspaper, the Daily Northwestern, reported allegations by two former players. "I've seen it with my own eyes, and it's just absolutely egregious and vile and inhumane behavior," the player, who asked to remain anonymous, said.

The paper also obtained images of whiteboards from the team's locker room with incriminating information and a video the player said indicated the kind of hazing taking place. According to the paper, a second player who also asked to be anonymous said he could confirm the other player's account.

News Tips

Sometimes sources will approach reporters via phone call, email, or direct message with information that could result in a news story. This is what's called a "news tip." Even if it's a trusted source approaching you with the tip, however, the tip needs to be vetted through primary sources, secondary sources or behind-the-scenes sources.

Vetting news tips is always essential, but especially so during "silly season" — sports journalist slang for when the coaching carousel is up and running. The University of Michigan was on the hunt for a new coach after Lloyd Carr retired, and one of the potential candidates was Kansas coach Mark Mangino, according to the Lawrence Journal World. In its story, the Journal World reported that Mangino's agent said Mangino was in "serious negotiations." The man quoted in the story, however, wasn't Mangino's agent. He had hoodwinked the newspaper into believing that he was. The Journal World ultimately had to run a correction and apologize for the error. Had the reporter attempted to verify the source, the embarrassing gaffe could have been easily avoided.

While the Journal World's error occurred before Twitter (now known as X), it's a cautionary tale. Fake social media accounts pretending to be well-known and well-trusted reporters pop up all the time to mislead social media users and local reporters. And now with verification being reduced to a status symbol people can pay for, it's even more important to confirm before running what could be incorrect news.

GOING BANANAS

Remember those three-hour baseball games? They're going, going, gone, thanks to a series of rule changes adopted in 2023 designed to speed up play. The biggest change was a pitch clock that limits how long pitchers can twitch and scratch before throwing. The change, which seemed to gain universal approval, shaved about half an hour off game times.

Other changes were afoot, too, although they were designed to put more fun back in the game—time passes quickly, it was said, when you're laughing, dancing or singing. That's where we find the Savannah Bananas. The Bananas are baseball's answer to the Harlem Globetrotters, a raucous band of barnstorming comics and entertainers who make the game light-ning fast and side-splittingly hilarious.

In "Banana Ball" no one bunts, no one makes a visit to the pitching mound and there's a two-hour time limit. If someone in the stands catches a foul ball, the batter is out. Eccentric rules are only part of the circus atmosphere. The first base coach dances, and the team celebrates home runs by racing into the stands for high fives. When the Bananas are on the field, they might take a dance break between pitches, spinning and slide-stepping like the Four Tops in cleats, only to resume play as if nothing hap-pened. "A lot of moving parts," Bananas first baseman Dan Oberst says. "You can't blink or you'll miss what happens."

It was no secret the sport was lagging behind a quick-twitch world, young fans antsy to avoid sitting through games that stretched past three hours. Jess Cole, owner of the Bananas, and his staff started asking them-selves, "What if? We looked at every boring play," says Cole. "And we got rid of it." The Bananas have been a hit wherever they've played. In a game in Kansas City against the Monarchs, they drew fans from across the region. "I like baseball games but, for me, they're just a little slow," says Will Denton, who brought his family three hours from East Missouri. "This thing is like sensory overload."[2]

CONTACTING SOURCES

Now that you've begun to get sources of your own, there are several questions. How do you reach them? When do you talk to them? How often? The answers depend on a num-ber of factors, but things have changed compared to previous decades. Obtaining sources' cell phone numbers is the new norm. Arranging interviews with high school athletes may still go through coaches at practice, but those can also be arranged with the athletes them-selves through social media direct messages — depending on the high school's protocol.

Contacting college and professional coaches and athletes is usually more involved. Generally, reporters are not allowed to reach out to athletes and coaches directly. Instead, they rely on sports information directors (SIDs) and public relations (PR) personnel who have their own specific rules to follow about contacts. Typically, SIDs and PR staffs arrange set times for interviews. And though you may request a player or a coach, that does not mean they will be made available.

A common restriction, for example, is to ban all media contact for true freshmen and redshirt freshmen players. An extreme example of this restriction came in 2012 with Texas A&M's star redshirt freshman quarterback Johnny Manziel. Then-coach Kevin Sumlin, following in the footsteps of many coaches around the country, had a strict no-freshmen policy — even if the player was a starter. Manziel was dazzling as the Aggies' starter and made a meteoric rise as a Heisman candidate, yet he was not allowed to speak with the media until late November that year — two weeks before he won the Heisman.

Relationships With Coaches

It's a necessity for beat writers to have working relationships with the coaches they cover. You'll be working with them closely, likely seeing them more than they see their spouses. How do you establish a strong relationship? First impressions are important. When you arrive on a beat, or your beat has hired a new coach, it's imperative to introduce yourself. The conversation doesn't need to last long, but allow enough time to shake hands, tell them who you are and maybe bring up some commonality (if there is one). In press conferences, ask questions. The more the coach sees your face and hears your voice with regularity, the better.

Some coaches will give you their personal cell phone number. Others will prefer to communicate over third-party apps like Signal or WhatsApp. Still others will do everything in their power to keep you from getting their number or will change their number with regularity. Regardless of how a coach feels about the media, they'll gen-erally lay down some ground rules about contacting them — whether they want you to text before calling or if they prefer you go through the sports information director.

Not every interaction with a coach needs to be an interview. Sometimes it's good to build off-the-record rapport while talking about other things, like TV shows or concerts or something happening in the news that isn't political. That doesn't mean reporters should cross the line into friendship. Being seen as too friendly could create conflicts of interest. It's imperative, though, to understand what's appropriate and what's not.

Potential conflict between reporters and coaches is not out of the question. How that gets resolved, though, depends on the situation. When a problem does arise, it's always beneficial to talk it out and attempt to come to a resolution. It's not good for anyone if there's constant strife between a coach and a reporter.

Relationships With Athletes

Reporters and their relationships with athletes look very different depending on the level of sport a reporter is covering. High school athletes might not be the most mature or insightful, considering their age. Because they're in school full-time, the majority of your contact might be after athletic competitions or practice.

As a high school reporter or a recruiting reporter, developing sources among high school students is the job. While there might be fewer rules for covering a high school program compared to a college program, there are some potential personal rules to follow — such as not texting them after 9 p.m. They are minors, after all, and they have their homework to do.

For a college reporter, developing relationships with athletes is a delicate dance. Many sports information directors discourage reporters from talking to athletes outside of sanctioned interviews. If you're new to the job, introduce yourself to as many athletes as you can. If there's a new athlete, introduce yourself to them, too. Reporters typically have media access before or after practice several times a week, depending on the school's media protocol. If there's an open practice, be there. Athletes and coaches, regardless of the level, notice who is there and who isn't. They also notice who is asking questions and who isn't. They may not say anything to you about it, but they're aware.

For many athletes, being the subject of an interview is stressful. Be friendly and conversational. The more at ease they are, the more insightful they will be. Don't just talk to star players. Walk-ons and practice squad players have good stories, too, and make great sources.

Athletes, like coaches, will likely build better relationships with some reporters than others. That happens. If there's a spot of tension with an athlete based on your write-up of their performance or an off-field incident, the best option is to give them space. It's not ideal to be on the outs with a player, especially if it's a star quarterback or the captain, but they'll usually come around. And, as with coaches and every source, don't burn them. And don't get too friendly with any of them either.

WORKING WITH MEDIA RELATIONS

Reporters are obligated to produce unbiased, thoroughly reported stories for their readers. Meanwhile, media relations professionals—otherwise known as sports information or public relations—are required by their employers to present their team in a positive light no matter what information they may need to distribute to the media.

The job description for media relations has changed plenty over the years, but the core mission remains the same: serving as the middleman between a school's athletic department and the public. Even though their jobs are very different, both media relations and the media need one another. Sports information directors assist reporters by

PRAIRIE WOLF
WEEKLY

ATHLETICS SCHEDULE

Women's Tennis
Nebraska Wesleyan hit the road and escaped Dubuque with an 8-1 win over the University of Dubuque.

Volleyball
Against the Luther Norse, the Nebraska Wesleyan volleyball team recorded 48 kills en route to a three-set victory (25-23, 25-14, 25-15).

Football
Entering enemy territory, Nebraska Wesleyan fell to the University of Dubuque, 28-56.

Women's Golf
Nebraska Wesleyan women's golf finished eighth at the 2023 American Rivers Conference Women's Golf Championship.

UPCOMING HOME EVENTS

OCTOBER 10
6:00 PM - VOLLEYBALL VS. BUENA VISTA

OCTOBER 14
1:00 PM - FOOTBALL VS. LORAS

OCTOBER 16
6:00 PM - VOLLEYBALL VS. GRINNELL

OCTOBER 18
6:00 PM - WOMEN'S SOCCER VS. BUENA VISTA
8:30 PM - MEN'S SOCCER VS. BUENA VISTA

OCTOBER 21
11:00 AM - VOLLEYBALL VS. WARTBURG
1:00 PM - WOMEN'S SOCCER VS. CENTRAL
3:30 PM - MEN'S SOCCER VS. CENTRAL

OCTOBER 24
4:00 PM - MEN'S SOCCER VS. BETHEL

X @NWUSPORTS

 @NWUATHLETICS

 NWUSPORTS.COM

The sports information director and staff typically provide lots of information for the media and the student body about upcoming events.

© Nebraska Wesleyan Sports Information.

coordinating interviews and maintaining the stats and information about their team. Members of the media help media relations by writing stories about their team.

"With the explosion of the media corps here, the job has changed a lot," said Keith Mann, Nebraska's associate athletics director for communications. "It's more managing players' and athletes' time. It'd be great if the starting quarterback could talk to everyone individually, but it's just not practical anymore.

"This isn't just media, but every coach, athlete, administrator is under more scrutiny now because it's more of an open book with social media. So, it's hard to still try to keep a good rapport with the media where there's still more relationship-driven conversations. But it's hard when everything's under a microscope."

With more media coverage comes more staff in Nebraska's communications office. The team includes six full-time sports information directors, an administrative assistant, the director of photography, a host of undergraduate students and two full-time interns. That doesn't include the creative and emerging media folks who work closely with communications but are housed in an entirely different department.

Mann's office is responsible for interview coordination, media guides, weekly and daily news releases, game and meet programs, statistics, record maintenance, event planning, game and match administration, general communications, speaking engagements, basic social media account maintenance and so much more. Plenty of his day-to-day work happens behind the scenes with planning discussions, such as those for the Volleyball Day in Nebraska event in Aug. 2023. Volleyball Day drew 92,003 spectators, setting a world record for the largest crowd at a women's sporting event.

Writing for Sports Information

Those who work for sports information departments generally put a positive spin on things, even when that may seem difficult if not impossible. For Mann, it's a balance. "You can't always sugarcoat everything," he said. "If we're 3-8, I'm not going to sell 'Everything is great.' But there's always good things going on with any team, whether that's individual performances on the field or 'Hey, we've got a young roster.'

"You just try to find the positives. You have to be more selective about what you celebrate. But when you're invested with the team and the coach and the athletes, you really feel an obligation to make it a positive experience for them, too. It's easier that way because you know them individually and personally."

When Nebraska lost to Ohio State by 41 points in 2019, the game recap posted to Nebraska's website didn't sugarcoat the loss. But instead of leading with the Huskers' faults, the story hyped how talented the Buckeyes were.

> No. 5/6 Ohio State produced a complete game in all phases to post a 48-7 win over Nebraska on Saturday night at Memorial Stadium.

The Buckeyes improved to 5-0 and 2-0 in the Big Ten, while Nebraska slipped to 3-2 and 1-1 in the conference. The Buckeyes showed that they may be one of the nation's best teams, rolling for 580 total yards, including 368 on the ground, while holding the Husker offense to just 231 total yards.

When speaking about the Huskers' woes in the game, the story did not avoid them, but didn't dwell on them either.

Two plays into Nebraska's fourth possession, Martinez was intercepted at midfield — this time by OSU senior free safety Jordan Fuller. Three plays later, the Buckeyes were in the end zone on running back Master Teague's eight-yard touchdown run to give OSU a 24-0 lead with 8:26 left in the half.

Mann and the other full-time staffers in the office help provide guidance for the students who work in Nebraska's communications office for situations such as that. His biggest piece of advice: "Remember who you're working for. You're working for the team. Even in a scenario where the coach may not be there the next year, you're working that team until something changes. But if there's scenarios where you don't know how to handle it, don't try to do it on your own."

SPORTS NEWS RELEASES

A sports news release is a familiar material source for journalists, and it's how communications offices relay information about their teams to the media. Sports news releases are written from the perspective of the team sending out the release, so republishing those releases verbatim is a journalistic no-no. Check and confirm the information.

Email is the most popular way reporters receive sports news releases, though sometimes the information in the news release is posted to social media or to a team's respective website first. While reporters may delete many news releases, some useful story ideas can come from these releases. Local storylines are generally a hit in reporters' respective markets — especially unique ones.

Those working for Nebraska's communications office work diligently on sending news releases and information updates. Mann shudders to think how many emails his office sends out per year. Take October, for example. Football is its own beast, with releases sent out with game notes, practice reports and game recaps. Then there's volleyball, which plays two (or sometimes three) matches a week, which results in match previews and match recaps. And that doesn't factor in potential accolades or releases about team rankings.

"There's some Saturdays where you can get 14 press releases," Mann said. "And it's all necessary. Does everyone on that email list need every one of those? No. But does every one of those things that's written need to be available, posted and shared on social media? Ninety percent of them, for sure."

The information included in these releases generally pertains to three specific categories:

- Events, breaking news and personnel changes.
- Accolades.
- Off-the-field good works.

Not all news releases sent by communications offices are positive. Coaches get fired, a notable player or coach from decades ago dies or players leave via the transfer portal. Releases pertaining to these sorts of events are devised to make the announcement official without grandiose language. Be factual and straightforward.

Media Guides

One of the largest projects for any communications office is handling the planning, production and execution of the annual media guide for each sport. Some sports, like football and basketball, are more labor intensive than others, but hundreds if not thousands of man-hours go into those books. Media guides are the encyclopedia for each team — containing records, bios, summaries of previous games, schedule information and much, much more. While reporters use them to do their jobs, prospective student-athletes also read them as recruiting guides. Before the NCAA mandated page counts for media guides, some of Nebraska's older guides were the size of actual encyclopedias. In 2002, Nebraska's football media guide was 448 pages long.

Nebraska remains one of the few athletic departments that still prints and sells hard copies of the media guides for multiple sports, including football and volleyball. Many departments share their guides on their websites without printing the book.

Credential Requests

How do reporters get access to the press box? By requesting credentials in advance with a team's communication department. Each team sets specific guidelines on how people and media outlets are allowed access to their events. Anyone can apply for credentials, but that doesn't mean they will be approved. Writers and columnists from the local paper will be granted access, but fan podcasters will need to cross their fingers and not hold their breath. Check with your team's sports information director for credential application protocol.

UPON FURTHER REVIEW

1. You've been assigned by your school newspaper to the track and field beat. What steps would you take to prepare for the job? What is on your to-do list before the season begins?

2. Look at a media guide or two. (You can access them online on athletic department websites.) Is there any content that surprised you? What couldn't you find that you were looking for?

3. Interview a sports information director for a nearby team — maybe a small college or small professional team. Prepare a list of questions. Write a feature story about them.

Go to a college team's website and look for their news releases. (They should all be posted to the "news" tab.) Conduct an analysis. Look at the subject lines. Are they formatted in any specific way? Look at the quotes. Is there something notable about them? Note the things you would find helpful and not helpful as a reporter.

NOTES

1. Information drawn from a story by Emmanuel Morgan, *New York Times*, Sept. 26, 2023, and reporting by Maureen Dowd.

2. Material drawn from David Wharton, "Meet the Savannah Bananas, Who've Captivated Fans and MLB," *Los Angeles Times*, May 16, 2022.

Navigating Social Networks

The time is 5:30 a.m. You're still asleep, but daylight is breaking, and perhaps you hear the "thud" your Sunday newspaper makes as your neighborhood carrier throws the heavy bundle of newsprint against the screen door of your front porch. Or maybe you were born after 2000 and have no idea of what used to be known as "newspaper delivery." Truth be told, you probably get your news these days from the internet or, more specifically, social media sites like X, platforms that link and aggregate stories.

"It's almost like throwing it on somebody's doorstep," said Austin Meek, a sports columnist for the Eugene Register-Guard in Oregon. "You give them a link on X, and they wake up in the morning like I do and check their X feed. That's how they find things they're interested in." Meek said he's embarrassed to admit how much time he spends on his phone each morning when he opens X. "It's a big part of how I gather news, for sure," he said. "Most of the things I read, and certainly any breaking news, I usually see it first on X. It's the first thing I look at in the morning, to catch up on whatever happened when I was asleep."

A WRITER WHO SCALES THE HEIGHTS

Basketball fans often talk about a "height advantage," a situation where one team's players might be somewhat taller than the other team's. The average height for an American man, for example is 5 feet 9 inches; for a woman, 5 feet 3 and a half. The average height of an NBA player is 6 feet 6 inches, but average means there's lots of room above and below.

Is there a height advantage for sports writers? One person who would know is Mirin Fader, a senior staff writer for the Ringer, who navigates her way around the social media universe to write long-form human-interest sports features. On a good day Mirin might stretch up to just south of 5 feet tall; her subjects, they're in another

Giannis Antetokounmpo.
© ALL ACCESS / Alamy

stratosphere entirely. Fader has already written two books about NBA stars and has another in the planning stages. Her first, a New York Times best-seller, "Giannis: The Improbable Rise of an NBA Champion," profiled a 6-foot-11-inch Nigerian-Greek playing for the Milwaukee Bucks. Her second book was about Hakeem Olajuwon, a seven-footer, who played for the Houston Rockets. A third book, about one of basketball's all-time greats, concerns Larry Bird, a mere 6 feet 9.

Mirin Fader

Fader doesn't focus only on tall people. She's profiled some of the world's best athletes across all sports, including Bryce Young, Coco Gauff and Puka Nacua. She has been a staff writer for Bleacher Report and freelanced for ESPN.com. She got her start writing sports features at the Orange County Register after graduating from Occidental College. That path could be described as "traditional," but students looking to break into sports journalism may need a new approach. "I think what I would do if I was a student now is start my own Substack," Fader says. "I would use my own platform to try to pitch stories. So, if I'm in LA, I would see what teams are coming to town. I'm going pitch a story to whatever paper or national outlet is wanting to cover that game and say, hey, I'm here. I can do that feature for you. It would require a lot of hustling, a lot of scheduling, but that's how I would get my start. Almost like getting the clips for yourself."

Fader has established her voice in the marketplace, so to speak, but it takes just as much work to stay in the game. Here's how she describes her work habits: "I think the coolest part of the job is that every day looks different. Sometimes you're going to have big reporting days where you're in the field all day interviewing people. Other days you're locked in your apartment with a lot of caffeine trying to make deadline. You've got this feature that you have to figure out, and you're not going to leave your apartment till you do.

"I'm a morning person," Fader says, "so I like to write in the morning. I usually have two stories going on at one time. If I'm writing one story, I'm reporting for the other. I think that's good because it gives your brain some space. So, if I'm writing in the morning, I'll probably report in the afternoon and just call a bunch of people or do the interview in person." On this particular day, for example, Fader was headed an hour south from her home in Los Angeles to the University of San Diego to do some reporting. She had only just learned that her interviewee would be available: "They just told me that I could go like an hour ago," she said, "so it is very much on the fly."

One of her most important challenges is constantly discovering new and interesting stories. Much of Fader's time is spent thinking of stories that audiences might want. "I think an underrated part of the job is the hours you spend trying to come up with ideas and story pitches. I go through local newspapers to see what's happening in the world. What's interesting? What should I pitch?"

The Toil of Transcription

Fader is a master of the interview, often conducting hundreds for each of her books. The interviews, however, take a toll because of the mind-numbing and laborious task of turning an audio conversation into a prose transcription. Fader often saves the late afternoon hours of a day for this task: "I spend a lot of the 3 p.m. time when your brain stops working just for mindless transcription."

Fader's second book is on Hakeem Olajuwon, and it led her into a severe time crunch. "I was having trouble balancing that deadline and handling my regular job and dealing with a lot of other things," she said. "I got so behind on transcribing that it was insurmountable. Every time I would complete a few transcripts, I would fall behind again. I interviewed over 260 people for this book. What do I do, I wondered. Should I hire a student?" Fader's difficulties with transcription ultimately led her past human help and into the mysterious realm of AI. "I tried to hire students," she recalls, "but they quit after the first week. It's not a sexy job. Transcribing is not fun. I was in a desperate time crunch when a friend steered me toward an AI transcription service, and it saved me. I used it for about 50 interviews."

As a sports journalist, however, Fader said she has deep concerns about AI. "It's something that we're all thinking about, even sports broadcasters and statisticians. Every level will be affected. I saw a sign during the Hollywood writers' strike that really hit me. The sign said, 'Your robot doesn't have my trauma.' And I thought that's so true because my vantage point, where I come from, my history with sports, my life, impacts my journalism. It's why I try to write such deep human features. I know in my heart that this robot cannot do that."

Fader reluctantly discovered another use for AI. "I was at the coffee shop with a friend, and I really needed to come up with a podcast idea. None of my ideas had been accepted. What do I do? And he's like, let's ask ChatGPT. He asked for a pitch, and I was horrified at how good the pitch was — how detailed and how thoughtful. So, there's that existential dread of, am I complicit in doing something that goes against my industry? It's a weird paradigm to manage. But it's part of how you leverage ever-evolving tools."

One of those tools is social media, especially a platform such as X. "I would say my approach has been a little bit different in the sense that I don't really put forth any opinions or takes. I don't engage with trolls. I don't dunk on people. I ignore haters. Mine is a completely positive space. I tell myself, just tweet something you care about in writing once a day so people know you're alive and you're on there."

Fader says that she prefers using social media for networking. "It's been an incredible tool for that. I tell students to use it for networking and not socializing. There's such an emphasis on branding now, but you should use it as a journalistic tool. I have found so many sources simply by reaching out and saying, hey, I'm a staff writer for the Ringer. Can I DM you for this question? And boom, the interview happens."

Fader also found a mentor, the writer Jeff Perlman, on Twitter. "I just DMed him one day and said, I saw that you moved to Orange County. I just began at the Orange County Register. You're my favorite writer. Would you have a moment to talk? And he became one of my closest friends. None of it would have happened without Twitter. So, I acknowledge the positive parts and the networking that can come from it."

Branding

Branding is a big part of establishing your identity in the sports industry. Fader says her brand derives from her stories and not her presence on social media. "I think what really changed for my perspective on social media was when I saw people getting laid off that had 50,000 followers, 100,000 followers. I just said to myself, okay, so it doesn't matter how many followers you have, everyone's getting laid off. That's not going to insulate you. My editors tell me that social media doesn't really matter the way that it used to, that having a large number of followers doesn't insulate you from failure. That freed me from this feeling that I have to be something I'm not. Now I can showcase the genuine me, which is just a big nerd that loves books and writing."

KEVIN VAN VALKENBURG ON GOLF

What started as a group text among college friends has now grown into one of the most popular podcasts in the game of golf. No Laying Up is a company built around the goal of entertaining, informing and connecting a community of avid golfers around the world, and their archives include appearances from the biggest names in the sport. No Laying Up also produces a video travel series, coverage of the PGA and LPGA Tours, and a robust social media presence. Kevin Van Valkenburg joined No Laying Up as editorial director in 2022.

Van Valkenburg played football at the University of Montana, where he also studied journalism and wrote for the student newspaper. He moved to Maryland to work for the Baltimore Sun and eventually the Ravens. In 2012, he joined ESPN as a senior writer for ESPN the Magazine and ESPN.com. He lives in Baltimore with his wife and three daughters and is endlessly searching for ways to overcome the chipping yips.

Van Valkenburg has some advice for young journalists trying to find a foothold in the field although he acknowledged that the industry has changed dramatically since he entered it more than twenty years ago. "Breaking into media now is a bit like trying to have a career as a musician. You have to be hungry, and you have to grind, and there are no guarantees. You might have to hold down another job. The most important thing is that you have to create.

"Don't wait for an invitation. Maybe it's a blog or a podcast or a TikTok. You don't have to earn anyone's permission or get a job first. If you wait around for an opportunity, it's unlikely it will ever come. Establish yourself as someone worth following, and hopefully financial compensation will follow."

Van Valkenburg says he mainly works from home but spends about nine weeks a year on the road. That means "I'm watching golf and talking to players, trying to find insights I can share with readers and listeners. That's a lot of time in different cities and in hotel rooms." He said it's important to recognize the contemporary distinction between writers and "personalities." "ESPN doesn't want its writers to be personalities, and I think that's the right decision. The on-air talent are the personalities, and the writers and reporters need to focus on journalism."

Van Valkenburg said that writing for No Laying Up means that he's writing for a small audience, but one that is personally invested in his point of view. "There are a lot of golf fans who feel like I speak for them, that I capture how they feel about the game. There are also fans who don't like my perspective. Because I'm a fully formed character in their eyes, certainly more so than when I was just a byline, they might try

Following golf competitions across the country generally takes writers to pleasant green, leafy places.
© Nebraska Wesleyan Sports Information.

to wound me in ways that feel like they're striking back. So, the good interactions are way better, but the bad ones are way worse. It's a fair trade-off."

If we could somehow travel back in time, Van Valkenburg said he would tell reporters to only "tweet links out to the stories or news items you are reporting." Once every aspect of American life started to feel political, he said, tweeting about even basic human rights became controversial. The whole media landscape turned into a mess, "one that is almost unfixable. I think what people want with their sports coverage is authenticity, even if they don't agree with the speaker or writer. You might as well be authentic and hope it connects with an audience."

Van Valkenburg reminds young sports writers that "there is always going to be a place for people to be fair and ethical reporters. It may take different forms, but we can't have only personalities shouting at each other each day without reporting because there would be no substance to any of it. Three-fourths of what gets discussed on shows and podcasts is not based on original reporting done by the show's participants. So, I think for someone in my position, I'm always trying to make sure we acknowledge that without boots-on-the-ground reporting, we wouldn't have jobs. Or at the very least, we'd be way less informed."

RULES FOR SOCIAL MEDIA

To that end, how should sports reporters handle social media, and what rules should they follow? Here are some general guidelines:

- Use discretion in what you post. Steer clear of politics and profanity.
- Be accurate. You're a journalist. The usual rules apply.
- Engage with your audience. Respond to their questions. Don't simply repost your favorite thoughts.
- Maintain a positive, lighthearted approach. While not every news item you post will be good news, in general keep a positive outlook.
- Post at peak hours: normally before 8 a.m., over the noon hour and after 5 p.m.
- Wait until you have a link to a story before you post breaking news.
- Use good-natured humor, but do not use social media to become a stand-up comedian.
- Don't be snarky. While sarcasm is common among sports reporters, too much can turn off your audience.
- Use the block button sparingly. You don't want to develop a reputation as being thin-skinned. Only remove followers if they are rude, vulgar or threatening — not if they simply disagree. (The "mute" button is a possible alternative.)
- Don't overpost. While there's no steadfast rule on how often to post, use common sense in not flooding your followers' feeds.

Hot Takes

Before social networks existed in the late 2000s, the term "hot take" likely didn't exist in any sports reporter's vernacular. Today, the term is prominent. Loosely defined, a hot take is a strong opinion written for the purpose of promoting a reaction. Consider this example: "Field goals under 25 yards should only be worth two points." Was the poster getting a jibe at a team that won a recent game?

Sending hot takes may not be the most important thing a sports reporter or columnist does, the fact remains that some sports writers try to claim attention with outlandish opinions. "If that works for you, great," Meek said. "That's not how I have chosen to use it." Rather, Meek relies on social media outlets as a way to engage and inform readers. "I like engaging with people and I like having reasonable exchanges," Meek said. "I'm not looking to use it to just promote reaction or to get five million people posting back at me. If I really have something to say, I'd rather say it in a column where I can actually develop and support it, versus just kind of blobbing it out there."

ESPORTS ARE GROWING MORE POPULAR

Sports fans are used to wading through jargon in the games they love
to follow. Esports have a language all their own. The following story
describes the action in a "League of Legends" match, one of the more
popular electronic sports:

> NRG flipped the script in the finals, opting to focus Fudge heavily
> with pressure from their jungler, Juan "Contractz" Garcia, but occa-
> sional visits from NRG mid-laner Cristian "Palafox" Palafox and sup-
> port Lee "IgNar" Dong-geun. Fudge's play was certainly not the only
> factor in NRG's upset, but C9 was unprepared for such a strong top
> side focus and it showed in the difference in cohesion between the
> two teams on that side of the map.[1]

The description of the "League of Legends" game above comes from
Esports Illustrated, an online guide to electronic sports. "League of
Legends" is one of the more popular MOBAs, or "multiplayer online bat-
tle arenas." Other popular MOBA games include shooter games like "Call
of Duty," fighting games like "Super Smash Bros." and strategy games like
"StarCraft."

How popular are esports? Millions of people around the world follow
video game competitions, and in the United States about 200 universities have adopted them as varsity sports and added them to the cur-
riculum. "The esports industry is exploding, and we want our students
to be part of it," said Shari Veil, dean of the College of Journalism and
Mass Communications at the University of Nebraska-Lincoln. "By providing opportunities for students to engage with the industry, we're helping
to shape the future of esports and prepare our students for successful
careers."

To lead their varsity team, Nebraska hired Ahman Green, a former NFL
running back, and built a state-of-the-art arena in the student union for the
team to practice and play. For students interested in a gaming career, Veil
said, "The program offers hands-on experiences in livestream production,
broadcasting (known as shoutcasting in esports), digital graphics, event
management and more."

Live Posting

One of the most popular uses of social media among sports reporters is to update followers during a live sporting event or news conference. The reasons vary. Some fans enjoy following along while watching the event, either in person or on television, and look for insight on a particular play or call. They also want answers to questions they think the reporter may know because he or she is on-site. For example, "They are wearing throwback uniforms today."

Other followers, perhaps on the other side of the globe, may use social media as their only means of receiving live score updates. Or maybe fans are at work during the hastily arranged news conference of a coach's firing and can only glance at their phone now and then for updates. Here are five tips for live posting:

1. Tell your audience about your plans. Your followers appreciate a heads-up when you'll be live posting an event. Alert them at least an hour before your game begins. For example, when you arrive at Allen Fieldhouse at the University of Kansas, take a picture of the arena with a post to help set the scene:

    > This place will be packed 16,300 strong in another 90 minutes when No. 2 Kansas hosts No. 4 Duke in a key nonconference tilt. PG Grayson Allen (sore ankle) is suited and warming up and will likely play. Game starts at 7. Follow here for updates.

    You've not only promoted the event, but you've also informed your followers of some injury information. Other pregame posts could include who's officiating the game, television information or series history — any tidbit that helps promote what's about to happen.
2. Use hashtags. Many events have dedicated hashtags, and by using the right one, you will ensure that your post is added to the overall conversation. One quick search will typically turn up the event's official hashtag — and it might shed some light on unofficial hashtags that the community is using as well. For example, the post you sent out previewing the Kansas-Duke game could include #KUBBall to attract Kansas fans, or #GoDuke if you're seeking the Duke audience. Some events, especially bigger ones, will have neutral hashtags, like #SuperBowl or #WorldCup.
3. Provide insight. While it's acceptable to post periodic score updates and other statistical information, chances are that the majority of your followers are following some stat-tracking app that tells them individual point totals or team yardage. If you're only posting the numbers every five minutes, you're likely to lose your audience.

    But don't ignore statistics entirely. Remember, there's the dad stuck in a meeting or in the stands at a midget football game who might be sneaking peeks at his cell

Posting live information about players helps engage your followers.
© Nebraska Wesleyan Sports Information.

phone and depending on you for the score. So, in addition to score updates, provide some sort of analysis or information your followers may not know:

#Jayhawks seem perplexed early by the #GoDuke surprise zone defense. Kansas down 10-2 at the first media time-out. Looks like Bill Self is making multiple subs in this first break. Allen started and his ankle seems fine thus far.

4. Engage with your followers. That initial post you sent to preview the Kansas-Duke game may lead to questions or comments about Allen's ankle. Given that the game hasn't started, you should have time to reply. Other times, followers might be simply posting questions or comments about the game.

Whether you respond is up to you, but make an effort to engage with your followers. You don't want them to think you are unapproachable. You can reply directly to the post, repost it with your comment or answer at top, or send a private direct message, if needed.

5. Use professional language. Commonly used acronyms are acceptable, and so are abbreviations such as "pro" for professional or "biz" for business. But don't think a character limit means you can get away with "U" in place of "you." Err on the side of professionalism. Remember that every post represents the brand you're

cultivating and should maintain the voice you chose when you created your social media plan.

Quoting From Social Media

Live posting from news conferences can be especially tricky. If you're 100 percent certain you heard every word correctly and in order, then use quotation marks with proper attribution. If, however, the person speaking has a long thought that's pushing past your 280-character limit, it may be best to paraphrase what the source said. It's a safe way of getting the message across without the accusation of misquoting under hurried circumstances.

Direct quoting is obviously easier — and sometimes more effective — if the quote is short and easy to remember: "I guarantee we will win this game." And as always, only quote or paraphrase interesting thoughts or newsworthy items. Don't flood social media feeds with every single detail. Pick and choose the highlights.

Relying on Social Media as a Source

Social media outlets such as Facebook and Instagram help sports reporters have an easier time keeping tabs on recruits — the future athletes that fans love to hear about. Even current college athletes planning to jump into the transfer portal can deliver posts that turn into news. Any beat writer covering a college or professional team should follow as many athletes or coaches on their team as possible. You never know when a member of the team will drop breaking news — he's leaving the program, she's injured and having surgery — or deliver some controversial comments that turn into news.

In any case, following your sources on social media is an easy way to keep tabs on potential news, or as a means of contact in case you need an interview. A click of the button, and you can direct message a source rather than worrying about finding a cell phone number.

Scooping on Social Media

"Scooping" the competition means you have reported a story before anyone else. That takes dedication, hard work, solid sources and, sometimes, good luck. Today, in the 24/7 news cycle, a scoop probably won't last more than 10 minutes before others have the same story. "As soon as you break something, it's literally going to be everywhere five minutes later," Adam Jardy, a sports reporter for the Columbus Dispatch, said. "If you have it first or you have it second or you have it third, chances are it's all going to be within a very short time frame." The 24/7 news cycle has deemphasized the importance of "having it first," but having the story correct is, and always has been, most important.

SMARTWATCH TECHNOLOGY CHANGES THE GAME

The fun (and larceny) is over. Baseball and softball will never be the same.

The days of sneaking a peek to see how many fingers the catcher is holding up to know what pitch is coming will soon be over thanks to the emergence of smartwatch technology. Back in the not-so-distant past, the manager would send a sign from the dugout to the catcher, who would relay it to the pitcher. That meant a cat-and-mouse game where runners on base would try to steal the sign and tip their teammates off. Now, between every pitch, players look toward their wrists. They're not checking the time. They're watching for instructions from the coach.

Beginning with the 2024 season, for example, the Nebraska softball team has partnered with GoRout to implement an electronic system that allows coaches to send signals quicker (and more secretively) than ever. "It's been really nice," head coach Rhonda Revelle said. "We're able to personalize it for each pitcher's pitches and we can also put words on it like, 'Keep it low.' It's also nice that we can position the infielders and outfielders."

The technology became legal in 2017 when the NCAA granted waivers for college baseball teams to use electronic devices in fall exhibition games. Early versions were bulky and inconsistent. Soon, however, another vision emerged — what if players could have a wearable device that could receive a secure electronic signal from the bench? Thus, the electronic wristband began its journey into collegiate athletics.

Nebraska found a solution through GoRout, which uses cellular signals to communicate between the dugout and the field. Mandie Nocita, Nebraska's director of video technology, analytics and player development, set up the system shortly before the 2024 season. She used the company-issued tablet to load opposing lineups and scouting reports into the system before each game.

Revelle calls the pitches in the dugout, her input is quickly keyed on the tablet, then the players' watches show the message. "There's about a two-second delay for them to get the signal, but it's been handy and we're big fans," Nocita said. "Like any technology, there are times when it does glitch [because] it's not perfect, but it's been working really well for us."

Electronic communication devices are also helping to speed up the game. With a 20-second pitch clock in softball, the time it takes to glance at the watch and go to the plate is negligible for the pitcher. Other sports, including college football, are inching closer to implementing similar technology. Based on the ease of operations and the benefits the Nebraska softball team has found, it may be sooner rather than later that a similar setup arrives in other sports.[2]

Satisfying Your Social Media Audience

It's important to know your social media audience, whether your account has 500 followers or 50,000. Why are they following you? What information, analysis or opinion do they seek? As a beat writer for an area college football team, for example, it's easy to know what your followers want: recruiting news, injury updates and game analysis.

What happens, though, if you are covering a sport you are not familiar with? Jardy faced this challenge when he began covering the Columbus Crew soccer team. "I didn't have a soccer background," he said. "In the world of soccer, if you don't have that background, people are generally skeptical of you. I dealt with a lot of angry people who just had no belief that I would be able to cover the team they cared about. So I got a lot of angry messages at first."

Count this one reason a sports reporter might wish social media didn't exist: backlash from followers and "trolls" — users who simply send negative posts to elicit a reaction from the original person who posted. "It can hurt. It can be very frustrating," Jardy said. "People picking fights with you, or people taking exception to a phrase you might use. I remember I had an ongoing argument with a Crew fan because I was talking about the team's depth chart. This guy was like, 'You're a moron, there are no depth charts in soccer.'

"I feel these days you can't have a byline and hide behind it," Jardy said. "You have to put yourself out there. I don't mean from a 'I have to be a personality' type of thing but to occasionally post things about my kids, or 'I just bought this album.' Those kinds of things show your readers who you are, and they get to know you a little bit."

The 24/7 news cycle is now a fixture of sports coverage. Long gone are the days when a reporter could write a game story and head home or to the nearest pub. During the search for a men's basketball coach, for example, Jardy updated his X feed and the Dispatch website three to four times a day. The more a beat writer calls and texts, the more often he or she can update readers. "We want to have the newest information on our website to drive people there," Jardy said. "At noon, it might have been, 'These are the candidates they have expressed interest in.' Then 2 o'clock, 'They've interviewed one of the assistants,' and by the evening, 'They still don't have a coach.' By night-time, it was everything that had happened that day for print the next day. What have we learned since the last time we printed a newspaper?"

Are Message Boards Relevant?

Some sports reporters deny they ever visit message boards, a place where fans can express their thoughts and opinions, converse with other fans — or fans of the opponent — and do it all under the nice, tidy anonymity of a goofy name like "Bobcat-bob327" or "Weluvthedawgs!" Unlike chat rooms, the messages are often longer than one line of text and can be at least temporarily archived. Even high school coaches and athletes are not immune from taking a quick look at message boards.

The problem, of course, is that nobody is held accountable, whether the information is accurate or simply a hoax. Hence, many sports reporters say they would rather deal with a migraine on deadline or chew tinfoil than associate themselves with message boards. However, those beat reporters are probably fibbing. If they were really telling the truth, they would admit that anonymous message board posters — sometimes referred to as citizen journalists — are part of their job. For example, perhaps Bobcatbob327, a regular on his favorite fan message board, posts something he has heard about his team — the freshman quarterback has decided to transfer because he is unhappy with his playing time. The rumor spreads quickly. You, the beat reporter, receive a text from a friend who has read this hot item. The rumor has made the rounds on X, too. Can you afford to ignore this tip simply because it appeared somewhere anonymously? Probably not. As with any tip, you begin digging, asking, checking and verifying.

What if your late-night, last-minute digging is all for naught, and Bobcatbob327 turns out to be wrong? This might be the time to remind yourself that this is just a normal headache beat writers must handle. Ideally, they would have such information about freshmen quarterbacks before it finds the fingertips of a rapidly typing message board regular. But in a 24/7 news cycle, even the most astute and responsible beat writer can't possibly know everything before cyberspace does.

A thorough beat reporter will at least keep tabs on some message boards, whether for tips or just to gauge the pulse of the fan base. Some feature story ideas could result, too. None of this, however, means beat reporters should depend solely on message boards for information. Nor does it mean beat reporters need to interact on message boards, anonymously or not.

SOCIAL MEDIA AND MEDIA RELATIONS

For media relations departments at major colleges and universities, social media is a key part of their communication strategy. The University of Colorado media relations department, for example, has a handbook for coaches and student-athletes on the topic and also speaks to student athletes about what to post and — more importantly — what not to post. Even a post that exists for a mere seven seconds before being deleted will likely be nabbed on a screenshot and exist for eternity. Specifically, political, sexist and rude comments, or unflattering comments about the upcoming opponent, could have bad results for student-athletes.

Nick Burkhardt and Social Media Strategy

Many journalists step across the aisle, so to speak, to work for media relations. Nick Burkhardt, assistant athletic director and head of the Creative & Emerging Media Department at the University of Nebraska, leads the way for social media strategy. It's a massive effort. "With Nebraska athletics," Burkhardt says, "we have nine full-time staff members and roughly 30 student interns." His department works on two buckets of responsibility: "to amplify recruiting and to elevate the Husker brand while providing general communication to recruits and fans."

Burkhardt said the first bucket includes 24/7 oversight of each team's social media accounts, which at this writing include X, Instagram, Facebook, TikTok and YouTube. His department serves as the "voice" of the team, speaking on their behalf when needed. The staff also provides game coverage, keeps up with trends and breaking news, and engages with the university's many, many followers.

The other bucket, content creation, includes lots of production responsibilities such as graphic and print design, video production and photography. The staff also coordinates coverage of recruiting visits, game play-by-play and live streaming. "We use a project management tool to stay organized with all of these different tasks," Burkhardt says. "We have estimated our team as a whole faces upwards of 2,000 content/social requests annually."

Burkhardt's typical workday is delightfully varied. "The equally refreshing and stressful thing about working in college athletics," he said, "is that no two days look alike. With that said, we are constantly receiving requests from our coaches, administrators and staff. One day we may need to make a fancy commitment graphic for a recruit with an hour turnaround; other days we may need to find a red rustic barn in the area to shoot a teaser video for a Husker mascot."

Burkhardt has some solid advice for young journalists setting out in the field. "The number one thing we preach is having an open mind and a willingness to expand your skill set. Because we serve athletics in a number of different ways, the more versatile you are as a content creator or social media manager, the more valuable you are. Every athletic department in the country is looking for individuals who can check multiple boxes."

Burkhardt added that many staff members started their career paths in one specific area and then branched off. "This often works," he said, "because the core principles of being a creative person translate from one discipline to another." As far as interns are concerned, Burkhardt says his department is looking for people with a passion for sports and a passion for creating things, whether that be graphics, video, photography or even clever captions.

"In the social media space," he said, "having the ability to stay open-minded and learn on the fly is so important." These platforms are constantly evolving and so are the strategies one needs as a result. "This could consist of formatting photos in a certain way, editing video to a certain length, using hashtags, not using hashtags, the list goes on and on when it comes to solving the algorithm each company implements."

UPON FURTHER REVIEW

1. Think of a story you could pitch to a local sports media outlet. Describe the story and make the pitch, highlighting what you could bring to the story.
2. What are the pros and cons for a sports writer of engaging with followers on social media?
3. In what ways can AI be helpful to sports journalists? In what ways might it represent an unsettling trend?

NOTES

1. Nick Geracie, "Unpacking the Biggest Upset in LCS Finals History — NRG vs Cloud9 LCS Summer Finals," *Esports Illustrated*, Aug. 25, 2023, https://www.si.com/esports/league-of-legends/lcs-championship-2023-nrg-c9-recap.

2. Luke Mullin, "As NCAA Mulls Electronic Communication Devices in Football, Nebraska Softball Offers Shining Example," *Lincoln Journal Star*, March 14, 2024.

4

Covering the Game

The most exciting thing about reading about a sporting event is the feeling that you are in the midst of the action, even inside the players' heads. A story about the 2023 Women's World Cup begins this way:

> From where she stood, the ball looked to be headed straight into the goal, and Megan Rapinoe cursed loudly in her head.

And there's more. The story continues with the player having a flashback of her entire career as the ball hurtles toward the net:

> "My whole international career is over," she said she thought as a shot by Portugal whistled toward the net in the final minutes on Tuesday, threatening to end Rapinoe's final Women's World Cup.

How does the writer know this? Juliet Macur of the New York Times knows because she attended a press conference after the game and interviewed Rapinoe. Macur also knows because she was watching each moment of the game as carefully as she could from her seat in the stadium.

The next few paragraphs of her story supply the context missing from the high drama of the opening:

> Neither team had scored yet. The tie that loomed would mean the United States would advance to the next round. A loss would send the Americans packing their bags in what would have been the biggest upset in Women's World Cup history.
>
> And so Rapinoe swore as the shot delivered by Portugal forward Ana Capeta headed toward the goal, watching wide-eyed with players on both sides as it veered

just a smidgen too far to the right. The ball hit the right post and then, to the relief of Rapinoe and her team, caromed off it and away from the goal.

"Girl," Rapinoe said with a nervous laugh, "that was stressful."[1]

Macur's story is an excellent example of why we enjoy reading sports stories — they make us feel like we are part of the game. Macur moves us just outside the penalty box (at least in our imaginations) as the game comes to a thrilling conclusion. That's why "being there" is such an important part of being a sports writer.

COVERING THE WORLD CUP FROM 7,000 MILES AWAY

The world's largest sporting event, soccer's World Cup, set precedents in 2022 with an unusual time — winter (November through December) — and an unusual place — Doha, Qatar. But that didn't stop an enterprising Minneapolis reporter from covering exuberant fans — he found plenty of them in downtown sports-themed bars.

Brit's Pub in Minneapolis, for example, opened its doors at 6:30 a.m. on the first day of the tournament, and general manager Shane Higgins found an England fan and a USA fan already in line. "I let the England fan in first," Higgins joked. By 7 a.m. about 100 fans were seated for the match between England and Iran. Those fans joined an estimated five billion people worldwide who would tune in to watch the matches over the next few weeks. And the Minnesota fans were ready. Bars and restaurants throughout the Twin Cities were prepared to open at odds hours — the Black Hart in Saint Paul showed some matches that began at 4 a.m. — because the event was being held half a world away.

When England took a 2-0 lead in the 45th minute, someone yelled, "It's coming home," as in, the English are bringing the cup back to the birthplace of the game. "That was probably me yelling," Higgins said with a laugh.[2]

A NEW KIND OF SPORTS REPORTER

It might take a little chutzpah these days to be a sports writer. Those who cover sports are sometimes prone to making outrageous claims. Dave Portnoy, podcast host and founder of the sports blog "Barstool Sports," bragged that he could play a round of golf just as well as the top pros so long as he could have unlimited mulligans. A mulligan is a free shot; in other words, Portnoy, an average golfer at best, would be allowed to hit the ball over and over and over again until he found a shot he liked.

Sure enough, the ruling authority of professional golf, the USGA, offered Portnoy a chance to play at Shinnecock Hills, the venue for that year's U.S. Open. Portnoy could have as many mulligans as he liked, so long as he finished the round in 5 hours 15 minutes. Insane prediction or something achievable? Portnoy ended up with a score of 66 (four under par), estimating that he used about 10 mulligans per shot, or nearly 700 shots for the round! This publicity stunt was great for Portnoy's blog, but it was also a dose of reality for pro golf after some of the players had complained that the course was just too hard. Now none of them wanted to say that they couldn't beat Portnoy.[3]

Portnoy's career as a radio broadcaster offers a good clue as to what the next generation of sports writers might look like. Most will be mojos, "mobile journalists," professionals who can compose blogs, shoot video and continue to handle all the traditional responsibilities of print journalism.

The American Sports Fan

Sports fans are changing, too. Fans have obsessed over their favorite teams, no doubt, for as long as there have been fans, but the internet has helped create a new generation of committed followers. Take Will McDonald, for example. McDonald, a University of Iowa doctoral student, painstakingly recorded an account of each game played by his favorite team — the Kansas City Royals — on his blog, a popular hangout where Royals fans could follow the action and swap opinions. Many posted comments such as:

> "$3 million a year doesn't get you much these days."
> "Never before seen this batting order, the 67th of the season."
> "Ha Ha Ha!!! I love it! Right off Pujols' dome."[4]

This interest, one shared by millions of fans across the country, has blurred the line between sports fans and professional journalists. Chris Thorman, who runs a Kansas City Chiefs' blog,[5] said, "It's totally changing the landscape for sports fans. What separates the mainstream media from the typical blogger is the access. The *Kansas City Star*'s beat writer will have more access, will have nuanced conversations with players, and see things we can't." But the major media's advantage may not last forever.

Today, major sports teams rarely give credentials to bloggers. That could change. "I think the time is coming when bloggers will be credentialed and at games," said Will Leith, founder of Deadspin.com. In what may be a precedent-setting move, the New York Islanders are planning a bloggers' box for an upcoming season — a press-like area set aside just for them.

In fact, nearly all print journalists are facing the same paradigm shift. According to David Dunkley Gyimah, a pioneering video journalist in the UK, they must learn to understand "visual narrative" and allow it to drive storytelling. As Gyimah puts it, "Vloggers [video bloggers] will undoubtedly rule the net. Their short, sometimes idiosyncratic productions are well suited for a medium where time is compressed, and users' attention spans shortened."[6]

And that's not all. Increasingly, sports writers are finding it necessary to cover a whole range of stories far outside the normal bounds of playing fields and arenas. To read sports now is to read about the Supreme Court, the Menninger clinic and the Harvard Business School. Sports writers must become pharmacists, for example, to understand the bewildering array of legal and illegal performance-enhancement drugs. They must add the police beat to their repertoire as a significant number of college and pro athletes run astray of the law. Joanne Gerstner, a sports reporter for the Detroit News, noted, "Sports writing is a lot more than a home run or a slam dunk. I have to be able to decipher contracts. I have to be able to describe a knee injury."[7]

Sports writers must also be prepared to follow their sport into whatever bizarre territory it takes them. On one windy morning, for example, a college rowing team needed rescue after wind-whipped waves started to swamp their boat. The reporter soon found himself at the edge of a lake examining what was left of a racing shell.[8] But just because sports writing has evolved to include new electronic-based media and a wider field of play does not mean that the essential standards have changed. The age-old principles of good journalism — accuracy and objectivity — still hold.

Any moment in a basketball game can be the one that changes momentum.
© Nebraska Wesleyan Sports Information.

Irrational Pastimes

Most people acknowledge that America is a nation of sports nuts. Sports, too, get nuttier and nuttier. From motorcycle racing on ice to rattlesnake rodeos, fans turn out each weekend for the next dubious sport. Battle of the Monster Trucks, anyone? John Cherwa, associate sports editor at the Los Angeles Times, explains: "Trash sports, that's our official name for them. Because they're not traditional and, in many cases, they're not real. Supposedly, in Atlanta, they have a thing called cat chasing. They throw a cat out of an airplane and then different parachutists try to chase and catch the cat. I don't know if it's true, but I've heard of it."[9]

The Olympic Games may represent the ultimate slate of what people consider sports, a collection that itself seems to change with each new set of games. Flag football, for example, will make its Olympic debut in Los Angeles in 2028, along with the reappearance of squash (last contested in the Olympics in 1900) and lacrosse (1908).[10] Not all these activities actually involve sweating. "Poker players used to be guys avoiding their wives," comments author Michael Lewis. "Now, apparently, they are professional athletes."

And yet sports are one thing that gets Americans fired up. Sure, some Americans like C-SPAN, but their numbers are overwhelmed by ESPN addicts. As Lewis writes, "For every little boy or girl who wants to grow up to be a member of Congress there are, oh, about one million who intend to become major league baseball players or professional basketball players or ice skaters or gymnasts."[11]

For this chapter, we'll turn our focus to the main event: the sports contest itself. For all the hoopla, color and spectacle, the sports writer's first obligation is to get out to the ballpark, to report, in other words, on the game. The three major types of game stories include the advance, the recap (or gamer) and the postgame analysis. Sometimes these stories may be composed days apart, but in the harried life of an electronic sports journalist, they may all be due within a 24-hour cycle.

ADVANCE STORIES

A preview of an upcoming game that compares teams and players, discusses team records and gives lineups is known as an advance. The advance story requires diligence, but the deadline pressure is light. Athletes will tell you that games are won or lost in practice. Sports writers say the same thing — the key work is doing research before a game. The reporter tries to find out all they can about the teams, the coaches and the issues. "Background is the one time when I don't have to worry about asking the right question," sports writer Steve Sipple explains. "It's the one time when I'm able to relax and have fun while I familiarize myself with an athlete or an issue."[12]

Prepare, Prepare, Prepare

How can you prepare to write an advance? In this respect, sports writing is similar to news writing. "You're looking for documents," explains Michael Wilbon, sports columnist for the Washington Post and cohost of the talk show "Pardon the Interruption." "You're looking for anecdotes. You're looking for good quotes. You're looking for something the competitor doesn't have."[13]

First, read all the relevant information you can from local sources, including your rival school's sports website. In so doing you might discover possible angles you can use. What happened in last year's game? What's the history between the two schools? Second, get to know the team's vital statistics. This knowledge will not only give you insights into how the game might play out (i.e., one team often gets a fast start) but also give you something to talk about during interviews.

Finally, get to know the people you'll be covering. Go to practices and remain afterward to speak with players, coaches and trainers. Try to establish a good working relationship with them. Once these people feel comfortable coming to you with their story ideas, they should also be confident that you will represent their comments fairly and accurately.

It's crucial that you prepare well for interviews. Athletes and coaches are often too ready, willing and able to respond to generic questions with pat answers. How often have you heard a coach say, "It was a really big win for us" or "We are playing the games one at a time"? This information is of little use to you or your readers. Be prepared to ask as many specific questions as needed until you get the information for a genuine story, one with something new or insightful. Look for trends. If you're observant, before long you will spot changes you can develop into thoughtful, well-informed questions.

Pregame Tips

Mark Derowitsch, a sports writer for the Lincoln Journal Star, once quipped, "You could train a chimpanzee to write an advance." Indeed, professional sports writers sometimes seem to be monkeying around when their previews of upcoming games are painfully predictable. The lazy sports writer merely notes the time and place of the game, mixes in a few statistics and adds a quotation from each coach. This formula produces the same stale story week in and week out.

Don't let your advances serve as sedatives for your readers. In fact, make them have exactly the opposite effect. Think about the anticipation your audience shares for the contest ahead. Typically, the next game is the most talked-about topic on campus — among the players, the general student body and even the faculty.

How can you add flavor to your advances? Find an angle that your readers might not know. For instance, Kelaine Conochan, a freelance writer for ESPN the Magazine and Runner's World, offered a portrait of her mother's toughness in a first-person account of running the Badwater 135, known as one of the most challenging races in the world:

> "No wimpy women in this house." A catchphrase, a vibe, a lifestyle that my mom bestowed upon my sister and me while growing up. She'd say that, flexing her biceps after accomplishing some feat of strength that ordinary moms wouldn't dare, like dragging thousands of pounds of wet carpet up the basement steps and onto the front lawn to dry after an unfortunate storm. My mom was not waiting around for anyone's assistance. In fact, she probably found your offer patronizing. She'll do it herself.[14]

Each advance you write should include something fresh, something new. Put simply, try to spice up your advances to keep them from sounding the same. Of course, don't forget to include the basic information. The following are some of the things you might include in an advance:

- The significance of the matchup. Will this game decide who goes to the playoffs? Will one team finally win its first game? Is either team ranked?
- Who are the coaches? What are their records?
- Key players, key statistics, injuries and starting lineups.
- The series history (i.e., "This will be the 10th meeting between these programs," what was last year's score?).
- Where to find live video, stats and social media.

Don't overlook advances for sports besides football, basketball and baseball. The tennis, golf and wrestling teams might not attract the same crowds that the big-ticket teams do, but they are putting forth as much effort — and often have as much at stake — as the teams that are more visible. They can also attract large crowds; at Iowa and Oklahoma, wrestling teams fill large arenas even for dual meets. Moving indoor sports outdoors helped the University of Iowa set a women's basketball attendance record at 55,646, and the University of Nebraska set a women's volleyball record at 92,003. Both games were played in 2023 in football stadiums.

Make sure to balance your reporting on men's and women's teams. More women sports journalists have entered the field, and their voices are helping to change the sports landscape. The popularity of U.S. women's soccer, for example, led to a historic collective bargaining agreement in 2022 that stipulates equal pay for men's and women's teams in FIFA World Cup competition. That is a sign of just how much your audience cares, so be sure to cover these events as diligently as men's sports.

■

SOFTBALL ISN'T BASEBALL WITH CURLS

Softball is not just baseball played with a bigger ball. Tennis isn't out-door ping-pong. Volleyball and beach volleyball? Two different sports. Sometimes knowing the subtle differences between sports is crucial to covering them effectively.

Take softball. Obviously, the ball is much larger than a baseball and, as a result, the field dimensions are significantly different. The outfield fences are not as distant since a larger ball does not carry as far, and the bases are 60 feet apart, 30 feet closer than on a baseball field.

The game is also played much more quickly than a typical three-hour major league baseball game. Softball games go seven innings, two fewer than professional baseball, and the game moves at a faster pace. Pitchers do not spend much time worrying about runners, who cannot leave a base until the ball leaves the pitcher's hand. So they just concentrate on batters.

"We don't always rely on the three-run homer like many baseball teams," said Kelley Green, then softball coach at Lock Haven University. "You will have more sacrifice bunts in softball than baseball to move run-ners into scoring position."

Pitching is also vastly different. In baseball, teams require a rotation of four to five pitchers as starters, who need several days for recovery time. Baseball pitchers rarely go beyond 100 pitches in a single game. In soft-ball, pitchers often pitch on consecutive days, if needed. The underhanded motion does not put as much strain on the shoulders and arms, but the windmill delivery results in pitches that are just as fast.

As with anything, you need to fully understand a sport before you can properly cover it. Read the NCAA's rulebook. Watch some practices and speak to coaches and players for background information. Obviously, the more you cover games, the more you will learn.[15]

GAME SUMMARY

As a sports writer, you often have the best seat in the house. You might be on press row (usually at courtside), in the press box (high above the crowd) or on the sidelines. Your job depends on your ability to see all the action with minimal distractions. Your goal is to write a game summary or recap of what happened. Part of that job will take you deep inside the game.

Lee Barfknect, a football and basketball beat writer for the Omaha World-Herald, describes his duties this way: "My job is to take fans where they normally can't go — the sidelines, the field and the locker rooms. And I have the opportunity to interview the athletes and coaches they don't get a chance to talk to. You have to know how to use the amount of access that you're given."

With great access, though, comes great responsibility. Fans depend on you to provide insight into the bad news (the cause of the crucial fumble or why the star volleyball player was benched) as well as the good (a wind-aided home run). Most likely, if you're curious about something, your readers will be, too. Almost anything that grabs fans' attention at a game deserves at least a brief description or explanation in your story.

The key plays may call for more elaboration. How, then, should you decide which plays are crucial? The first step is taking detailed game notes that highlight the momentum swings and key performances. It may seem a bit old-fashioned to "keep the book," but keeping careful notes forces the reporter to pay close attention. For example, look for moments when a basketball team goes on a 10-2 run or when a tennis player wins 12 straight points. Then, decide how to fit this into the context of the entire game. Prepare to ask pointed questions about those key moments.

Writers must stay alert for a run of points in a tennis match.
© Nebraska Wesleyan Sports Information.

When the game ends, a writer on deadline needs to get good quotations quickly. To get these quotes, the writer must ask tough questions — especially after a tough loss. In fact, a coach or player may not like many of the questions that he gets, but don't be afraid to do your job. Sometimes you won't get an answer. Sometimes you'll get an angry response. Generally, though, if a question is legitimate, coaches and players will be willing to cooperate.

A Front-Row Seat, but Keep Your Yap Shut

A press pass gets you into the inner sanctum, the holy of holies — the press box. Usually situated high above the stadium, the press box affords a great vantage point and munchies galore. Sounds like a fan's dream, right? Wrong. "Sports writers don't root for teams; they root for stories — the more unusual, compelling and head-scratching the better," explains Omaha World-Herald writer Lee Barfknecht.

Sports writers can certainly be emotional in the press box, but it's not the place for shouts of glee or heart-rending moans. Working in this venue leaves reporters with only one option: be professional. Cheering for one team or another is a sure way to find yourself getting tossed out of the press box, probably on the widest part of your anatomy. If you cheer, your copy might also be one-dimensional. So remember: the press box is only for the cheering-impaired.

Objectivity?

But a sports writer doesn't have to be completely neutral either. Don't readers expect the local writers to be rooting for the home team? An Omaha writer describing his team's game put it like this: "Bright spots abound with a little squinting." Sports reporters try to be objective, but they also stress what the players on their team did or didn't do. Depending on where you're sitting, in other words, two accounts of the same contest might seem as if each reporter was watching a different game. Writers should try to be as evenhanded as possible even if they focus on one team or the other.

Like all the rest of us, perhaps, sports writers can't help but feel sympathetic toward the underdog. Many of the best sports stories pit David against Goliath, with the writer pulling for David and his slingshot. Here is a story from the 2022 World Cup when one of the tournament favorites and a former champ, Spain, faced one of its former colonies, Morocco.

> AL-RAYYAN, Qatar — For two hours, the noise had been building. It had started out at incessant and gone from there, passing by ear-splitting and head-spinning until it leveled out at somewhere beyond deafening. The constant, percussive roar seemed to emanate not so much from the tens of thousands of Morocco fans inside the Education City Stadium on Tuesday, but from the concrete and steel itself.

Achraf Hakimi walked into that wall of sound, his head bowed, as though all of the noise and all of the tension was bearing down upon him. He would take the penalty shot that could not only end Spain's stay in Qatar, eliminating one of the tournament favorites, but that could take Morocco to its first World Cup quarterfinal.

The noise rose another octave. The pressure dropped another bar. And then Hakimi — who was born in Spain, raised in Spain and might have played for Spain — stepped forward and, with a slight, deft touch of the ball, nothing more than a brush of silk, gently stroked his penalty past Unai Simón, a moment of utmost calm before unbridled chaos descended.[16]

Sports Jargon

Good sports writing depends on the same reporting and writing techniques as any other area of the news. But, in addition to following basic style rules, sports writers must also deal with the unique terminology of each sport. If you've ever been thrown a curve, pulled a punch or played the field, you can chalk it up to the world of sports. In baseball, for example, the writer is expected to use sport-specific terms such as "bullpen," "ground-rule double," "walk-off," "pitchout," "pickle," "rundown" and "sacrifice." In volleyball, fans expect to see "dink," "kill" and "overhand pass." As odd as it sounds, a "klaxon" is the device that makes the warning sound at a basketball game.

On the other hand, beginning sports writers too often rely on clichés. Clichés are trite, overused words or expressions. When you write "split the uprights" or describe a close game as a "barn burner," "squeaker" or "nail-biter," you are merely echoing other worn-out writing. Avoiding clichés will help your stories stay fresh and lively.

Highlights and Heroics

Dick Enberg, a sports commentator for NBC, once said that "The beauty of all sports is how grown adults can act like little kids." Indeed, sports can bring out the same emotions in 30-year-old professional baseball players as they do in 8-year-old Little Leaguers. Sports writing is about reporting those emotions.

Whether it's a blowout or a close game, every sports event produces at least one prevailing emotion. Capture that emotion and make it the theme of your story. Support it with descriptions and quotations. You'll rarely find a sporting event that doesn't produce some sort of drama you can write about. In addressing that issue, Daryl Moen, a journalism professor at the University of Missouri, tells his students the story of a blind newspaper publisher. The publisher would ask reporters to come into his office and tell him about their stories. Often, they would just tell him the facts — the who, what, where, when, how and why of the story. Patiently, the publisher would ask about the emotions that were evident on the faces of the people. He'd leave each reporter with one piece of advice: "Make me see. Make me see your story."[17]

But don't just make your readers see. Make them hear the crack of the bat, the rip of the basketball net and the roar of the crowd. Make them smell the locker room after two-a-day practices. Make them feel the volleyball slam against the floor. Make them taste the bitterness of defeat. In other words, use all your senses — sight, sound, touch, smell and even taste.

An unfortunately gruesome accident gave Lincoln Journal Star reporter Ken Hambleton a chance to test his descriptive powers. Hambleton was covering an arm wrestling match during the Nebraska State Games, a sort of amateur Summer Olympics. "This has proven to be one of the most interesting things I've done," he said in an understatement, as we will see in his story about the contest:

> Two well-matched guys, both rookies, were first up.
>
> After grunting, straining and pushing for more than three minutes, one guy's arm broke. Snapped. The loud crack. The blood. The bone sticking through the skin.
>
> The injured guy was too shocked to move. The other competitor got sick. Many in the room ran in panic.
>
> I remembered my first aid training and helped the guy until the paramedics arrived. I got a pretty good interview, too. The injured guy said he'd try again next year — left-handed.

One way to tap all your senses is to draw on specific details to evoke a scene. Sports Illustrated writer Rick Reilly employed this approach in describing a memorable golf shot. At the Augusta National golf course, any ball that lands on the bank in front of the iconic 12th green inevitably rolls back into Rae's Creek. Reilly put it like this: "A ball has about as much chance of stopping on that bank as a marble does of stopping halfway down a drainpipe." On one occasion, however, the ball didn't fall into the creek and somehow, miraculously, stayed dry. Take a look at Reilly's description of that moment (the player, Fred Couples, by the way, went on to win the tournament). Note how he imagines all the possible ways that the laws of physics might be suspended. Those reasons — explained through concrete details — make the writing unforgettable.

> One less drop of rain. One more run of the mower. A cup less of fertilizer last fall. One more breath from a nearby butterfly. A blade of grass with weak knees. An eyelash less luck. Any of these things could have cost Fred Couples the Masters. But somehow, some way, Couples' golf ball hugged the steep slope at Augusta National's 12th hole, clung to it the way a sock clings to a towel fresh out of a hot dryer. The ball steadfastly refused to fall into the water.[18]

If Reilly can make a golf shot, of all things, come alive, just think how dramatic you can make your stories.

How Big Is Big?

Another way writers can use description is to suggest the scale of what some team or individual has accomplished. For example, Linda Robertson of the Miami Herald wanted to give readers a sense of the size of pro football players, so she found a few familiar analogies: "Like American houses, Hummers, and hamburgers, football players are a reflection of the bigness of our society." In 2023, for example, the average weight of an offensive tackle in the NFL was 317 pounds. Quarterbacks have gone from an average of 175 pounds in 1920 to 223 pounds today.

But don't overdo it. Make sure you support your descriptions with facts. For example, writing that the volleyball players were "down in the dumps" is questionable; unless you're a volleyball player, you don't know how they feel. Instead, ask the players about their disappointment. Describe their distraught faces and the tears streaming down their cheeks, but then support the emotion with revealing quotes.

COVERING PROFESSIONAL EVENTS

Imagine you're a college reporter who has covered a few events on campus. Usually, you wear jeans and a T-shirt, blending in with the other students. Suddenly, you receive an unusual assignment: cover the U.S. Open. You're scared to death. How do you act? What do you wear? As one college sports reporter put it, "I guess my biggest fear is when I go to pick up my media credentials, they'll figure out I'm not a pro yet."

In the case of the country's largest golf event, a writer would probably head for the USGA's Media Center, an aircraft-carrier-size collection of tents. One tent contains the cable-connected desks of 350 journalists who never need to leave the tent to cover the tournament. In fact, they'll probably see more of it if they don't. That's because their desks face a scoreboard 100 feet wide that presents the hole-by-hole progress of each player. On either side of the scoreboard are two smaller TV screens where the writers can follow the action. Does all this work make you hungry? No problem. In one of the tents, you'll find a dining area with a dozen TV screens so you won't miss a minute of the action.

After players finish their rounds, some agree to do a short press conference called a "flash interview," which takes place just outside the locker room. If a golfer has an unusually notable round, he might be invited to a more formal news conference in the Media Center. But what if you miss a key interview because you're finishing your peanut butter, pickle and olive sandwich? No worries. A stenographer takes notes at

A cheese pimento sandwich at the Augusta National Golf Club.
© UPI / Alamy

each interview, and with breathtaking speed, transcripts of the interviews will have been typed, stapled and placed in wall racks where you can pick them up.

Observe the other professional journalists as they work. In most situations, you'll find journalists swarming around the players after their rounds. Feel free to do the same. You are allowed to record comments made to other journalists, but don't interrupt if a reporter and player are clearly off to the side in a more private setting. You can stand nearby and wait your turn to jump in with some questions.

You should try, however, to seek out angles no one else has found. Before the round begins, select two or three golfers to follow — at least for a few holes — so you can get details that won't be visible to the writers all watching the leaders. Make sure you get out on the course to capture that firsthand flavor (and try those pimento cheese sandwiches).

POSTGAME ANALYSIS

Once the dust has settled and the game recap has been completed, the sports writer has a chance to, as Wordsworth might say, reflect in tranquility, or in other words, analyze what the heck just happened. An analysis is the third kind of game story reporters typically write and one that features opportunities for the most writerly kind of prose.

NO SHIRT, NO SERVICE

That pile of dirty laundry next to the player's bench at the U.S. Open Tennis Tournament is a good indication of how deep into the match the players have reached. If the pile is stacked as high as 20 dirty shirts, we must be in the final set.

The owner of that pile is probably Frances Tiafoe, an up-and-coming American tennis star who insists on wearing a clean shirt for every possible point. "You want to be as light as you can on the court," Tiafoe said after a second-round victory, adding that if he feels even a small amount of moisture on his shirt, he'll change it. "I'm very adamant about that."

Whether Tiafoe's decision to be a quick-change artist is strategic or superstitious is in the eye of the beholder. Many athletes have quirks. Baseball players hop over foul lines to avoid bad luck. Rafael Nadal, the multi-Grand Slam champion, insists on having two water bottles by his bench, carefully positioned diagonally from each other with the logos facing the court.

Many players change into a clean shirt a few times each match. But Tiafoe has taken freshening up to an elite level. If he feels uncomfortable, he wants a fresh top. "I don't want to feel like I'm playing with really sweaty clothes just because I'm not prepared," Tiafoe said. "I know how much I can sweat."

Players are allowed to change tops from their benches during a match. Men may leave the court for a complete outfit change twice in a best-of-five match, and women are allowed one change of attire in a best-of-three match. "Shirts, socks and shoes should be changed on court," the International Tennis Federation rule book says.

At the 2023 U.S. Open, Tiafoe wore a teal, sleeveless top patterned with shades of baby blue, coral, peach and maroon. He completed his ensemble with teal shorts and a pair of bright red shoes with his nickname, Big Foe, across the heels. He said he packs two extra pairs of shoes in case a pair becomes too sweaty.[19]

Roger Angell, baseball correspondent for the New Yorker, often filed stories months, if not years, after the events had taken place. He was going for something besides who won and lost:

> When I began writing sports pieces, it was clear to me that the doings of big-league baseball — the daily happenings on the field, the managerial strategies, the celebration of heroes, the medical and financial bulletins, the clubhouse gossip — were so enormously reported that I would have to find some other aspect of the game to study. I decided to sit in the stands — for a while at least — and watch the baseball from there. I wanted to concentrate not just on the events down on the field but on their reception. I wanted to pick up the feel of the game as it happened to the people around me.[20]

A sports analyst writes for true aficionados, fans who don't need to have every reference explained. But those fans do appreciate a sense of perspective, something writers can offer through their experience and the use of appropriate context. They might compare, for example, current performances with those of the past. So Angell tries to find a way to measure one pitcher's great year: "Many observers believe that Bob Gibson's 1.12 earned-run average in 1968 is one of the Everests of the game."[21] Comparing a pitcher's achievement to climbing Mount Everest gives vivid testimony to the scale of his accomplishment.

Sports writers love adjectives, and an analysis piece is just the place to use them. Many invent hyphenated modifiers such as "pennant-winning," "ear-wrenching" and "one-base-at-a-time." Writers can also indulge their taste for humorous exaggeration. The artificial turf of a football field might have the "consistency of an immense door-mat," while a normally gruff manager might turn from a "grizzly bear to Gepetto."

Analysis pieces open the spigot on the full range of punctuation from dashes to italics and parentheses, not to mention the occasional sentence fragment. Sentence structures become exceedingly flexible. Take the following passage, for example, from a description of a Detroit Lions exhibition game by writer George Plimpton. Plimpton was allowed to play quarterback for five snaps, and he steadily moved his team backward toward its own end zone. On his final play, he pitched the ball to a halfback who was tackled on the one-yard line. After the play, as Plimpton trudged wearily toward the bench, he noticed that the fans started to applaud. At first, he couldn't believe the people in the stands were clapping for him and then he began to understand:

> I thought about the applause afterward. Some of it was, perhaps, in appreciation of the lunacy of my participation and for the fortitude it took to do it; but most of it, even if subconscious, I decided was in relief that I had done as badly as I had: it

verified the assumption that the average fan would have about an amateur blundering into the brutal world of professional football. He would get slaughtered.[22]

Plimpton's description probes deeply into the psychology of the game — the certainty fans have, for instance, that what they see players do is impossibly hard.

Finally, analyzing a game, season or player gives the writer a chance for sheer exuberance. Why not, for example, stretch a metaphor throughout an entire paragraph as Roger Angell does here:

> Steve Garvey always seems to be standing at attention in the batter's box. As he waits for the pitch, his back is straight and his bat shows not a tremor of anxiety or anticipation. His feet are apart, of course, but perfectly parallel with the back line of the box. When he swings, his head snaps down, as if he were checking the shine on his tunic buttons. What he is doing, of course, is watching the ball — really watching the ball. He swings exactly the same way at every pitch: perfect swings. Last year, he batted .304, which is exactly his lifetime average in eleven seasons with the Dodgers. Garvey is a soldier of hitting.[23]

Long before the reader reaches the punch line, he knows he is being carefully set up. The physical description of Garvey, as if he were in a military inspection, the repetition of "perfectly" and "exactly," and the listing of his hitting statistics all suggest a machine-like consistency. Garvey isn't a player; he is a soldier.

Other metaphors are useful when describing the techniques of each game — throwing, catching and hitting, for example — skills that are simple to the point of banality and yet breathtakingly complex (physicists have yet to fully explain how a curveball works). A split-finger fastball, for example, could be described as "baseball's Rubik's Cube"; fielders must deal with "bazooka shots that are lined past them or at them" or cope with a sneaky bunt, "baseball's shiv in the ribs."

Settling back with one of these analyses, the reader feels the arm of a favorite uncle wrap itself around their shoulder and senses the joy of yet another trip out to the old ballpark.

UPON FURTHER REVIEW

1. Describe the key elements in writing an advance story about a game.
2. What are the biggest challenges for a sports journalist in covering a game in person?
3. Can a sports writer take sides? Why or why not?

NOTES

1. Juliet Macur, "Back from the Edge, U.S. Tries to Focus on What Comes Next," *New York Times*, Aug. 1, 2023.

2. La Velle E. Neal III, "Twin Cities Soccer Fans Fill up World Cup Watch Parties," *Minneapolis Star Tribune*, Nov. 21, 2022.

3. El Presidente (Dave Portnoy), "History at Shinnecock — El Pres US Open Unlimited Mulligan Challenge," *Barstool Sports*, June 14, 2018, https://www.barstoolsports.com/video/1010031/history-at-shinnecock-el-pres-us-open-unlimited-mulligan-challenge.

4. See the Royals Review website, www.royalsreview.com, for similar comments.

5. The blog can be found at www.arrowheadpride.com.

6. David Dunkley Gyimah created ViewMagazine.tv to illustrate how one person could create online broadcasts. This quote appears in "InsideSolojos: Videojournalism" on his website, www.mrdot.co.uk/videojournalism_today.html.

7. This quote appears in Ed Finkel, "Getting into the Game," *Medill*, Summer 2004.

8. The college rowing team's mishap was recounted by Algis J. Laukaitis in the *Lincoln Journal Star*, April 16, 2007.

9. Cherwa is quoted in *Funny Times*, an American humor newspaper (http://funnytimes.com/).

10. "Flag Football, Cricket among Sports Poised to Join L.A. 2028 Olympic Program," *Athletic*, Oct. 9, 2023.

11. The quotes from Lewis appear in his introduction to *The Best American Sports Writing 2006* (Boston: Houghton Mifflin, 2006).

12. Steve Sipple is a sports writer for the *Lincoln Journal Star*.

13. Quoted in Finkel, "Getting into the Game."

14. Kelaine Conochan, "Badwater Ultramarathon: What I Lost and Found During 135 Miles of the World's Most Impossible Run," *ESPN the Magazine*, Nov. 26, 2021, reprinted in J.A. Adande, ed., *The Year's Best Sports Writing 2022* (Chicago: Triumph Books, 2022).

15. Many of these thoughts come from Joe Gisondi's blog, OnSportz.Blogspot.com, an excellent place to find information on how to cover virtually every sport.

16. Rory Smith, "Morocco Knocks Spain out of the World Cup on Penalty Kicks," *New York Times*, Dec. 6, 2022.

17. Daryl Moen says that "the goal of all writers is to make readers see and smell and feel and taste and hear." Find more tips on his website at web.missouri.edu/~moend/writing/index.htm.

18. Reilly's article on the Masters, "Bank shot," appeared in *Sports Illustrated* (April 20, 1992).

19. Jesus Jimenez, "No Sweat. Frances Tiafoe Would Like a Fresh Shirt Now," *New York Times*, Sept. 4, 2023.

20. Angell's description can be found in the foreword to his collection of baseball pieces, *The Summer Game* (Lincoln: University of Nebraska Press, 2004).

21. Roger Angell, "Distance," *New Yorker* (Sept. 22, 1980).

22. This description comes from George Plimpton's book *Paper Lion* (New York: Harper & Row, 1966).

23. Angell's account of Steve Garvey appears in the *New Yorker*, May 4, 1981.

5

Asking the Questions

Journalists exist to ask questions, the central function of their profession. Much of the time, they ask those questions during an interview, a conversation at the heart of just about every story. When you interview someone, you're acting as a proxy for readers who would themselves like to sit down and chat with this man or woman. Your task is to ask the questions those readers would like to know. This ability to anticipate what readers or listeners want is part of what makes an interview successful.

INTERVIEWING AS A CONTACT SPORT

An interview is a seemingly casual but directed conversation that opens locked doors, organizes scattered memories and penetrates private chambers. The craft is both art and science. Being a reporter gives you a license to be nosy, but remember that subjects are doing you a favor by talking to you. Reporters work at the mercy of their sources. Think of yourself perhaps as a hair stylist or bartender — someone with great listening skills and plenty of patience.

Keep in mind that while many public figures enjoy being interviewed, some don't. The toughest people to speak with are probably certifiable stars who guard their privacy. But even then, there are ways. One reporter happened to run a limousine business on the side. He got the job of transporting Bruce Springsteen's entourage to the venue, picking them up later and taking them wherever they wanted to go. He eventually spent several hours with Springsteen himself, having fascinating conversations en route to one place or another. If you really want to talk with a famous person, and have a legitimate reason for doing so, there's almost always a way.

Let's divide the challenge of mastering this task into three parts: what to do before the interview, what to do during the interview and what to do after the interview.

BEFORE THE INTERVIEW

Preparing for an interview is a critical and strategic process. Choose an interesting topic and ask yourself whom to interview. Who can add life to the story? Who is the person closest to the topic you're really interested in?

Tips and Techniques

- *Pick a good time and place.* Most interviews are arranged in advance — ideally, at least 24 hours. The people being interviewed will appreciate knowing the topic ahead of time, mostly because it gives them an opportunity to prepare. Occasionally you may want to offer your subject a few questions in advance to get them thinking about the topic you want to explore. A star athlete, for example, might be happy to talk about her quest for a school record but not be willing to discuss a close friend's death. If that means your interview request might be denied, it's better to know sooner than later.

  The best setting is someplace where you won't be disturbed, where you can have your subject's undivided attention. Many people like to be interviewed where they do their activity — at the practice field, for example. That's good for them, but it might create problems for you. Other players or coaches might stop by to chat, and your subject can be easily distracted. Getting your person off somewhere private can do your interview a world of good.

- *Ask your subject for half an hour.* You can probably get a good interview in less time than that, but you run the risk of not getting the information you need. Also, by asking for half an hour, you tell your subject that you have a number of questions to ask, that you are anticipating substantial answers and that you feel the subject has some valuable and worthwhile comments. Of course, sometimes your subject may be so busy that only a few minutes will be available, or perhaps there will be only time for one question, as in a busy press conference, but those are special cases.

- *Do your homework.* Don't waste your source's time. If you have only 15 minutes with the newly hired assistant coach, do not spend the first 10 minutes asking basic background information that, in most cases, you could have found on your own. Instead of asking, for example, "Where was your previous job?" ask, "When you coached at Central, how did you manage the substitution rotation?" Not only are you asking an insightful question, you're also showing the coach that you care enough to do some work. Sources notice. Don't pick up a phone or knock on a door before you have researched your subject.

- *Don't make a script, but pre-think the interview.* Jot down a few questions in advance. This can help clarify the purpose of your interview. Your success will depend in large part on the quality of your questions. The main thing is to think out your questions carefully. This will help make each minute count, and it's also your best chance to steer the interview in the direction you want it to go.

Wrestling is one of the less well-known sports that may require some educational investment by the reporter.
© Nebraska Wesleyan Sports Information.

Many experienced sports reporters say they can think of questions on the fly, especially for general, day-to-day interviews. But there will occasionally be an exclusive, sit-down interview with a hard-to-reach athletic director or perhaps a famous athlete visiting the area. Writing specific, prepared questions becomes more important in those situations.

Recording the Interview

Take your digital recorder along, but use a notepad, too. Recording devices allow you to pay more attention to the person and be more personable yourself. They are also more accurate and offer proof for a quote. But batteries can die, or a recording can be lost. Use the recorder as a supplement to your notes, not as a substitute.

Another problem with recorders is that they don't make your job any easier. You still have to make a transcript of the recording to see what you have, and that is a time-consuming and tedious process. Many reporters find that taking notes during an interview is a natural editing process. It forces them to think about the story as they go and take down only the essential information.

Display your notebook as if it were a fishing license. It shows that you're prepared, and it encourages talking. When someone sees you actually writing down what they are saying, it's a real ego boost. Try not writing anything and see how their behavior changes. By the way, not many reporters know shorthand, but they all have their own shortcuts. Some omit vowels and endings. Most use abbreviations. Whatever system you use or devise on your own isn't important; what matters is that you can talk, think and take notes all at the same time.

PUTTING THE PAST IN THE PRESENT

How can you manage a story when one key element lies many years in the past? That was the problem Graham Hill of CNN faced when he wrote a story about a remarkable surfer who recovered from a horrific shark attack. In 2016 Hawaiian surfer Bethany Hamilton finished third in the Fiji Women's Pro competition, beating the six-time champ and world no. 1 Stephanie Gilmore. Thirteen years earlier, Hamilton had lost her arm in a shark attack in Kauai.

In 2003, when Hamilton was 13 years old, she was badly bitten by a shark while surfing. She lost nearly two-thirds of her blood, putting her life and any kind of athletic future in serious doubt. But miraculously, she recovered and just 26 days after the attack was back on her board. Two years later, she was a national champion.

"When tough times come my way," she said, "I definitely rely on my faith in God and just say 'hey God' I don't know why I lost my arm but I'm going to trust you and know that good can come from this situation."

Getting back in the water was a memory the reporter needed. So he asked Hamilton to recall her thinking: "I guess my passion for surfing out-weighed my fear of sharks, and I was just waiting until the doctor gave me the OK to get in the ocean." The occasion for this new story on Hamilton was the debut of a documentary film, "Bethany Hamilton: Unstoppable." The film shows her remarkable journey, including her surfing with one arm and raising her two young sons. Keen to encourage others to "live an unstoppable life," she says she feels "privileged to be a role model."[1]

DURING THE INTERVIEW

Now it's time to get on with business. The most important thing to do while conducting an interview is actually the simplest: listen well. Good listening improves your accuracy and your attention. It is also a great encouragement to the person you're listening to. He or she is much more likely to say something quotable if it's clear that you are listening intently. By the way, maintain a polite but professional distance.

At the Beginning

- Identify yourself and state your reasons for the interview. Be sure your sources know they're on the record.
- To build rapport, ask a few brief questions that the subject can easily answer. Show some interest and enthusiasm to help the subject warm up to you. Don't be a phony, of course, but find something that genuinely interests you in what the person is saying.
- Empathize. Try to see the interviewee's side. Be sympathetic, but don't join their side. Don't argue either, just press for logic.
- Provide a forewarning if yours is going to be a tough interview. Say something to the effect that, "Look, I have some tough questions to ask, but I think it would be unfair to write a story without asking you to speak to these questions."

LET'S GIVE LOSERS THEIR DUE

As fans, we all know the victors in sports are going to get their due. The world's greatest athletes stretch and bend the limits of human potential. No wonder we watch them with awe. Sports writers naturally gravitate to winners, but feature writers often head somewhere else, knowing that there's glory, too, in defeat. Losers make athletes more relatable to the rest of us.

Tennis player Wang Xinyu of China, for example, thought she could win a game. Surely, she could put four points together before her opponent did, but such was not the case. Xinyu lost 6-0, 6-0 in the 2023 French Open, a dreaded double bagel in tennis terms. Xinyu's opponent, by the way, was no slouch. She was Iga Swiatek, the event's defending champion and top seed. But perhaps there's honor in the journey, not the destination.

Think about the basketball player who tosses an air ball in a crucial situation or the goaltender in hockey who slips and lets the winning shot whiz by. Let's give a cheer for nerves that wilt under pressure, for reflexes that aren't what they used to be. Those who lose in so many different ways occupy the more relatable corner of big-time sports. There's comfort in knowing that finely tuned athletes can tire, cramp, succumb to pressure and suffer stinging defeat. So we take solace in the legendary struggles of the Chicago Cubs and, of course, Mighty Casey's Mudville Nine. And losing provides a gold mine of opportunity for sports features.[2]

After You've Broken the Ice

- Let your personality shine through. Don't be a blank wall. It helps sometimes to tell people about yourself.
- Strive to find the seeds for the next question in each answer. By carefully drawing on what the person has already said, you can lead them smoothly toward the next question.
- The order of your questions matters. As a rule, ask questions in reverse order of importance. That way you and your subject have begun to trust each other before the going gets tough.
- Be sure to ask tough questions in the same tone as your other questions; don't broadcast that the "bomb" is coming, and don't react when you hear something big. The subject will freeze up if he thinks he said something he shouldn't have.
- Use slow motion. When people reach the important part of the interview, slow down so you don't miss an important detail.

The intense emotion generated by sports is one of the aspects that creates so much fan appeal.
© Nebraska Wesleyan Sports Information.

- Don't interrupt. When the person finishes speaking, don't jump straight into your next question. Pause in case they have something more to add. Sometimes people hesitate before they say something especially important. Remembering takes time.
- Use silence to your advantage. If you sense that the subject is reluctant to talk, simply be quiet. We all hate to sit next to someone and be still (you may have had that experience on a date). Let your subject break the silence.
- Beware of the person who is "overinterviewed." Sports administrators, for example, might be easily accessible, but they might also be selling instead of telling a story.
- Don't hesitate to ask the source to repeat, slow down or clarify. Ask, "Did I get that right? Is there more?"
- If the subject resists answering a question, try to show some way the interview can work to the person's advantage (i.e., "Don't you want your side told for a change?").
- Be prepared to move away from your list of questions when necessary. Your subject may say something far more interesting and valuable than you expected — if so, follow it.
- Be polite. No matter how rude someone may be to you, keep your cool. You never know when you will need to interview him or her later for another story.
- Be an active listener. Encourage the subject by gesturing or nodding and by repeating some of their words back to them. Without being obnoxious, mirror their body language to encourage connection.
- When a source rambles, gently prod them back on track. At the same time, don't mentally leave your own interview — stay focused.
- Sometimes people will misunderstand your question or perhaps even ignore it. Don't be afraid to ask the same question again. You can rephrase it or ask it the same way again if you weren't satisfied.

Nearing the End
- Near the end of an interview, ask the person what else he or she might like to say. Give your person one last chance to get their two bits in.
- Before you leave, check any numbers or fuzzy details. Tell the person you may get back in touch if you need to check a fact or discover you left something out. Leave the door open for future interviews.

ASKING THE RIGHT QUESTIONS
The goal of an interview is to get a person to talk about something you think your audience will want to know. That means asking plenty of thoughtful questions. TV and radio host Larry King said that nearly all his best questions begin with "why." Your goal is to craft short questions that produce long answers. You can also think of your list of questions as a safety net when an interview begins to lag. Any question that

elicits a colorful response, an interesting anecdote or useful information is considered productive. Of course, it's hard to tell in advance which question will produce those results.

- Your first question goes a long way toward telling the other person just how serious you are, how much work you've put into it and how much respect you have for them. Make sure that question shows your interest and professionalism. For example, the following question was so good the subject couldn't wait to answer it:

Five games.
Will Bolt gave the answer so quickly that it interrupted the end of the question. How close was Nebraska baseball this spring to what it was supposed to look like?
The Husker coach sat alone at a table underneath Charles Schwab Field in Omaha. NU had just seen its season end with a 4-2 loss to eventual champion Maryland in the Big Ten tournament semifinals.[3]

- Drop a curveball occasionally if the interview is starting to sound less spontaneous.
- Don't be a pushover for the easy answer or the nonanswer. Respond to "No comment" by saying, "You know, I feel bad about putting a 'no comment' in this story since the readers will think you are hiding something. Let's find a way to talk about this. Tell me, for instance . . .'"
- If someone wants to go "off the record," they mean they're willing to keep talking so long as the reporter promises not to repeat or publish the information. Try to resist, at least at first. If a subject insists on talking "on background," take notes anyway. At the end of the interview, pick out a good quote from your notes and say: "Now what about this thing you said here. Why can't you say that on the record?"
- Make your questions brief and to the point. A multipart question such as, "What is your position on the college playoff plan? And how will it affect your school? And what would you personally propose to make the system fairer?" can confuse a subject. Which should he answer first? Give the person you're interviewing a chance to bite off one question at a time.
- Ask lots of follow-ups. Remember that the list of questions you wrote out in advance are merely something to get the interview rolling. Don't be afraid to stray from that path. Any question, for example, might trigger a series of other questions you hadn't planned. Follow-up questions might be needed to clarify a response, encourage the source to expand on a thought or help you seek further information. For example, "You just said your foot has been bothering you. What's wrong with it?" Sometimes a simple follow-up can change the course of an entire interview, and perhaps the angle of your story. When you find an idea that's new or unexpected, follow up with several good questions, questions you may have to manufacture on the spot.

- Use open-ended questions, especially if you're after an opinion or interpretation. This gives the source an opportunity to respond any way he or she chooses. If you ask the coach, for example, "Did your offense have a difficult time adjusting to their zone defense?" and the answer is "Yes," you haven't moved your story very far forward. On the other hand, if you ask, "What difficulties did their zone defense give your offense in the second half?" you might get an insightful answer.

Questions to Avoid

- Avoid yes-no questions because they give people easy outs. They can also lead to unquotable quotes and even stop a conversation in its tracks. If you ask, "Do you deny . . ." or "Will you . . . ," the person may just clam up. Almost any yes-no question, however, can be recrafted to produce a better response. Instead of asking, "Did you see the flagrant foul?" try, "What did you see?"

- Avoid leading questions that put words in people's mouths. For example, "Isn't it true that you once enjoyed Justin Bieber songs?" The question almost coerces the subject into a preconceived answer. Sometimes, leading questions are obvious clues that a sports reporter has already drawn their own conclusion and is merely trying to gather quotations to support his or her point. For example, "Joe, you're probably happy to see a change in coaching staffs, aren't you?" This question is leading Joe toward what the reporter perceives as a positive change. Sure, Joe is free to dispute the question, but he might go along and give the response the reporter wants. Instead, the sports reporter should make the question open-ended: "Joe, what are your thoughts on the change in coaching staffs?" Now Joe is able to respond freely.

- Resist the temptation to make statements in your questions. Statements are usually not questions at all. For example, "Coach, your running game really stalled in the fourth quarter, and your offensive line looked tired." How is a coach supposed to respond? Sometimes, he might elaborate and bail out a reporter. Other times, however, a curmudgeonly coach might respond with, "That's a statement. Next question!"

  OK, so let's rephrase. "Coach, why did your running game produce only four yards in the fourth quarter?" Remember that reporters are not there to tell a coach what went wrong in the game. With this question, the coach still might be a little grumpy, but at least he might give the reporter more than a blank stare.

- Avoid "talk about" questions. A growing trend among sports journalists — and not necessarily a good one — is the "talk about" question, which, of course, isn't really a question at all. This strategy represents a passive-aggressive demand of your source that usually leads to canned answers.

  "Talk about your game-winning basket."
  "Talk about your decision to go for two points in the third quarter."
  "Talk about the electric atmosphere."

Instead of using a fake prompt that gooses your source in hopes that something interesting will pop up, ask genuine questions. You are much more likely to get genuine answers.

Pay Attention and Observe

Sometimes, sports reporters become so focused on asking the right questions that they miss something in front of their nose. Interviewers should always pay attention to nonverbal signs. A roll of the eyes might indicate disgust. A smile might be a sign of sarcasm. A player answering questions while staring at the ground might be distraught. These are all signs of emotion that sports reporters could describe in order to give life to a story.

Observations should not be limited to the interviewee. Look around. The coach's desk might be cluttered with game film and scouting reports. That might help describe the coach's frenzied week in preparing for the big game. Fans might be gathering outside the locker room, waiting for the player you were interviewing to finish and sign autographs.

INTERVIEW SETTINGS

The type of questions sports reporters ask might depend on the interview setting. If the conversation is only between you and your source, you can ask questions in a more conversational tone. News conferences with a large group of reporters usually require more general questions and might limit the number of follow-ups.

Most colleges and high schools conduct postgame interviews in a designated room or area and do not allow reporters into locker rooms. The policy differs in professional sports, where locker rooms are usually open to reporters, men and women. Sometimes reporters might try to corner athletes in a hallway by the locker room, outside the team bus or even underneath the stadium bleachers. The setup is not ideal, especially when the marching band goes by or fans for the opposing team stop to yell obscenities. Be ready to deal with distractions.

One-on-One Interviews

What if the interview is just you and your source? That is the best possible setup for a sports reporter but one that requires the most work and research. You are the only one asking questions, so you better have a good plan. The advantage is the exclusivity: no other reporters are present, so there is always a chance for a breaking news item or scoop, even if the interview was meant for a simple feature.

Many reporters, especially columnists, go to great lengths to interview sources one-on-one. "The harder you work to get a person one-on-one, the better your work is going to turn out, especially when so much of what we do is in the group setting, whether a press conference or scrum," said Austin Meek, a sports columnist for the Register-Guard in Eugene, Ore.

"I think readers can tell when you put in the effort to get something that not everybody else has. If you can get somebody away from the group, I think that comes through in the way they talk, and when you read the quote, people pick up on that."

How do you coax a source off to the side to speak with you alone? It's not always easy, and it's especially difficult for high-profile sources. A high school coach may be much more willing to visit with a reporter than somebody with the popularity and demand of, say, the starting quarterback. "Part of it is having the courage to stop somebody and say, 'Hey, can you talk to me for two minutes?' It doesn't have to be a 30-minute, face-to-face, one-on-one," Meek said.

Reporters hoping to grab a source after a news conference or small group setting are always scouring the territory. Where will the source go after the main interview? Where will he or she walk? Where should the reporter be so as not to have to run after the source in some awkward, obvious way? And don't be offended if the source brushes off your request. It's happened to all reporters at some time or another. "You develop the ability to just shake it off," Meek said.

Small Group and Postgame Interviews

Have you ever seen a television interview where an athlete is standing in front of his locker with a bunch of tape recorders and microphones in his face? Postgame interviews can truly be a mad scramble, and a hectic time for sports reporters on deadline.

For newcomers, postgame interviews that involve a small to medium group of reporters can be intimidating. Squeeze your way into the huddle with your tape recorder or camera. Be assertive but polite. Speak up, and don't let other reporters ask all the questions. In some instances, you might be hopping from player to player, from huddle to huddle, scrum to scrum, trying to gather information from as many sources as possible. The experience can be stressful and, at the same time, exhilarating.

News Conferences

A form of collective interview, the news conference is designed as a way for sources to share information simultaneously with a group of reporters. News conferences are more tightly structured and organized than regular interviews. The source, not the sports reporter, is in control. Most conferences begin with an opening statement from the coach or athlete. Sports reporters will follow with questions. News conferences can last anywhere from five minutes to half an hour or longer, depending on the circumstances. On some occasions, the source will simply appear long enough to make a statement and not take any questions.

Reporters should realize that what they ask in a group setting is fair game for all competing reporters to use. If you ask a question that elicits breaking news, realize that you don't have exclusive rights to what was said. "I think we've all been there, where we've gotten to ask a question that elicited some great response, and you're like, 'Ugh, I wish only I had that,'" Meek said. "But we've also been on the other side, where somebody else asks something that we used. In some ways, we all borrow from each other and depend on each other."

Some tips for dealing with news conferences:

- Arrive ahead of time. News conferences might start early, and it's awkward and a little embarrassing if you are scurrying around the room, finding a place for your tape recorder and searching for a place to sit while the coach is already talking.
- Pay attention. Sometimes those weekly media luncheons with the football coach might be a little boring and make you sleepy (especially after eating the free pizza) but stay alert. Never ask a question that has already been asked.
- Be considerate. Do not dominate the news conference by asking a string of questions. Keep the follow-ups to a minimum. There might be more time to spend with the subject after a news conference, but don't depend on it.

Many times, postgame news conferences are broadcast live via closed-circuit television, with a feed going directly to the press box. This allows sports reporters on a tight deadline to gather a couple of quick quotations before filing their story. The drawback is those reporters are merely listening to questions and answers and not participating. But when a trip to the interview room and back might take too much time on deadline, watching a telecast is a good option.

Role Reversal

Sports reporters sometimes find themselves on the other side of the table. Talk radio hosts, for example, love to pick the brains of the local beat reporter the week before a big game to get inside information, insight and predictions. Sports reporters might ask each other questions about a hotshot recruit on a weekly vidcast or podcast. Fans might even have an opportunity to ask questions of sports reporters on a live internet chat or through X. Sometimes being on the receiving end of questions is good practice for future interviews. And it's kind of fun to be the one saying, "No comment."

AFTER THE INTERVIEW

Write your story as soon as possible after the interview. Your notes will make much more sense to you now than a few hours or days later. You still have the person's exact words echoing in your mind, you have the sense impressions of the subject you were

REPORTING FROM THE SIDELINES

Most of what viewers learn about a televised game comes from a couple of people in the broadcast booth, usually high above the field. But, especially in football, someone else is working hard to tell us about what we are watching — the sideline reporter.

Reporting from the sideline is a challenging assignment. Veterans advise newcomers to wear sneakers because they can expect to race at least five miles around the stadium during a game. "I'm all over the place," said NBC's Melissa Stark. "What it boils down to is we really want the observations on the sidelines because you can't get that anywhere else. Of course, if there's an injury, I'm sprinting over to that, if someone is in the medical tent or the athletic trainers are looking at them."

Sideline reporters must navigate bad weather, grumpy coaches and boisterous fans to bring breaking news to a television audience. The reporter typically conducts flash interviews with players and coaches. "Coaches are pretty fiery," said Stark. "They're intense. They're in the moment."

Erin Andrews reporting on the sideline during an NFL game.
© Zuma Press, Inc. / Alamy

The idea for a sideline reporter grew out of a sports tragedy. According to Jim Lampley, who was covering the 1972 Munich Olympics, it was the Israeli hostage crisis that challenged ABC to put its new wireless technology to work. After the games, producers wondered if the technology would work in a football stadium. Using that equipment, Lampley himself became the first sideline reporter during the UCLA-Tennessee game in 1974.

Andrea Kremer, an Emmy-winning sports journalist who spent five years on the sidelines for NBC's "Sunday Night Football," estimated that maybe 1 percent of the reporting she did leading up to the game made it onto the air. Reporters are challenged to find just the right question for a tiny time frame. "It's tough, and I try to make it feel urgent," Stark said. "I try to keep my questions very short. A lot of times it's based on what you just saw. It's a matter of whatever the big themes are going in."

The sideline job didn't start as one that would be staffed chiefly by women although it has turned out that way. Laura Okmin, an NFL broadcaster for Fox, was drawn to the job in the early 2000s because it gave her a chance to cover the game from an access point no other reporter had. "Somewhere along the way, it's turned into having to justify the value and the worth of this role," Okmin said. "And not so coincidentally, it really became a role for women."

That identity has led to a few cases of sexism. Fox's reporter Charissa Thompson created a stir in November 2023 when she said she made up a report during a Detroit Lions game after the team's coach, Rod Marinelli, told her he liked her perfume instead of answering her question. But no game would be complete anymore without a postgame coach's comment collected by the intrepid sideline reporter.[4]

observing, and you have a good idea what the gist of your story will be. It might be relatively easy to get back to your subject to check a fact. When you start writing, you may discover that your notes are incomplete. Was that figure $10 million or $10 billion? Don't hesitate to check and recheck a fact to be sure it's accurate.

One thing you should not do is promise to give your subject a copy of your story *before* publication. You are responsible for what you write, and you don't want to cede that right to anyone else. Naturally, most people would prefer to see themselves portrayed in a positive way; thus, they may object to any phrase that makes them appear less than charming, gracious or brilliant. To be fair, your story should portray the person as he really is, and that may not always be flattering. People also have faulty memories. That is one of the reasons people may feel they have been misquoted. They remember what they think they said or what they meant to say but forgot what they actually did say.

If a source is treated fairly and earnestly, that person is likely to be more cooperative with others who wish to interview him the next time. On the other hand, if you bungle the job, the person may be off-limits to reporters in the future. So, remember, others have gone before you and others will follow. You can ease their path a bit by doing a good job.

ELECTRONIC INTERVIEWING
Occasionally the only option for a personal interview is via electronic means. Telephone calls are one of the most common forms — sports reporters can ask questions and generate responses, and thanks to various video apps sometimes see nonverbal signs, too. Interviews via email or any form of social media should be used as a last resort. When a source responds to a written list of questions, the answers are often wordy and sound scripted. Follow-up questions might not be possible, and there are no nonverbal signals. Of bigger concern is the interview's authenticity. It is hard to be certain your source is the one who provided the answers to your questions and not an agent, coach, friend or sports information director. Inform your readers when you have conducted an interview via email or social media.

UPON FURTHER REVIEW
1. The university athletic director has called a news conference to begin in two hours. You know only that the topic is "a change in direction for the baseball program." What steps should you take to prepare for this news conference?
2. Your editor returns your story on a freshman All-American gymnast and says it's filled with too many quotations. How do you determine which quotations to keep and which to omit? What are other options?
3. A Los Angeles Dodgers pitcher is in town for a fundraising event and is gracious enough to do a 10-minute one-on-one interview with you. How do you prepare? What types of questions will you ask? Give three specific examples.

NOTES

1. Story includes material from Graham Hill, "She Lost Her Arm in a Shark Attack, but Surfer Bethany Hamilton Is Living 'an Unstoppable Life,'" CNN, Oct. 25, 2019.

2. Material used from a Kurt Streeter, "Winners Get Their Due. But Losers Are Wonderfully Human," *New York Times*, June 6, 2023.

3. Evan Bland, "Five Games: Nebraska Baseball's Fine Line Between the NCAAs and Staying Home," *Omaha World-Herald*, June 4, 2023.

4. "Melissa Stark Q&A: On the Art of On-Field Questions, Eagles Fans and Taylor Swift," *Athletic*, Oct. 21, 2023.

Writing the Story

Of all the universities that play major college football, only one — Iowa State — has a stadium named after an African American. The stadium's namesake is Jack Trice, Iowa State's first Black athlete, who played football for the Cyclones in 1923. He majored in animal husbandry with the intention of helping Black farmers just as the university's first African American student, the scientist George Washington Carver, had done three decades earlier.

Instead, Trice died two days after being trampled during a game against Minnesota and sustaining severe bruises to his intestines and inflammation of his abdomen. He was one of 18 college, high school and semiprofessional football players to die in October and November 1923. For 50 years, Trice was largely forgotten at Iowa State. Then students, Black and White, led a years-long campaign to get the stadium named in his honor while university officials resisted. The dedication came in 1997, during a period of racial polarization on a predominantly White campus. "People persisted because they viewed it as a compelling story, an injustice, but one that had been lost from Iowa State's memory except for a dusty plaque in an old gym," said Mike Reilly, student government president.

Jack Trice is now no longer lost and forgotten. "Iowa State did the right thing," said Jeff Johnson, president of the Alumni Association, "at a time when this was not seen as something that you would do."[1] Finding stories like this are what make sports writers more than just reporters.

BECOMING A STORYTELLER

Sports writers are storytellers. They tell stories of action and conflict, stories about real people in exciting, tension-filled moments. They share facts, quotations and numbers, but their ultimate goal is to create accounts of athletes as human beings with whom readers and viewers can identify. To a true sports storyteller, it's not enough to say who won, who lost and what the score was. The storyteller also focuses on how people interacted to reach that end and uses descriptive details to bring the event to life. But first, to decide what makes an event truly worth a story, the sports writer considers its news value.

Find an Angle

Sports fans want to read and hear about their favorite teams. They're interested in stories about games they've seen so they can compare their idea of what happened and what it means through the eyes of the players and coaches. Fans also want to know about games they've missed and how player performances will affect their seasons. They want to know more about their favorite athlete's life away from sports. Sometimes they just want to see or hear their child's name in the news.

To clarify those sometimes conflicting desires, sports reporting shares a common set of priorities with other kinds of coverage. Those characteristics, or news values, are the ingredients that make a story newsworthy. The values are the same in print, on air and online. Here is a list of seven commonly recognized news values in no particular order:

- Conflict
- Timeliness
- Prominence
- Proximity
- Impact
- Human interest
- Novelty

Let's take a look at how these values play out in sports coverage.

Conflict

Every sport from curling to beach volleyball has its version of the final confrontation: the Master's Golf Tournament, Wimbledon, the Final Four, the World Series. These competitions are all based on conflict. Perhaps two old rivals are preparing to play again, or an experienced athlete fights back against a health problem or an injury. In any event, competition is inherently dramatic, even if all that is at stake is a dog and a bun. Joey "Jaws" Chestnut won the Mustard Belt at the 2023 Nathan's Hot Dog Eating Contest, easily besting his rivals by consuming 62 hot dogs in 10 minutes. Miki Sudo continued her run of dominance in the women's event, winning her ninth Mustard Belt with 39.5 hot dogs and buns.

Conflict makes news off the field or court, too. Basketball star Brittney Griner was arrested and jailed in Russia for possession of illegal substances. The conflict became an international standoff until officials finally negotiated a prisoner trade. During the back-and-forth, sports writers shared the stage with diplomats, presidents and policy wonks.

Timeliness

As a news value, timeliness refers to the immediacy of a story. The story itself doesn't have to be entirely new, but some new information must have emerged that makes it timely and relevant again. The continuous deadlines of online media have boosted timeliness from anything that's happened yesterday to what's happening in real time. The key is the frequency with which information can be added to the original entry. Online reporters know people are checking news sites often during the regular work or school day and that headlines, news blurbs and one-sentence summaries attract attention. A short lead or an update to a changing story often satisfies users' needs better than a fully developed story held until all the details are in and the interviews completed.

Timeliness is different for each medium and influences the perspective from which the story is presented. In a newspaper, for example, timeliness can mean a story about yesterday's game. Timeliness for broadcast is the next regularly scheduled newscast,

Fans celebrate a big moment, such as a volleyball game hosted in a football stadium.
© Lincoln Journal Star.

or, if the news is important enough, "We interrupt this broadcast for . . ." Timeliness for online stories is immediate, with updates as soon as new information becomes available. Reporters and bloggers upload game commentary in the online equivalent of play-by-play. Each story update is marked with the exact time it was posted.

Deadline differences dictate content differences. A game played tonight will be updated several times online during the game with a complete story available as soon as the final shot is taken; another update will appear after interviews with the coaches and players following the game. Tomorrow's newspaper will carry a detailed game story with quotes from the coaches, statistics and an analysis of how this game changes the season for the team.

TEN BEST THINGS ABOUT BEING A REPORTER

10. You never need to know anything. Just ask questions.
9. You never need to dress up or even shave. It's not expected.
8. You never need to grow up — you can be a smart aleck for life.
7. You can call anyone in the world, demand info and when you don't get it call back, then write a self-righteous "so-an-so failed to return telephone calls seeking comment" story.
6. You never need a license, certification, continuing education or even acceptable social skills.
5. You never have to sell anything, be nice to anyone or buy flowers for any favors done.
4. Even though you're in the thick of things — games, matches, meets — you risk nothing, have no stake, are not responsible for anything and have nothing to lose.
3. If you get a good beat, you get a front-row seat to the best games.
2. Attention deficit disorder is an asset. If you get complaints, you can blame an editor — "I wrote it. Someone must have taken it out."
1. If you can write, you'll never have to work again.

Consider these leads for a story about the announcement of a prestigious award. The time of the announcement and the names of the candidates were released in advance so reporters could gather background for the story before the winner was announced.

- 6:36 p.m., Monday. The first story posted after the 6 p.m. ceremony in New York by USAToday.com had a lead that reflected background research:

  > Nebraska volleyball star Sarah Pavan maintained a 4.0 grade-point average in biochemistry while leading the Cornhuskers to a 33-1 season and the NCAA title. Those achievements earned the junior from Kitchener, Ontario, the 31st annual Honda-Broderick Cup as the nation's female college athlete of the year Monday.[2]

- 7:18 p.m., Monday. About half an hour later, after the postannouncement interview, USAToday.com updated their lead to reflect Pavan's comments:

  > Nebraska volleyball player Sarah Pavan was shocked to win the Honda-Broderick Cup, which was announced Monday in New York.[3]

- 10 p.m., Monday. By 10 p.m. viewers of a TV station in Nebraska heard the news in this lead, which emphasizes the local connection:

  > Even before she was named Collegiate Woman Athlete of the Year, University of Nebraska volleyball player Sarah Pavan had already won some great honors. Pavan helped lead the Huskers to the National Championship and was selected NCAA Volleyball Player of the Year and the Academic All-American Player of the Year.[4]

- Tuesday afternoon. The following day a central Nebraska daily newspaper put the story in a regional context:

  > She has achieved "celebrity status" in Nebraska, UNL volleyball coach John Cook said. "When she shows up to speak to grade school kids in her sweats, the kids shut up and listen."

  > Nebraska's Sarah Pavan on Monday won the Honda-Broderick Cup becoming the nation's female athlete of the year and the first Nebraska athlete to be named in the 31-year history of the award.[5]

Prominence

Prominence means having name recognition, or "authority" in online parlance. Community athletes have prominence in their local media; professional teams and athletes have national prominence; Lionel Messi and LeBron James have international prominence and make news just because people know their names whether they follow sports or not.

Hollywood good looks help, too, and if you happen to marry a supermodel and break just about every record in football, you're going to be front and center. That's the case with Tom Brady, the NFL's GOAT (greatest of all time). Statistically speaking, Brady is on top of the heap: he has the most touchdown passes, the most wins and the most come-from-behind drives. Some of those achievements, however, don't easily lodge in your memory, but one number that might stick was something Brady notched in 2022 when he reached 100,000 yards passing. In other words, he threw complete passes up and down the length of 1,000 football fields. That sort of thing is certain to give a player prominence.

If you're already prominent and your career takes a turn no one expected, you're still going to be big news. At the 2020 Tokyo Olympics, seven-time medal winner Simone Biles suddenly withdrew from the women's team gymnastics final, citing mental health concerns. Biles said she had a case of the "twisties," where her mind and body felt out of sync. "It just sucks when you're fighting with your own head," she said. The U.S. gymnastics team said the situation should remind fans all over the world that those competing weren't just athletes. "We're people at the end of the day."

Proximity

Proximity means nearness, especially in relation to the target audience. Audiences will pay more attention to stories that take place in their own backyards than in crowded stadiums across the world. The bowling team down the street who call themselves "Generation XXX" is on the radar of local fans much more than the cricket champions in New Delhi.

College athletic directors do what they can to heighten proximity. For years, the Boise State Broncos have played their home football games on bright blue turf in Bronco Stadium. Anyone channel surfing on a Friday or Saturday night in the fall is sure to pause when that electric blue rectangle pops up on the screen.

Impact

Impact is gauged by the consequences of an action or change. This type of story helps explain how something may change the future. Talk shows and blogs, for example, often focus on the possible impact that an action by an individual or a governing organization might have. Reactions and repercussions invariably follow any change, and it's the reporter's job to keep the public informed of the impact.

Human Interest

Human interest addresses people's natural curiosity about each other. From pictures on cave walls to text messaging and Instagram posts, human beings want to learn how others think, feel and overcome obstacles. This value can help you put a human face on a big story. Human interest stories stir emotions and make people feel the urge to take action, if only by blogging their opinions or support.

What could be more stirring than a story about life-or-death competition? Viewers thrilled to a Netflix documentary in 2023 called "The Deepest Breath" about a young Italian free diver who risked her life by diving more than 100 meters deep on a single breath of air. In the film we meet Alessia Zecchini as a 13-year-old already beating older and often male competitors; to win one competition, she swam 105 meters underwater. But then the Italian federation banned divers under 18 from competing. When Alessia was finally again eligible in 2011, she began to set world records. Her unique fearlessness — divers sometimes lose consciousness on especially deep dives and need the help of rescue divers to make it back to the surface — and her desire to push the boundaries of human endurance made for a must-see program.

In profiles, sidebars and sports features, readers and viewers are looking for the human side of the story: which side of the field does grandmother sit on when she has a grandchild on each team, what kind of therapy does it take to rehab a player's injury, or perhaps how does it feel to play the last game of a collegiate career?

Novelty

An old journalistic adage goes like this: "When a dog bites someone, it's not news. When someone bites a dog, that's news." In other words, people enjoy reading about unusual situations. The drivers in a car race, for example, plan to cross the finish line right side up, with all four tires on the track. That's why when NASCAR driver Clint Bowyer's Chevrolet slid across the finish line upside down and on fire at the Daytona 500, it was unusual; we might call it a novelty. Even though Bowyer placed 18th, his finish stole the headline from winner and teammate Kevin Harvick.

French tennis player Tatiana Golovin's choice to wear red shorts at the very traditional Wimbledon tennis tournament was unusual enough to attract attention from the audience, the referee and the media. Somewhat befuddled, the referee consulted the rule book before declaring that the red shorts were underwear, not part of Golovin's white tennis dress, and therefore acceptable attire for Wimbledon's all-white dress code.

ASKING QUESTIONS IN REVERSE

Does the order of your questions change when your subject is the world record holder for doing things backward? Aaron Yoder, a track and cross-country coach at Bethany College in Kansas, is the fastest person to ever run backward. On Sept. 4, 2020, Yoder ran a backward mile on a stretch of road near Marquette, Kansas, in 5 minutes and 30 seconds. Yoder chose a flat stretch of road with no potholes and little car traffic because, of course, he couldn't see where he was going.

If you were to interview Yoder, one of your first questions, naturally, would be "Why?" Yoder says he used to run like everyone else until an injury to his knee put him in reverse. "I hope this can inspire others to set goals and go for their dreams," he said. "I am proof of that."

Next, you may wonder whether it is actually less stressful to run backward. Yoder cites research showing that backward running alleviates knee pressure and shortens strides. That strengthens the hip flexors and improves posture. "The one challenge is you can't see behind you," he said. "I've fallen down quite a few times, but I've always just bounced back."

Finally, you may want to ask, "OK, you can run backward in a straight line; can you run around in a circle?" Yoder says he plans to attempt running a backward mile around a track. He thinks he could do 5:40. "If the griddle is hot," he said, "I need to keep on cooking."[6]

WRITING THE LEAD

The lead is the beginning of a story — sometimes a sentence, often a paragraph, occasionally more. In essence, it tells readers and viewers what happened. In sports news, the lead often hints about what led to the outcome. A well-written lead assures readers that no matter where they exit the story, even after the first paragraph or two, they will have the basic information they need.

News values help sports writers determine what goes into the lead. If a fight breaks out on the court, conflict will almost certainly be in the lead. If someone breaks a record, impact is likely to be the lead. If that record-breaker is well-known, prominence will be key. If the record is broken in the player's last game, human interest will also play a role.

The major difference between a lead and a toss (a broadcast teaser that previews a story) is that a lead reveals the outcome. Traditional leads aren't mysterious — they tell people how the game turned out. The best ones, however, do so in such a way that even someone who saw or listened to the game will be intrigued. Here's how USA Today, for example, captured readers in a story about the 2023 Super Bowl:

> On one leg, Patrick Mahomes finished the job. His reward, other than resting an oft-injured ankle this postseason, is a second Lombardi Trophy for the reigning NFL MVP.
>
> The Kansas City Chiefs defeated the Philadelphia Eagles 38-35 in Super Bowl 57 on Sunday, the team's second title in four seasons.[7]

The job of the lead is to summarize the key information. To do so, the reporter typically identifies the 5 Ws and an H first, as in this example from a baseball game:

Who: the UC Irvine Anteaters.
What: defeated Arizona State 8-7.
Where: College World Series.
When: Tuesday.
Why: the Anteaters hope to win a national championship.
How: in their final at bat in the 10th inning.

Some of this information is available before the game begins, but most won't be known until it ends. Once you have identified the key facts, compare them to the news values. Which fact has the highest value for your audience? Is it a prominent person? Was it the championship game? Was there a key play that clinched the game?

From this list, the reporter should be able to summarize the story in a sentence or two, beginning with the most appealing news value. For example,

> The UC Irvine Anteaters won in their final at bat for the third time in four games on Tuesday night, knocking off Arizona State 8-7 in 10 innings in an elimination game at the College World Series.

The "how" of the story dominates this lead, a value usually found more often in the second or third paragraph. "When" is rarely the factor with the most audience appeal; it often appears just after the main verb.

When Should You Write the Lead?

Sometimes you write the lead first. Sometimes it will be the last thing you write. When sports reporters are covering a game or a news conference and have short deadlines, they often write the body of the story as the game unfolds and add the lead later. When writer's block strikes, as it does for everyone at some point, the cure may be to skip the lead and write the rest of the story. The lead usually reveals itself as the story develops. A forced or contrived lead always sounds like what it is: the writer attempting to make the story fit the lead instead of the lead setting up the story.

Tease the Reader

Readers make quick decisions about whether to read a story or move on. That makes writing the lead one of the biggest challenges in sports journalism. You must convey enough information to tease readers and viewers into the story while not giving away so much that they are content with what they've learned.

Two Types of Leads

Leads fit into two general categories: direct and delayed. Advances, gamers and briefs usually have short, direct leads, while features, profiles and in-depth stories are more likely to have longer, slow-developing delayed leads. But they're not mutually exclusive: gamers may have delayed leads and in-depth stories may have direct leads.

Direct Leads

Direct leads, also called summary leads, present information quickly. If readers stopped at the end of a direct lead, they would know who played, who won, what the score was and where and when the event happened. Reporters on deadline use direct leads because they're quick and easy to write. Readers and listeners like direct leads because all the key information is readily available. Editors like direct leads because they know if there's not enough room for the whole story, it can be shortened from the bottom without losing important facts.

One drawback to direct leads is that they begin to sound alike. The last thing readers want in a sports story is dull and boring. One way to pique their curiosity is to add a short teaser sentence that slightly delays the real news. A CNN story, for example, about an unlikely soccer player ran with this lead:

> Breathing heavily, Oleksandr Malchevsky puts on his prosthesis and hurries home to his wife and son.
>   The 39-year-old has just lost a soccer game, but he isn't too upset. For him, the sport is more than just a game — it's about helping his rehabilitation as he adjusts to civilian life. Malchevsky is a Ukrainian soldier who lost part of his leg fighting in Eastern Ukraine.[8]

This combination of a teaser ("puts on his prosthesis") with a direct lead has a good chance to draw lots of readers into the rest of the story.

Delayed Leads

Leads that wait to summarize an event are called delayed leads. They often work well in feature stories that don't have a timely element. Rather than quickly clarifying the 5 Ws and H, delayed leads use visual details and emotional appeals to urge readers to keep reading.

A delayed lead may take the form of an anecdote — a short, self-contained story with a point to make about the subject. This might set up a scene that invites readers or viewers to imagine what lies ahead. For example,

> Reporters covering a college football team's opening game thought they had asked just about every possible question until someone asked the team captain if he would be calling heads or tails at the pregame coin flip.
>
> The captain took the question in stride and said he had been practicing since "I messed it up in church softball this summer." For the record, the captain said, "Tails never fails."

That anecdote sets up a story about the role of luck in football games, but the reader won't know this for several paragraphs. Eventually, the delayed lead will transition into the body of the story by telling the reader what theme the story is going to explore.

Here's an anecdote that sets up a story about one of the nation's best 70-and-over slow-pitch softball teams. It transports readers to the field, where they feel the summer heat, meet the players and ultimately want to stay to watch the game.

> LIBERTY, Mo. — Think heat, motion-stifling, odor-producing, nap-inspiring heat. Think of sitting in an attic in the Sahara with a space heater under your rump. Think of eating Grandma's chili with her wool quilt over your head.
>
> Records will show the temperature on July 6 in this Kansas City suburb topped out at 93, but if you think it was a day to swing a bat instead of playing pinochle down at the coffee shop, somebody poured a few shots of something in your chili.
>
> "You know every spring the robins come hopping along," said 71-year-old Lee Leriger of Norfolk. "Well, it's the same thing with us. We'll play 'til we can't."
>
> They call themselves the Omaha Spirit and they don't just play, they win enough to earn distinction as one of the nation's best 70-and-over slow-pitch softball teams.[9]

Leads to Avoid

Some writing strategies that work in other contexts might not be good choices when it comes to writing a lead. For example,

Don't begin your story with a question. This would seem like an easy way to pull readers in, but the fact is, they expect answers, not more questions. It's too easy for a reader to reply "yes," "no" or "I don't care" and move on. If, for example, your story begins "Why did it take so long last night for the Turtles' offense to get rolling?" many readers will be lost — "What game? What result? Why should I care?"

Don't begin with a quotation. Readers like to know what people said, and that makes quotations tempting to use as leads. But finding a quote that captures the essence of the story is rare. It's better to use a quotation to embellish the lead. Of the 28 stories featured in *The Year's Best Sports Writing* (2022 edition), for example, only two begin with quotations.

STORY STRUCTURE

Sports writers use the same structural patterns as news writers to organize stories. Once the facts have been identified, the background research done and the sources interviewed, the writer plans how to tell the story.

Inverted Pyramid

In most stories, journalists begin at the end and then backtrack. That's the concept illustrated by the inverted pyramid organization pattern. The first questions fans ask should be answered at the top of the story. After story basics are taken care of, the supporting information flows down from the most interesting or significant to the least. The writer's judgment makes the determination of what is most important to the greatest number of people.

"Who won?" and "What was the score?" are the first questions most readers ask. If they watched the game, they still want to be reminded, but they might like to be teased with the reason the game turned out as it did. Here's how one writer described a Super Bowl game:

> GLENDALE, Ariz. (AP) — Patrick Mahomes was magical when the Kansas City Chiefs desperately needed him to pull off another Super Bowl comeback.
>
> Playing on an injured ankle, Mahomes threw two touchdown passes in the fourth quarter and scrambled 26 yards on the go-ahead drive before Harrison Butker kicked a 27-yard field goal with 8 seconds left to give the Chiefs a 38-35 victory.

Readers, reporters and editors like inverted pyramid stories because they are quick and efficient to read, to write and to place on the page. The information of most interest to the most people is in the first paragraph or on the first screen. The least important information is at the end, so the reader who doesn't scroll to the second screen won't miss a key point.

The Super Bowl story cited above continues like this:

JUST HOT AIR?

For about 70 years, a vital part of sports reporting has been a big bag of hot air — the Goodyear blimp. The blimp has been to just about every major sports event you can imagine — the Olympics, the Super Bowl, the NBA Finals, the World Series, the Kentucky Derby and the Indianapolis 500, just to name a few.

That list is subject to change. On Dec. 3, 2023, the Blimp floated over an athletic resort in San Clemente, Calif., to cover the professional pickleball finals. That's right: pickleball is now "blimpworthy," right up there with the Rose Bowl and all the other greats.

What the blimp provides for us is live aerial coverage of the sports event, a point of view that has charmed television viewers for decades. Goodyear was founded in 1898, but it wasn't until the 1950s that the company started to make a name in sports. As television was growing in popularity, NBC asked Goodyear if it would be possible to place a camera on board an airship for the Rose Bowl. Once NBC had installed camera and microwave transmitting technology on the blimp, it was no trouble to fly over both the Rose Bowl parade and the game itself.

The blimp is about 250 feet long and weighs nearly 20,000 pounds. It holds enough helium to fill more than 1 million balloons and costs Goodyear about $100,000 for each trip, depending on the price of helium. Goodyear agrees to cover all its expenses in exchange for marketing during on-air TV broadcasts. Most fall weekends, a fleet of three airships flies to various college games. Pilots must navigate the wind, sun and other atmospheric conditions to get a shot of the game without casting the blimp's shadow on the field. "During a typical week," according to Forbes, "prep for the game begins on Wednesday with the television technicians departing on Thursday. On Friday, the rest of the crew leaves with the blimp. Depending on the distance to the game, there might be two travel days, as the blimp flies to the location and tops out somewhere at 70 miles per hour."

But the bad news, for blimp lovers, is that drones can now provide similar coverage at a much lower cost. And blimp pilots are getting harder and harder to find.[10]

Inverted Pyramid

Lead/Nut Graf: 5 Ws, Score

Highlight/Key Play

Impact of Event on Season

Quotes: Coach, Player

Details of Important Plays

Penalties/Injuries

Quotes

Numbers/Statistics

Quotes

Background on Teams

Previous Meetings

Next Contest

Order of information will vary with story

Inverted pyramid diagram

The Chiefs won their second NFL title in four years and two-time NFL MVP Mahomes earned his second Super Bowl MVP award.

"I thought guys just embraced the moment," Mahomes said about rallying from a 10-point halftime deficit. "In that first half, we were playing and doing some good stuff, but I felt like the guys were getting consumed by everything around us."

Mahomes and Jalen Hurts excelled in the first Super Bowl matchup featuring two Black starting QBs. But Mahomes turned it up in the second half after reaggravating a sprained right ankle.

Here the writer slowly integrates material, including quotes from a key player, the game's rhythm (a second-half comeback) and historical tidbits (the Super Bowl's first two starting Black quarterbacks).

Sports reporters like the inverted pyramid because they can work more efficiently. Reporters working on short deadlines or with continuous online updates find the pattern especially helpful because they can start the story during the event and insert information anywhere in the story as it becomes available. The lead will probably change as the game develops, but it doesn't need to be finalized until the clock runs out.

For online readers, the pyramid works well, too. The story becomes a stack of "information chunks" descending from the lead. Each chunk may stand alone, presenting a small part of the story for readers who just want to scan the page for highlights or quotes, according to media writing expert Janet Kolodzy.[11]

Circular Organization

Broadcast media prefer a circular organization pattern for their stories because sportscasters must tell the whole story in a tight time span. They use a strategy something like this: "Here's what I'm going to tell you, now I'm telling it, and let me remind you what I just told you." Game stories, for instance, begin with a direct lead, details or sound bites in the middle, and end with a wrap that ties content back to the lead. The wrap might also anticipate a future story, such as when the teams will meet again. If circular stories need to be shortened, they must be carefully edited in the middle so the tie-back is not lost.

Tips for Writing an Interview Story

- Make it a habit to leave the question out of the story. Instead of writing, "Asked when he knew . . ." just use the quote — it will almost always be self-explanatory.
- You only need one attribution per paragraph if the same person is speaking.
- Use quotations often. They add flavor, detail and emotion. Without them, stories would be nothing but play-by-play accounts of games. Breaking stories would just be a string of facts and numbers. Fans want reaction and insight. What did the coach think of his decision to go for the two-point conversion in overtime? Why did the wrestler suddenly change his strategy? How did the volleyball players react when learning they qualified for the state tournament? Quotations allow sports reporters

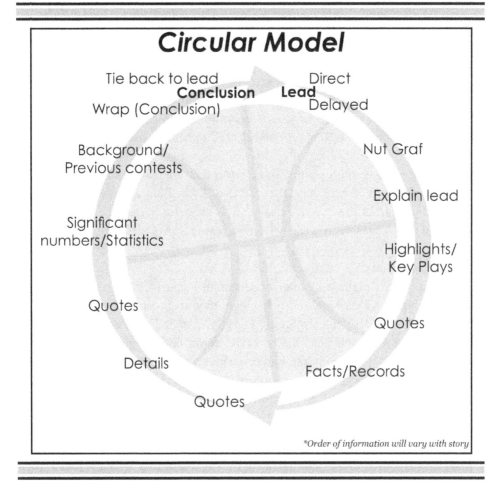

Circular Model

Tie back to lead
Conclusion   **Lead**   Direct
Wrap (Conclusion)   Delayed

Background/
Previous contests   Nut Graf

                                            Explain lead

Significant
numbers/Statistics   Highlights/
                                            Key Plays

Quotes   Quotes

Details   Facts/Records

            Quotes

Order of information will vary with story

Circular model diagram

to tell a story through the voices of their sources while they can remain on the sidelines.

USING QUOTATIONS

A direct quotation is an exact, word-for-word account of what a person says. It is enclosed within quotation marks and attributed to the source. Direct quotations should be used to convey a person's emotion or opinion, the more colorful, the better. Consider these, for example:

> "The pitcher has got only a ball. I've got a bat. So the percentage of weapons is in my favor and I let the fellow with the ball do the fretting."—Henry Aaron

"It's just a job. Grass grows, birds fly, waves pound the sand. I beat people up."—Muhammed Ali

"Excellence is not a singular act but a habit. You are what you do repeatedly."—Shaquille O'Neal

Of course, not every quotation will be lively or entertaining. Still, try to use quotations that reveal something interesting. Avoid cliches — you don't want to write one, so why quote a coach or player using one?

"We've got to take it one game at a time."
"He really brings a lot to the table."
"This was a total team effort."

Such quotations add nothing to your story and might bore your reader to sleep.
Quotations that include numbers and statistics are also unnecessary:

"Tatum scored 18 points, but 10 of those came in the fourth quarter and gave us a lift. He made all six of his free throws."

If you are covering that game, you should know how many points Tatum scored and when he scored them. You don't need the coach to repeat that information in a post-game interview and instead can go for something that will spice up your story.

Paraphrase

A paraphrase summarizes what a person says but in the writer's words, not verbatim. Because it is not word for word, a paraphrase does not have quotation marks. Reporters might paraphrase to shorten a long quotation or to help explain a quotation that was otherwise confusing.

If a quote, for example, is long and convoluted, the writer can ditch the quotation marks and state the essence in a paraphrase. For example, consider the following quotation from Duke basketball coach Mike Krzyzewski.

I think the experience of having been in those situations in the conference, really in over half of our games, we have been losing or just about to lose. It is tough to simulate those types of situations and you have to experience them. So far this year we have experienced them in a positive way and again you're experiencing them today. Our team turned it into something positive, which is good toughness on our part.[12]

Asking a player about a specific play can help you get a good quotation.
© Nebraska Wesleyan Sports Information.

The general thought that this coach is trying to convey can be better presented in a paraphrase.

> Krzyzewski said his team has benefited from playing in many close conference games and has become tougher as a result.

Here the writer used just 20 words to explain what it took Krzyzewski 76 words to say. This paraphrase gives you more room to describe the game-winning basket or squeeze in an interesting sidenote.

Attribution

Attribution is the term for giving someone credit for saying something. When reporters attribute, they are indicating who said what. Direct quotations and paraphrases are always attributed, using the preferred verb "said." For example,

> "If a tie is like kissing your sister, losing is like kissing your grandmother with her teeth out," baseball player George Brett said.[13]

Why stick with "said"? It is clear, concise and neutral. It does not imply, offer an opinion or leave room for misinterpretation. It is safe and all-inclusive. Using other attributive verbs can change the meaning or inadvertently suggest an emotion that might not be intended. For example:

"This is the worst game I've ever seen this team play," he snapped.
"We have got to be more aggressive in the second half," she insisted.
"Bygones are bygones. The hard part is over," he exclaimed.

Did he really "snap"? "Insisted" sounds like she was pretty tense, and "exclaimed" suggests that he shouted.

Words are not actions, and they cannot be "grimaced," "sighed" or "growled." Let the reader decide from the context of the story how the speaker might have sounded. If it is necessary to indicate speaking and facial expressions, use both.

Avoid: "That play worked well for us," Coach Hobson bragged.
Instead use: "That play worked well for us," Coach Hobson said with a grin.

Punctuating Quotations

Here are some style rules for punctuating direct quotations:

- Place a comma between the quotation mark and the attribution.

    Incorrect: "Coach always says if you set a good screen, you're the one getting the wide-open shot." Perry said.

    Correct: "Coach always says if you set a good screen, you're the one getting the wide-open shot," Perry said.

- This strategy applies to exclamation marks and question marks, too.

    Incorrect: "How many times is this going to keep happening to us?," he said.

    Correct: "How many times is this going to keep happening to us?" he said.

- For direct quotations longer than one sentence, it is best to insert the attribution after the first sentence, then continue with the quotation.

    Incorrect: "Football is what I've got. Football is what I love and what I'm good at. What you have and you love, you need to embrace," Sam Keller said.

    Correct: "Football is what I've got," Sam Keller said. "Football is what I love and what I'm good at. What you have and you love, you need to embrace."

- Use single quotation marks to indicate quotations within quotations.

  > Correct: "He came to me and said, 'I don't know,' and he said he didn't feel good. So I said he wasn't going to play."

- Sometimes, direct quotations may be several sentences or paragraphs long. If your quotation runs longer than one paragraph, use quote marks at the beginning of each paragraph but skip the closing quote marks until the quote is finally finished.

  > Correct: "I thought it was an extremely hard-fought game," Roy Williams said. "Both teams really wanted to play well, but their team played better than we did.

  > "The team that did most of the little things won the game. Whether it is shooting the ball in the hole or making free throws in the second half or getting a hand up on the outside shot — the team that won the game was the most disciplined.

  > "They did the best job of doing what their coaching staff wanted them to do."[14]

Cleaning Up Quotations

Not every "umm," "yeah" or "ya know" needs to be included in a direct quotation. Sports reporters are allowed to omit the stumbles so long as the meaning is not changed. The Associated Press stylebook says, "Never alter quotations, even to correct minor grammatical errors or word usage." In other words, this quote might be acceptable: "We was happy to win the game," he said. But realistically, that might sound like fingernails on a chalkboard to some. Much of the time, local style may override this rule.

Sometimes, direct quotations may include profane words. AP Style holds that you should not use obscenities in stories unless they are part of direct quotations and, even then there should be a compelling reason for them. Most of the time, writers try to find a way to give the reader a sense of what was said without using the offending word or phrase. Writers might also want to shorten a long quotation. It is OK to take out repetitive, unnecessary words — as long as the quotation's thought or meaning stays the same; use an ellipsis to indicate omitted words.

Quote Sheets

Transcribing your interview — a task you accomplish by listening to your digital recorder or iPhone voice memo and typing out every word your source said (or using a transcription service) — can take time, sometimes twice as long as the interview itself. That is still time well spent.

Using your transcript, compile a quote sheet — a set of direct quotations from an interview that will help you choose the best quotations for a story, those you would rather paraphrase and those which will probably not make the final cut. While writers create their own quote sheets for personal use, sports media relations staffs often release quote sheets after news conferences and events. These quote sheets can be helpful when you don't have time to transcribe a 45-minute news conference or perhaps weren't able to attend. Usually, the questions and answers will both be on these quote sheets.

UPON FURTHER REVIEW

1. Find a sports story for each of the seven news values. In other words, select one story that is news primarily because it is timely, one that is based on conflict, one that is unusual, one about a prominent person and so forth. Which news values do most of the sports stories you read highlight?

Is It Newsworthy?

Given the story ideas in the chart below, mark which values of newsworthiness apply to each idea. Keep in mind: it's possible that all or none will apply.

Story Idea	Conflict	Timeliness	Prominence	Proximity	Impact	Human Interest	Novelty
University makes portal offer to defensive lineman							
Star basketball player commits to college							
Basketball team is on the bubble for NCAA tournament							
MLB reduces pitch clock rule by two seconds							
Recap of your favorite NFL team's season							
School announces layoffs of four assistant coaches for budget cutbacks							

2. Choose three stories you think are written in inverted pyramid structure. Discuss places where you agree or disagree about the writer's prioritizing of information.
3. How would you handle a few direct quotations from a source who routinely uses profane language?

NOTES

1. Jere Longman, "A Stadium at Iowa State Says His Name: Jack Trice," *New York Times*, July 20, 2020.

2. Drew Costley, "Nebraska Volleyballer Pavan Takes Honda-Broderick Cup," *USA Today*, June 25, 2007, https://www.usatoday.com/sports/college/2007-06-25-pavan-honda_N.htm.

3. Costley, "Nebraska Volleyballer."

4. Ed Littler, KHAS-TV, 10 p.m. newscast, June 18, 2007.

5. Eric Olson, "NU's Pavan Is Female College Athlete of the Year," *Hastings Tribune*, June 26, 2007, 1C.

6. Material drawn from Zachary Kussin, "The World's Fastest Backward Runner Smashes His Own Record," *New York Post*, Sept. 7, 2020, and Andrew Dawson, "Aaron Yoder Smashes His World Record in the Backwards Mile," *Runner's World*, Sept. 8, 2020.

7. Steve Gardner, Safid Deen and Chris Bumbaca, "Chiefs Top Eagles 38-35 Thanks to Late-Game Magic from Mahomes," *USA Today*, Feb. 12, 2023.

8. Daria Tarasova-Markina, "'Relief From Everyday Life': How Soccer Is Helping Ukrainian Soldiers Who Have Lost Limbs in the War Against Russia," CNN, Feb. 14, 2024.

9. Dirk Chatelain, "Spirit of the 70s," *Omaha World-Herald*, July 15, 2007, 1C.

10. Kristi Dosh, "The Goodyear Blimp and College Football: More Than 60 Years of History," *Forbes*, Dec. 30, 2016.

11. Janet Kolodzy, *Convergence Journalism: Writing and Reporting Across the News Media* (Lanham, MD: Rowman & Littlefield, 2006), 194.

12. Quote from postgame news conference, Feb. 6, 2008, Duke University Sports Information.

13. Quote found on the website BrainQuote.com.

14. Quote from postgame news conference, Feb. 6, 2008, Duke University sports information.

Choosing the Words

Every sport has rules, and every player knows the penalties for breaking the rules. Step out of bounds and the play ends. Commit too many fouls, and you will be out of the game. Break an NCAA rule and your team may have to forfeit a bowl game. Sports writing has rules, too: grammar rules, spelling rules, punctuation rules. You may not be thrown out of the game for breaking one of these rules, but there is usually a penalty. With each mistake, you lose credibility with your audience and your employer. Make too many mistakes that someone else has to fix, and you might lose your job.

Not only are there rules to learn, but you must also master a sports idiom. This language is a combination of sports terminology, slang and cliché that has grown up within the world of sports over the last century or more and has become sports-speak, particularly in play-by-play announcing. The idiom is so pervasive that some of it has leaked into everyday conversation. For example, "par for the course" comes from golf, "to strike out" or "touch base" comes from baseball and "photo finish" is from horse racing. You make a "pit stop," "spin your wheels" or "win by a nose." Or you might be "thrown a curve," "driven up the wall" or find yourself "behind the eight ball."

Consider, for example, a story about a baseball game. If a reader doesn't already know a plethora of terms, they will be hard-pressed to understand what happened.

> OMAHA — The new No. 1 beat the old No. 1. Now Wake Forest is on the brink of the College World Series title round.
>
> A clash of the top-ranked baseball teams this season lived up to its lofty billing and then some in a CWS game stuffed with strikeouts, drama and big plays. The Demon Deacons made the last ones — Bennett Lee's rolling RBI single to left in the bottom of the eighth gave the No. 1 seed its first lead in a 3-2 win in front of a sellout crowd.

A thrilling eighth inning provided the difference Monday in a brisk 2-hour, 50-minute contest. A Tre' Morgan leadoff double and fielding error in the top half put the Tigers at the corners with no outs. Then Brock Wilken, the third baseman, gloved a hard grounder off the bat of Cade Beloso. Wilken double-clutched, moving into foul ground and fired home to the catcher Lee, who corralled the one-hopper in front of a sliding baserunner to apply the tag at the plate.

One video review and two pitches later, Wake Forest was out of the frame in a tie game as reliever Camden Minacci coaxed a 5-4-3 twin killing.[1]

Professional writers take language rules seriously because they know both their audiences and their editors respect good writing. Bloggers, emailers, tweeters and sports writers also make correct grammar and spelling part of their professional practice. In addition to knowing and using grammar rules, sports writers face the complexity of their audiences. They must craft stories informative and entertaining enough for the novice to enjoy but technical enough to hold the attention of the die-hard sports fan.

Winding up for a pitch, a Nebraska Wesleyan pitcher is surely a sign of spring.
© Nebraska Wesleyan Sports Information.

WRITING IN SPORTS STYLE

Sports reporters base their stories on facts, information and quotations. Information is gathered from sources or observed by the reporter. If the information takes the form of a quotation or paraphrase, it is attributed to the source. Stories should not include the reporter's opinion. That opinion is reserved for columns where it can be clearly labeled. In broadcast, opinion segments are introduced as opinion and often delivered in a setting with audio and visual cues to identify opinion as different from game coverage or sports news. The difference between a fact and an opinion can be as simple as a few words.

> Fact: The game went two extra innings, during which the Cubs changed pitchers three times.

> Opinion: The game went two extra innings because the Cubs' manager made three questionable pitching changes.

Facts can be verified. Opinions, on the other hand, are often expressed as sweeping generalizations laden with superlatives: "most famous," "best ever," "greatest play."

> Fact: Nick Saban has coached seven teams to the college football national championship.

> Opinion: Nick Saban is the greatest coach in college football history.

Blogging, tweeting and Instagram posting have opened other venues for expressing opinions, for both the sports journalist and the participating public. Newspapers and television stations have multimedia websites where they invite people to participate in community conversations via social media, written entries, photos and video.

Verify Information

The first rule for journalists is to be accurate. That means that journalists never assume anything. They always verify information before putting it in a story. A generally accepted guideline is to check information with three unrelated sources. If all three agree, the information is probably correct and safe to use. Note the word "probably" in the last sentence; if there's any doubt in your mind or you have a gut feeling that something is not quite right, don't use it until you're satisfied that it is correct.

One way to gather facts and information is to attend a sporting event, observe the activity and take notes or record the action yourself. What you observe may be reported without attribution. To ensure the accuracy of your story, compare your notes after the event to stat sheets from the sports information office. If you cannot attend an event, contact the sports information director ahead of time to get background on both teams. Make arrangements with the coaches or media relations director for phone interviews after the game and ask for game stats to be uploaded as soon as they are available.

WRITING THE STORY, SENTENCE BY SENTENCE

What makes a story easier to read? According to readability tests, the average sentence runs about 16 words long. Not every sentence should be 16 words, of course. Using a variety of sentence lengths gives writing a more pleasing rhythm. Subject-verb-object is the preferred sentence organization pattern because that is what readers expect. It makes the subject do the action and helps the reader move through the story quickly and easily.

This lead from the USA Today Sports Weekly, for instance, uses 38 words — more than twice the length of the average sentence — to include almost all the basic information:

> Patriots wide receiver Trey Brown [who] spent time playing defensive back [what] over the last three seasons [when], and it prepared him [why] to make the critical fourth-quarter play [what] that helped turn an apparent Chargers victory into a 24-2 Patriots comeback win [how].[2]

Daily publications, however, usually prefer short, punchy S-V-O sentences. This summary lead from a wire service tells the whole story.

> AUSTIN, Texas — Texas' [where] Destinee Hooker, the two-time defending NCAA high jump champion [who], will skip track [what] this season [when] to train with the U.S. women's national volleyball team [why] before the Olympics.[3]

S-V-O is the preferred sentence order in broadcast as well because it creates easy-to-say units of thought that the listener can understand and absorb. Online readers, too, are looking for easy-to-read, easy-to-understand information, and that's what S-V-O sentences deliver.

Short Paragraphs

In journalistic style, one- and two-sentence paragraphs are the norm. Paragraph indentations create small white notches along the left margin that make stories easier to read by opening small windows of light in the text. Online reading has its own challenges with frequent distractions (pop-up ads, for example) and the light from the screen that can fatigue the eyes.

Every Word Counts

Short, simple words are easier to comprehend for a reader scanning a story or someone listening to a broadcast. They also take up less space on a page or screen and less time on air. When there's a choice, choose the shortest, simplest word that works without diminishing the meaning. Replace technical terms and long words with shorter ones. For example, use "cuts and bruises" instead of "abrasions and contusions" and "knee injury" instead of "torn meniscus."

Action Verbs

Readers rely on the writer's choice of verbs to help them see how the player moved and feel the difference between a stroll, a strut and a sprint. They want to sense what it's like to dive for a ball, to feel the texture of the bat in their hands, to run the bases and slide in to score.

The Language of -isms

Three -isms — sexism, racism and ageism — present serious pitfalls for the writer. Even though the Constitution states that we are all "created equal," more than two centuries later, women, minorities and older people are still struggling to achieve equal treatment. Sports, where female and minority athletes have long excelled and been recognized for their achievements, may be on the leading edge of equity.

Strive to write about people as individuals, not as representatives of a group. Generally, ageist language, for example, reinforces stereotypes by expressing surprise over those who do not conform to them. Straightforward, factual writing free of descriptive adjectives and stereotypical labels is probably the best way to eliminate accusations of -ism bias in writing.

MISSPELLED WORDS AND USAGE ERRORS

"A misspelled name is second only to an incorrect score as the most obvious — and unnecessary — error," says noted AP writer Steve Wilstein.[4] Spell check and grammar check are your friends. Visit them often. But remember that, like people, they're not perfect. Spell check will not flag a correctly spelled but misused word. It won't change "no" to "on," "how" to "who" or "tea" to "tee." Unfortunately, spell check won't work on names either. Correct spelling remains the writer's responsibility.

Grammar check may identify what it suspects are incorrect uses of a word, but again the writer must decide. Homonyms such as "there," "they're" and "their" sound alike but are spelled differently and have unrelated meanings. If you have trouble remembering which is which, create a memory trick to help, such as "They're sitting over there with their boyfriends."

SPORTS METAPHORS

Just before the Oregon football team ran out onto the Rose Bowl field to start the game, a distressed fan shook his head pityingly: "Poor devils! Don't you think they ought at least to blindfold them?"

His point was, the game that followed was supposed to be a drawn-out execution, with the Ohio State Buckeyes on the business end of the firing squad. The worst defeat in Rose Bowl history was freely predicted for the Oregon Ducks. As it turned out, however, in the words of writer Jim Murray, "the doughty Oregon team was still staring its 'executioners' resolutely in the eye right up to the final gun."

Sports metaphors, like the one above by Murray writing in Sports Illustrated, "can be traced back to the 5th century B.C.," notes Robert Palmatier, author of a book called "Sports Talk" — a dictionary of 1,700 sports metaphors. "In fact, Shakespeare used them in some of his plays." Indeed, sports metaphors permeate all walks of life. "When someone asks you how you made out — in the old-fashioned sense," he said, "you'd either say that you struck out or you couldn't get to first base — or you scored."

Knowing the history of popular sports metaphors might help you as a writer put the right one in the right context. For example, can you define the following terms that have come into everyday use?

- "Hat in the ring." Back in the day, boxers and even spectators who wanted to get in the ring for a bout would signal their intention by tossing in a hat. The expression is used now in the world of politics to announce that someone is running for office.
- "Wild goose chase." Shakespeare used this expression first, according to the Oxford English Dictionary. Mercutio, in reference to a duel of wits with Romeo, said, "Nay if our wits run the wild goose chase, I am done." It was used later in the 17th century to describe a sport where riders would set one horse off on a ramble and then chase after it, setting off at intervals, to follow as closely as possible. Eventually the term became used for any hopeless quest.
- "Throw in the towel." In boxing, a fighter's cornerman throws a towel into the ring to indicate a sign of surrender. Other terms we still use from boxing include "down for the count," "saved by the bell," "take it on the chin" and "below the belt."
- "Out of left field." Why is left field the spot where kooky ideas come from? No one is quite sure. A colorful explanation is that behind the

left-field wall at the Cubs' ballpark was a mental hospital whose patients could sometimes be heard making bizarre remarks during the game.

- "Hands down." An easy decision, not close at all, requiring no effort, is called "hands down." When a jockey has a race in the bag, he can relax his hold on the reins and stop urging the horse forward.[5]

Collective Nouns

Collective nouns describe more than one person, place or thing as a unit: a class, committee, team. "Team" is the collective noun most often used in sports. A team, whether it has two members or 200, is one entity and requires a singular verb or pronoun: "The team is leaving Friday." If the members of the team are acting individually, "team" requires a plural verb or pronoun: "The team are expected to work out for an hour each day, sometime between noon and 6 p.m., and log their times on this form." To avoid any potential confusion, use "team members" or "players": "Team members are in the weight room working out." "The players are warming up."

Accurate times and distances are a critical part of reporting on track and field.
© Nebraska Wesleyan Sports Information.

The same principle applies to the names of teams. If referred to by the name of the university or the home city, a team is singular: "The University of Arkansas is favored by 17 points." If the team is referred to by its mascot, use a plural verb or pronoun: "The Dolphins are favored in their season opener."

Misplaced Modifiers

Modifiers should be placed as close as possible to the words they modify. If they aren't, they can distort the meaning of the sentence. "Dangling participle" is a fancy name given to a modifying phrase that begins with an "–ing" verb bumping up against the wrong noun. For example, dangling participles can create unintended humor as in this headline: "Complaints About NBA Officials Growing Ugly"

Weasel Words

Some words — even short, simple ones — just don't say anything. The question "What is 'fun'?" might elicit "winning" from an athlete or "watching my team win" from a fan. Perhaps an imaginative fan will say, "Fun is seats on the 50-yard line at the Rose Bowl on a 66-degree New Year's Day watching my team complete the winning touchdown after the clock runs out!"

In other words, "fun" is normally a weasel word, something that wastes space and doesn't move the story ahead. If a word does not pull its own weight, it is a weasel, one you should replace or omit. For example, instead of "a lot," use a specific alternative: "16 tons" or "90,000 fans." Instead of "a few," use something more definite: "the holes-in-one I've made in my lifetime" or "the members of my bowling team" or "the number of blind climbers who have reached the top of Mount Everest."

Quotes that don't add information to the story are just bigger weasel words. If a source says, "It was a great game," ask what made it great. A little more time spent asking for specific details means less time trying to write a meaningful story.

Clichés

"Down for the count," "throw in the towel," "snatched victory from the jaws of defeat" . . . well, you get the idea. Clichés are as dead as doornails. If you've heard it or read it 10 times, it's a cliché. Don't use it! A cliché is someone else's expression, perhaps once clever but by now trite and overused.

The more a cliché is used, the less power it has to engage people's imaginations. Instead, your goal should be to write the expression that becomes the new cliché (oops, sorry, that's an oxymoron) or to put a new twist on an old one as the following headline does. Lawrence Tynes, a kicker for the New York Giants, had missed twice in a playoff game but fortunately connected on a long game-winning field goal, leading to this headline: "Third Tynes a Charm for Giants"

CLICHÉ SPEAK

Could you write an entire story in cliches? Well, it's quite possible as demonstrated below by Isaac May, a journalism student at Hastings College. But would you want to? We hope that provokes a different response.

Sometimes as writers we have our backs against the wall. We have editors who expect our A game every time we metaphorically lace up the cleats. That's when I revert to what has been working: clichés.

Unfortunately, there are days like this. But what can you do? Sports are all about winning, and clichés are a proven winner. Who hasn't ever drained the buzzer beater to clinch the win in OT? Who hasn't wanted to punch one across the goal line for six? And who else but the media can add to the excitement with such bland, overused terms?

Don't get me wrong. Scored, made, missed, run — they all tell what happened, but they hardly take your writing to the next level. Some of us are wily veterans of the sports writing world and don't have to try the Hail Mary when we're down and out. But we freshman phenoms want to dive into the playbook for something fantastic.

We try to describe the things that don't show up in the stat column. We try to bottle up the emotion and capture the moment in words. Covering sports is a team effort and I'm happy making my contribution, but there has been a lot of trash talking out there.

Some bad words between writers have caused some extracurricular activity to take place on the field. I tip my hat to them. They made a point that clichés can be boring and useless.

I don't want to point fingers. I only have to look in the mirror to see who is to blame. I couldn't get it done in the clutch, and I shied away from the pressure. You just have to put the past behind you. My old arm isn't what it used to be. I hope I can become a living legend, go out on top. But you know, you win some, you lose some, and a tie is like kissing your sister.

So the moral of the story? Throw those old clichés out of your news stories. And if you're keeping score at home: that was 34 cliches.

Euphemisms

Once upon a time there was a reporter who was assigned to write a story about bananas. He thought readers would tire of reading "banana, banana, banana," so he substituted "elongated yellow fruit" each time the word "banana" appeared. The strategy didn't work. Unfortunately, sports writers who find themselves writing about the same old things continue to search for substitutes. Those substitutes are called euphemisms.

The sports page is the birthplace of many euphemisms, created when sports writers are trying to find a new, lively, colorful way to say the same old thing. Little has changed since Stanley Walker, editor of the New York Herald, wrote "that a few standard nouns and verbs become tiresome." Thus did a left-handed pitcher become a "southpaw," although, Walker observes, "For some reason, right-handed pitchers never were 'north-paws.'" A baseball became "the old apple," a football became "the pigskin" and a basketball shot that misses everything became "a brick" or an "air ball."

In most sports, for example, players run. If the ball carrier ran, he ran. For the sake of variety, however, sports writers now have the ball carrier "plow," "gallop," "break loose" or "trot." If the basketball player made the shot, she scored. But writers might have her "drain," "sink," "nail," "knock down," "swish" or "put two on the board." What would sports writing be without these euphemisms? Still, use them sparingly.

Redundant Words and Phrases

Redundant phrases say the same thing twice. Take the commonly used "all-time record." "All-time record" is a way of trying to make a record sound more important than, by definition, it already is. The record is the highest, fastest, most or best. No "all-time" is needed. Redundant terms like these often appear in sports contexts: "ultimate outcome," "close proximity," "new recruits," "end result," "favored to win." Even the football staple "sacked the quarterback" is redundant. After all, the quarterback is the only player who can be sacked.

Typos

It's worth remembering that no matter how hard you try, errors will still slip through. Typos are inevitable, just like death and taxes. But some are worse than others:

Twelve weeks of the college volleyball season are complete. The season started in August when Nebraska fans were wearing T-shits to the match.[6]

So strive for accuracy but don't expect perfection.

OTHER KINDS OF STORIES

After an Olympic athlete set a new world record, one of your friends says, "Records are made to be broken!" Your friend's point is warranted. Being the best in the world in an Olympic sport is, after all, an important story. But perhaps you wondered, are there some records not made to be broken? If you had then researched and written a story on unbreakable records, you would have produced a feature story.

Feature Writing

Features tell special or out-of-the-ordinary stories that entertain as they inform. They are often based on the human interest or novelty news values. The best feature stories tug at the heartstrings.

Ask most people what a feature story is, and they'll say something soft and puffy, written for the arts or fashion section of a newspaper or website. But, in fact, features can be about any subject, especially in sports. "Grabbing the essence of a feature is like wrestling a squid; it'll soon depart in a cloud of ink," said Richard Cheverton, editor at the Orange County Register. But there is a way to identify an important aspect of feature writing. A feature story usually has a personal presence (the author as spectator or participant). Here are some of the other characteristics that distinguish feature stories:

- *Pace.* Feature stories employ a more leisurely pace than news. Feature writers take their time to tell a story instead of rushing through it the way news writers often seem to do.
- *Focus on human interest.* If sports stories tend to focus on events, then sports features tend to focus on people. They are designed to bring the human element into the picture. So, if a news story recounts how 200 people are being laid off from ESPN, a feature story might focus on just one of those workers, portraying their grief at losing a job.
- *Style.* Borrow the techniques of short fiction, where you combine the rigors of actual reporting with the creative freedom of short story writing.
- *Build on a news peg.* A news peg connects a feature story to something timely in the news. For example, a feature on the safety of football equipment might build off a story that your school's quarterback recently suffered a head injury in a game.

Finding Feature Stories

Author E.B. White's advice to young writers is timeless: "Don't write about man," he said, "write about *a* man." Plan to tell your stories through the experiences of individuals in your campus community. A story about a classmate who volunteers at a local soup kitchen will engage your audience far more than a story about an antipoverty program in a nearby town. Would you rather read about a baseball card collection or a baseball card collector?

Profiles

One popular type of feature story is a character sketch, often called a profile. A good profile brings the subject to life by providing drama (through conflict) and mystery (what was the motivation?). Begin with an unusual or noteworthy detail — an inexplicable tattoo, for instance. Then try to discover what is unique about the person. Unfortunately, without a little imagination, profiles can turn into a tedious recounting of biographical facts: "She was born near Red Cloud and attended high school in Superior . . ." Lazy reporters might string a few unrelated anecdotes together with some quotations and call it good. But you can do better.

How to Organize a Feature

Feature stories differ quite a bit from news stories and consequently need a different kind of organization pattern to establish relationships between all the pieces of information, quotes and observations. Some common structures for feature stories are the hourglass, the spatial story and the story in scenes.

- The hourglass structure resembles the inverted pyramid: information is arranged in descending order of importance. Below the "waist" of the hourglass, however, the writer builds toward an ending that is as broad and comprehensive as the beginning. Readers should finish the story with a feeling of closure much different from what they feel at the end of a traditional news story.
- The spatial story uses physical space rather than logic to determine order. For example, you could describe a new building on your college using a room-to-room tour. Perhaps you could follow a maintenance person from task to task, and geography would become the roadmap of your feature.
- Writing the story in scenes is a good strategy for profiles. Show the subject of your story reacting differently in different situations. An advantage of this structure is that it allows the reader to see what you are describing through the eyes of many different people. For example, you might arrange a series of interviews with those who know your subject from different life situations.

No matter which structure you choose, the key is to provide the reader with logical connections. Think of each idea in your story as an island. Your task is to write bridges between the islands to keep your readers from drowning.

Nut Graf

Writers anchor their feature stories with a device called a "nut graf," a term drawn from the expression "in a nutshell." A nut graf is similar to a news lead in that it answers most of the who-what-when questions but differs in that it can float to a variety of locations in the story. Many features, for example, begin with an extended anecdote designed to intrigue the reader into hanging around. Once the reader is hooked, the writer uses the nut graf to summarize the essence of a story and tell readers why the story matters. With the nut graf under their belts, readers can then follow the story wherever its meanderings take it.

Sports Columns

Fans like to know what those on the inside think, and that's what columnists try to deliver. The sports column, a blend of personal perspective and solid reporting, is typically the most read part of the sports page. Written on a regular basis, perhaps weekly, it often develops a dedicated cadre of readers.

Readers and viewers are attracted to the voice, the style and the personality that come through in a columnist's writing. They think of the columnist as a friend, someone who shares similar ideas or makes them chuckle. Kim Ode, who writes for the Minneapolis Star-Tribune, says readers expect a columnist to feel passionately about something once a week and that she gets the greatest reaction to stories "from the heart." Unfortunately, being human, Ode says she can't generate that level of passion for every column. "If I'm writing about gardening, you know I have writer's block," she says.

Becoming the staff columnist is the pinnacle of sports writing, a coveted position earned over time as a beat reporter. Media give columnists space on the page or on the air and time to write on topics of their choice because their columns draw readers and viewers. Column writing offers you a great soapbox. Instead of annoying just your family and friends, you can irritate thousands with your rants and rages. Sometimes, columnists try to tie their columns to the news of the day. At other times, however, columnists relate personal experiences when they attempt to make the personal universal. That's what happened when Pat Forde realized he would be covering his own daughter in the Tokyo Olympics:

> This is my ninth Olympics, so I know what they're supposed to look and feel like. My situation was more complicated. With a child on the team, I would have loved to slip into the Team Dad role — but the rules prohibited that, so there would be no orange slices or juice boxes or food deliveries from me to them. Also, I had to work roughly 12-16 hours a day, factoring in bus time to and from Tokyo Aquatics Center. Most awkward of all, I had to attempt to objectively (and at times critically) cover the U.S. swimmers and their coaches while trying not to put my daughter in a difficult position.[7]

Other times columnists examine the past for clues about the present. It's easy to check what was happening a year, five years or 25 years ago. Checking those events might help you find a good topic. Thinking back on an old restaurant menu led Ellen Goodman to write this column about outrageous appetites:

> Once upon a time there was a restaurant in Harvard Square that sold whale steaks. Honestly. Whale was right there on the menu, along with cod and hamburger.
>
> I don't share this factoid of food history to send little children screaming out of the room. Or to satisfy the curiosity of the epicureans. (OK, it tastes like liver.) I serve it up rather to note how the ethical appetite has changed.
>
> Mind you, this was before Willy, and before environmentalism. Today a whale steak sounds like spotted owl pate or panda sorbet.

Columns provide the personality and passion that news reporting doesn't normally afford, according to Tim Harrower in "Inside Reporting."[8] It's OK to take a position if you're a columnist. It's acceptable to analyze and criticize. It's the one place you can use your imagination, create a persona, say what you think — based on the facts — and still be respected as a sports journalist.

Newspaper opinion columns are clearly labeled to separate opinion from regular sports content. Each has a column logo, a byline and usually a photo of the writer. Most use special typography to emphasize the difference from an ordinary story. Online opinion options such as blogs, personal web pages and instant messaging have increased people's expectations that columnists will help them understand how to think about issues and people. Perhaps most important, opinion writers write columns to show that journalists care.

UPON FURTHER REVIEW

1. The sports idiom used by insiders and fans alike is a language unto itself. Make a list of 10 words and phrases you find in sports news that you think are part of that idiom. Share your list with the class and discuss where you think a reporter should draw the line in a game story.
2. Find a few euphemisms or clichés in three sports stories. Revise the stories, replacing the euphemisms and clichés with more accurate, precise language.
3. As language evolves, usage changes. In some contexts, including media, the plural possessive pronoun "their" is becoming acceptable with a singular noun or pronoun antecedent. Example: "A player should work on their skills in the offseason." Can you find a sports story that uses "their" with a singular noun?

NOTES

1. Evan Bland and Mike Patterson, "College World Series: Wake Forest slips past LSU in winners game," *Omaha World-Herald*, June 19, 2023.

2. Jim Corbett, "Chargers Get Lesson in Playoff Pressure," *USA Today Sports Weekly*, Jan. 17-23, 2007, 15.

3. "Texas' NCAA High Jump Champ to Skip Track Season for Volleyball," *USA* Today, Jan. 22, 2008, www.usatoday.com/sports/college/2008-01-22-texas-hooker-volleyball.

4. Steve Wilstein, *Associated Press Sports Writing Handbook* (New York: McGraw-Hill, 2002), 112.

5. Jim Murray, *Sports Illustrated*, Jan. 13, 1958.

6. *Lincoln Journal Star*, Nov. 13, 2023.

7. Pat Forde, "I've Covered Nine Olympics. Nothing Prepared Me for Seeing My Daughter Win a Medal," *Sports Illustrated*, Aug. 5, 2021.

8. Tim Harrower, *Inside Reporting: A Practical Guide to the Craft of Journalism* (New York: McGraw-Hill, 2007), 130.

8

Following the Style

More than half a century ago, the Associated Press news organization recognized the need for a consistent style for stories flowing in from its bureaus worldwide. Today, the "Associated Press Stylebook" is the standard in American journalism. It offers guidelines on spelling, usage, grammar and punctuation and provides helpful formats for scores, times, distances, dates, addresses, names and titles.

Whether it's an editor, a sports reporter or the media relations director, anyone who writes for print or online media must know and use AP style. People in media recognize immediately whether the writer is a professional by the style used in a story or news release. Much less editing is required to prepare a story for release when it already conforms to AP style. That alone may make the difference in whether a story or news release is used or rejected.

READERS LIKE CONSISTENCY

Using a standardized style makes writing easier and faster for reporters once they learn the guidelines. It makes grasping information easier and faster for readers (who may not even realize a standard is being applied). It becomes a habit for the writer and a comfort zone for the consumer.

Today's "Associated Press Stylebook" is roughly 10 times longer than the first, published in 1953, and now serves not only journalists but also communicators in a wide variety of fields. The AP Stylebook is available both as a physical book and online. The spiral-bound book is published every other year, taking into account changes in usage. The 56th, and most current, edition spans more than 500 pages. Meanwhile, the AP Stylebook Online, updated in real time, often reflects input from regular readers. Both guides include the usual style tips plus sections on polls and surveys, social media guidelines and digital security. There are also special sections for those who write about business, health and science, religion and, most important for us, sports.

You can find a chapter on inclusive storytelling, too, an effort to help give voice and visibility to people around the globe. The chapter aims to help writers recognize and overcome unconscious biases, to be sensitive about specific words and phrases, and to reach beyond the usual sources for story ideas.

Language Is Always Changing

Language is remarkably fluid. Word combinations, slogans and phrases are being added to the language each day. "Because of the constantly changing usage," the very first "Associated Press Stylebook" stated, "no compilation can be called permanent." That modest claim set the tone for all that followed. The AP guidelines strive to be fair and not to offend any individual or group of people, according to Dr. Mike Sweeney, head of the journalism graduate program at Ohio University. It aims at "a general audience with a tone that is neither too elite nor too common," he said.[1]

Writers should remind themselves that there is no such thing as a definitive right answer. Some of the book's guidance falls into the many gray areas that confront a writer. Most media outlets have their own in-house stylebooks in addition to the AP guidelines that add rules for their own unique situation. Writers and editors still need to make judgment calls from time to time, often based on discussion with colleagues.

Many of the ideas for changes in the manual come from X and Facebook followers. Regular readers send emails with thoughts and examples. "Once we make our updates public," writes editor Paula Proke, "we pay close attention to the feedback. Nothing, of course, is universally applauded. The reaction — both positive and negative — can be intense." The end result, as the editors in 1953 noted with an eye toward the future, "necessarily represents many compromises between conflicting points of view."

Stylistic Formats

Recurring items are easier to read and understand if they appear in the same format each time. The date an event takes place, for example, might be written as a day of the week or as a date depending on the writer's habit, whim or mood. It could be written as "Sunday, Jan. 17, 2025" or "yesterday" or any of a wide variety of choices. AP style dictates that the date should be always written the same way — the day of the week or the date. The words "yesterday," "today" and "tomorrow," for example, make readers pause to calculate when the story appeared and consequently discourages them in most cases. If a story is delayed, such time references become inaccurate anyway and require further editing before publication.

Online sports news sites solve this problem by marking each story with the exact minute, hour and day of publication. Each time the story is updated, the time references within the story have to be adjusted accordingly — another reason for using the day of the week instead of "yesterday," "today" or "tomorrow."

Sports Style

The AP Stylebook has a separate sports style section that defines terms, indicates how scores, times and distances should be written, and offers help with spelling and punctuation. Numbers are all over the place in sports stories, so the rules for writing them are good to know. Single-digit numbers, for example, are written as words; anything larger is written as a numeral: one, nine, 10, 19, 119. Exceptions, and there are many, include ages, dates, heights, measurements, percents, proper names (i.e., Big Ten) and scores. The stylebook specifies the order in which scores and statistics are organized and gives helpful examples.

Broadcast Style

Broadcast sports departments also have stylebooks. Style changes when the reporter is writing for listeners who only have one chance to hear and understand the information. Because broadcast stories are shorter, it is even more important to omit extraneous words that take up airtime that could be used to report significant information.

PROOFREADING

"Accuracy, accuracy, accuracy" was Joseph Pulitzer's admonition to reporters and copy editors when he was the editor of the New York World in the 1880s. He might have added that a simple way to achieve accuracy is to proofread, proofread, proofread. Proofreading begins with the writer, who should correct errors before filing a story. The writer is the only person who can recognize some errors because they are the person who asked the source to spell his name or saw the coach put an arm around the shoulders of a player who was having a bad day. Which player was it — number 23 or number 32? Was the player's name Cheri, Shari or Sherry?

STRATEGIES TO WRING ERRORS OUT OF YOUR STORIES

Consult this process from time to time to improve the accuracy of your stories.

1. Use spell check and grammar check. Take advantage of these helpers built into your software. Even an eagle-eyed copy editor will never be as fast at finding and fixing errors as these electronic checkers. But use caution. The computer-generated correction may not carry the message you intended. If you mean "wood" and spell check suggests "would," your judgment still comes into play.

2. Read the story on-screen from beginning to end. The goal at this stage is to take a broad view: Does the story have all the necessary information? Does it flow easily? Are quotations in the right places? This is the time to add or delete information, reorganize paragraphs or insert a quote.

3. Print the story and read it again. This time pencil in corrections, changing words that don't seem quite right. This is where you'll catch errors that spell check didn't. Only the writer will recognize a misspelled name or know if the game was Friday or Saturday or whether the score was reversed.

4. Read the story aloud. You may hear mistakes in sentence structure or find sentences that need to be shortened. If a sentence is too long to read aloud without taking a breath, it's too long. Steve Wilstein, the author of the "Associated Press Sports Writing Handbook," calls this the mumble method. "I kind of mumble to hear what it's about and whether it makes any sense. By mumbling just loud enough, I can pick up the sound of sentences and the connections between them and better spot errors."[2]

5. Read the story to someone. Better yet, have someone read it to you. If the reader stumbles over a word, hesitates or stops midsentence, those are problems to fix.

6. Read the story aloud backward. Start with the last word and read from right to left. This is the ultimate test to make your eyes focus on each word. You will see phrases or groups of words in a new way and may realize that a word is repeated or missing, or that there's an "s" on the end of a word that should be singular.

Lining up a putt is one of the precision moves in golf.
© Nebraska Wesleyan Sports Information.

SPORTS HEADLINES

Typically, newspaper headlines are written by copy editors or page designers during the design process and not by the reporter who wrote the story. Headline writers have the task of reducing each story to a few words that will fit in the limited space above the text when the page is designed. A one-column story in a newspaper will accommodate two or at most three small words per line — and present one big challenge for the headline writer. Columnist Mike Sweeney described the challenge in the Fort Worth Star-Telegram:

> Names like Moe Iba [a longtime basketball coach] fit well in headlines and are appreciated by copy editors. When Iba was an assistant coach, the college newspaper ran a story saying he had turned down a job elsewhere. An editor who drew the page said the first proposed headline, "Iba rejects job," was just too long. The solution? "Moe no go."

Sometimes writers have advance warning of a headline they need to write. Amid the tension and excitement of the NBA Championship game between the hometown Bulls and the Utah Jazz, the Chicago Tribune staff was already preparing the front page that would run the morning after the game. If Chicago won, it would be the Bulls' sixth championship in eight years. Even if the Bulls lost, readers would expect a big headline.

Bill Parker, assistant managing editor, canvassed the newspaper's headline writers and gathered a list of ideas. He knew he had only four to six words to work with, words to capture the spirit of a sports-crazed city. As it turned out, the Bulls won 87-86 on a steal and field goal in the last five seconds. The streets of Chicago "erupted in an all-night celebration," excitement not lost on the Tribune's morning headline writer, who used the moment to wink at "another type of physical activity" and make an allusion to a popular New York Times best seller: "The Joy of Sex." The winning headline was simply "The joy of six."

Headlines Advertise Stories

You might think of headlines as a form of advertising that sells stories to potential readers by promising a benefit. That little "wink" of an allusion in the Bulls headline above implies the benefits of happiness, humor and satisfaction. Most headlines run four to six words, maybe more if there is space. In those few words, the writer must summarize the story in a way that is specific and accurate without distorting its meaning. Some readers are looking for stories they expect to see: last night's big game, who made the cut for the next round of the playoffs or which team is favored to win the Super Bowl. Some readers are in the market for any story about their favorite teams or players. Some readers are just grazing, looking for a good story to read. Each decides whether to read the story based on the headline.

The popularity of online news sites has made headlines even more crucial in getting readers' attention and drawing them into the story. Are they attracted first by the headlines, the photos or something else? Eye-tracking studies sponsored by the Poynter Institute showed that online readers notice and scan headlines first.[3] They check out the first two or three words of a headline or text block before making a decision whether to read or leave. The majority of online readers in another study, however, looked at the navigation bars and tools before reading the headlines. Print readers looked first at headlines and then at large photos.[4]

Names appear to be the secret to writing successful sports headlines. Names of teams. Names of mascots. Names of players and coaches. An informal survey of sports stories in newspapers and on sports websites showed that more than 90 percent of the headlines begin with the name of a team, mascot, player or coach.

Headline Tips

- Use conversational language. This example, "Sending a message," is from a story about LSU winning the College World Series.
- Use present tense for past events.

Not "Chastain won Ally 400"
But "Chastain wins Ally 400"

- Use action verbs: "wins" the match, "breaks" the record
- Replace "and" with a comma.

Not "Kenya and Australia qualify for semifinals"
But "Kenya, Australia qualify for semifinals"

- Be careful when you split a line so as not to separate subjects from verbs, prepositions from objects or modifiers from nouns.

Not "Baseball commission adopts new
policy to control drug use"
But "Baseball commission adopts
new policy to control drug use"

- Omit *to be* verbs.

Not "Olympic Games are headed to China"
But "Olympics headed to China"

Stylistically, most media prefer the "down style" where normal rules of capitalization prevail. The first word of the headline and proper nouns are the only words capitalized. For example,

UNK hammers Arizona State

Rain washes out Cup practice, jumbles schedule

Headlines omit articles (a, an, the), conjunctions (and, but, or) and most adjectives and adverbs. End punctuation is limited to question marks and exclamation points; even those are rare, but they do make the headlines on special occasions. For example: "Will Irish eyes smile in '24?" or "Pacman Jones getting ready to . . . wrestle?"

Action Verbs

Action verbs are the lifeblood of sports headlines. "McIlroy takes lead" or "McIlroy leads" would state the fact, but "McIlroy grabs lead" gives a stronger sense of the intensity and momentum. When choosing an action verb, make it fit the situation. A horse in the final leg of a race gallops to the finish line, a baseball player slides home and a player can be jazzed if he's just been traded to the Utah Jazz. How about this for an action verb: "Wildcats pounce on Tigers."

Punctuation and Style

Headline syntax and punctuation differ from standard grammar rules because of space limitations. Periods are not used, commas replace "and" and a colon connects a speaker's name and message. For example,

Seattle stymies Washington's rally, wins in NFC playoffs
Richardson: Landis fills stat sheet all the way across

Single quotation marks replace double quotation marks around words quoted in the story.

'Once-in-a-lifetime' shot sends Deuel to top

The dollar sign and symbols such as &, @, # and % appear in headlines as space-saving devices.

¢ turn into $ for baseball retirees' fund

SECONDARY HEADLINES

Secondary headlines add another layer of information between the headline and the text. They serve two quite different purposes: one, to encourage readers to read the rest of the story, and two, to give readers enough information to know a little more about the story in case they decide not to read on. Secondary headlines are set in type smaller than the headline and larger than the text. They are typically written as complete sentences. If the headline reads like this: "Destruction complete," the secondary headline may state: "Marvin Harrison Jr. paces quick-strike Ohio State in 38-3 rout of Michigan State."

Blurbs and Links

Blurbs are the online equivalent of secondary headlines. Blurbs tell readers what's in the news and help them decide what stories to read. More than one blurb may appear with a story or brief. Eye-tracking research showed that half of online readers are scanners who move quickly from one headline or blurb to another, seldom returning to read a story once they move away. By scanning the visual chunks created by headlines and blurbs, these readers gain an overview of the news.

Online stories have the added advantage of being able to use embedded links to lead readers to sites about related topics and give them more choices in finding the information they want. An online reader may never finish reading a news story yet have a thorough understanding of the event or subject because they are able to follow the thread of information from link to link. An online reader who wants to know

FIXING MISTAKES IS PART OF THE DEAL

"Almost every day when I come to work," said Kathleen Rutledge, editor of the Lincoln Journal Star, "I have a lot of fun. Almost every day, I take a little heat, too." The heat Rutledge refers to are the mistakes, large and small, that her staff prints each day in the paper. A perfect paper has never happened.

On one such day, Rutledge said, the paper printed a headline that misspelled a word ("turbulance"), moved a local tavern from its actual location to a mysterious spot across town, misnamed a film critic and put the legendary Battle of Iwo Jima into a time machine and dropped it into the Vietnam War.

Rutledge says everyone knows the paper makes mistakes, but not everyone knows "we hate to make mistakes. It hurts our credibility with readers. We know the little things damage our credibility as much as bigger errors of fact or judgment." Rutledge's paper, like most media outlets, makes sure that several newsroom staffers "touch" a story before publication. That includes the reporter, an assignment editor, a copy editor, a page designer and, finally, another editor who proofs the whole page before the negative is sent to the press room. At each stop along the way, staffers follow established procedures to help improve accuracy.

The paper also invites readers to call or email immediately if they see something wrong. Readers who help give the paper (or media source) the chance to correct the record also enable them to fix their archives too so that the next time someone on the staff writes about the topic, they won't look up the old story and get it wrong again.

The moral of the story: it's OK to make a mistake as long as you own up to it as quickly as possible.

more about a recent NBA championship game, for example, might link to the NBA Encyclopedia Playoff Edition to read a retrospective story about the game, to YouTube to watch video of the final shot, to Amazon to buy a book or to the New York Times archives for stories published about the game.

SPORTS CUTLINES

"A picture might be worth a thousand words," explains Texas writer and artist Austin Kleon, "but when it's paired with a caption that deepens, expands, or redefines its meaning, it can be worth a million." Important as they may be, however, captions are typically the last thing anyone in the newsroom writes or edits. Generally, photographers are responsible for gathering the information about the photographs they take, including the correct spelling of names, and filing it with the photographs for future reference, but someone else writes the caption.

"Caption" and "cutline," by the way, are interchangeable terms meaning the words that describe what's happening in a photo. Before photography and printing press technology converged in the 1800s, the only way to get an illustration in the newspaper was to carve or "cut" the image into a wood block. Images became known as "cuts," and the name has stuck through all the technological advances ever since.

Every photograph, including a mug shot, needs a caption. Whether it's online, on a page in a newspaper or magazine, or in a company newsletter, a photograph is just a graphic design element unless it's accompanied by a caption explaining who is in the photo, what is happening, when and where it took place and why it's newsworthy. The sports editor may know by looking at a photo that it's quarterback Tom Brady sweating out the last few minutes of the game, but do not assume everyone who sees the photo will have the same instant recognition.

Swimming is a little like track and field under water.
© Nebraska Wesleyan Sports Information.

What Captions Do

Captions identify the people in a photo and its context. As a general guideline, journalists go by the "rule of five": identify up to five persons by name if they can be recognized. Thus, in a photo of four players sitting on the bench, each should be named. But use good judgment — if the coach is pictured standing on the sideline shaking his fist at the officials in front of the players on the bench, only the coach needs to be identified. Note that the rule of five is flexible. If six or seven people in a photo wearing hard hats and holding shovels are poised to break ground for the new stadium, they should all be named.

Captions should also tell readers what they cannot see. A ground breaking, for example, is a ceremony formalizing a process that has taken months, maybe years, to reach this moment. The reader wants to know why these particular people are breaking ground for the new athletic complex, how much construction is going to cost and whether it will be ready in time for next season.

Posed team photos appear in special preseason sections and on posters. Every player, coach and team assistant should be named in the caption. The in-house stylebook should define how the caption will be written: for example, first initial and last name, first and last names, last name comma first initial, or some other way.

Captions can be as long as necessary to make the photo understandable without stating the obvious. "Coach Big Shot poses in his office" is easy to see from looking at the photo, but the reader wants to know more: Why is the coach in his office? What's newsworthy about this photo? This caption: "Coach Big Shot prepares to watch films and take notes for next week's game before meeting with the team Sunday evening" explains why the coach is taking notes as he watches the screen on the corner of his desk.

Photos capture the action as it is happening, and thus, captions are written in present tense: "Coach Big Shot *watches* . . . and *takes* . . ." The second or third sentence of a caption can be written in past tense if they explain the background leading up to this moment.

LIBEL AND OTHER LEGALITIES

Sports writers are subject to the same laws as all journalists when it comes to saying or writing words that are untrue or harmful to others. Writers are responsible for knowing and abiding by federal and state laws and the codes of ethics of their profession. A commitment to accuracy is the best protection. Failure to check facts, or the inability to support those facts, is the cause of most libel suits. At the very least, publishing an incorrectly spelled name or a mistaken score damages the credibility of the reporter and the publication. At most, reporters lose jobs and courts order millions of dollars paid to persons who have been libeled or whose privacy has been invaded. Here is a brief overview of the legal terms sports writers should know.

BASEBALL THE WAY IT'S SUPPOSED TO BE

Historians date the past using BCE (Before the Common Era) and CE (Common Era). Perhaps sports historians will someday use BT (Before Times) to indicate the long, long era that lasted before major league baseball changed its rules for the 2023 season. "It was tough watching the game," Hall of Fame slugger Andre Dawson admitted, referring to the Before Times. Now Dawson finds himself watching a game with a quicker pace and more athleticism. Suddenly, Dawson is interested again.

"It makes the game a little bit more exciting," he said. "And it's the best way to get the fan interest back. It's a good sign — and you're slowly starting to really enjoy the game again."

The new rule changes have brought back some of the charms of the past — base running and base stealing, to name a couple — but without getting gimmicky enough to where it felt, said one club official, like "you were creating a game show." "The game is faster now, and more athletic, and it drives forward with a momentum that maintains your attention," said Morgan Sword, Major League Baseball's executive vice president of baseball operations. "We haven't introduced something novel to baseball. We've really just chipped away at some of the delays and the dead time around what's always been a wonderful game."

More than any other rule, the pitch clock has shortened games. Prior to the change, baseball games averaged over three hours (putting fans at risk of not getting back home by midnight). After the change, games averaged 2 hours and 42 minutes, an improvement of about 20 minutes per game.

The most important changes in how baseball is played include these:

- The pitch clock: The new rule requires that pitchers have only 15 seconds between pitches with no one on base and 20 seconds with runners on. If a pitcher has not gone into his full motion by the time the clock hits zero, the umpire calls a ball. If the batter is not ready at eight seconds, he gets a strike.
- The shift: Another change made the game more fun to watch even if it didn't shave off any time. Baseball banned "the shift," a defensive strategy that allowed teams to overload one side of the infield. Hundreds of potential hits were swallowed up by shortstops playing behind second

base. Under the new rule, two infielders are required to stand on each side of second base.

- Stealing bases: We often hear the phrase, "It's a game of inches," and that applies to the new larger bases introduced to improve player safety and encourage more stolen-base attempts. The bases are now 18-square inches, up from 15-square inches. That puts home plate three inches closer to first and third base, while the corner bases are now 4.5 inches closer to second base.

Overall, the new rules lead to more action and less dead time. How much more action? Consider these facts from 2023:

- Over 1,600 more runs than the previous year
- More than 1,100 more hits
- Nearly 1,500 more baserunners
- Average time between balls in play — 30 seconds less than the year before

Hey, hand me that remote. I'm ready to watch some baseball.[5]

Libel

Libel is published defamation of character, an untruth that damages a person's reputation. A generalization such as "golfers are crooks" is not libelous by itself because it does not identify an individual, but "Dick Krapff is a crook" would be potentially libelous if Krapff sold used golf carts from the course and pocketed the money. But until he is charged with stealing from his employer, however, it would be libelous to say he is a crook.

The best defense against libel is the truth. If published information can be proven, through documentation or court record, it is a statement of fact and not libel. Many times, reporters run the risk of libel through their own negligence more than indulging in a vendetta against someone they don't like. Always verify information before using it. False information reported as fact, even if used in a quotation and attributed to the source, is still the reporter's responsibility and potentially libelous. Using the word "alleged" in some circumstances can serve as a defense.

Public Figures and Private Persons

Professional athletes and coaches, like entertainers, are considered public figures, and thus by voluntarily placing themselves in the public eye have a higher bar to prove libel than the rest of us so-called private persons. Access to the media has traditionally been considered a factor in determining who is a public figure. A person who has regular and open access to the media through news conferences with reporters is likely to be considered a public figure. This definition has expanded since social media platforms essentially give everyone access to the media. For a public figure to bring a libel charge against a reporter or the media, that person must prove the information was knowingly false. The injured party must also show that the reporter or media acted with intent to create ill will or to intentionally defame the public figure.

Private figures have more protection under the law. Most high school, college and amateur athletes, for example, do not have to prove malice when they believe they have been libeled. Negligence, which usually results from carelessness on the reporter's part, is cause enough for the court to award a libel ruling for a private person.

Corrections

Mistakes happen, and they should be corrected as quickly and publicly as possible. One way to avoid libel is to acknowledge factual errors without prompting. A show of good faith on the reporter's part does not undo the damage done to someone's reputation, but it may be looked upon favorably in court.

Privilege and Fair Comment

The ability of journalists to report information and statements made in official governmental proceedings, such as courts, without fear of being sued is protected by the right of privilege. Fair comment protects a journalist's right to express an opinion. A columnist who writes that a coach made a dumb decision or an official made a bad call, for example, is protected because those are observations and thoughts based on public performances. The same concept protects those who review plays, movies and TV shows. In turn, the journalist's obligation is to write commentary that is factually accurate and, as far as possible, fair.

Open Records and Open Meetings

Sports reporters occasionally have reason to attend a court session where an athlete is being arraigned or sentenced. They may need to see the police report on a traffic violation or an accident to verify information. There are many other examples of possible stories that would cause a reporter to cross the threshold of the judicial system. One of the reporter's best legal friends is the sunshine law, so called because it allows the "sun to shine in" on public records, public meetings and court proceedings. Laws vary from state to state, but almost all court proceedings and court records are open to the public. It's just a matter of finding them. Some traffic violations and accident reports may be on file at the courthouse and others at the police station, firehouse or city hall.

Not every public official or government agency, however, is eager to hand out information on a moment's notice, so plan ahead. Know where the information is located and get acquainted with the people in the offices. Even a sports reporter can benefit from reading the state and local statutes. A tour of local public offices will make finding the right place and the right piece of paper much faster when a deadline looms and the only way to get the official information is to go look at it. More public records are available online every day, but be aware that the websites may not be up to date or fully archived.

Fair Use

Fair use is a legal doctrine that allows reporters and other media producers to use small samples of copyright-protected material. No definitive rules exist to determine how much of any copyrighted work may be used, so when in doubt — ask. Examples of acceptable fair use, according to copyright expert James Tidwell, include

- A few lines of a song or excerpts from a book.
- A drawing of a copyrighted cartoon character in an editorial cartoon.
- News video in which copyrighted music provides ambient sound.
- Up to one minute of copyrighted audio or video to be used, for example, in the obituary of a famous athlete.

Copyright

Copyright is both a symbol and a law. Essentially, copyright is a tool to keep people from stealing work that others have created and claiming it as their own. For journalists, who often aggregate the work of others, copyright can be a minefield of trouble. Fortunately, the law allows the use of limited amounts of copyrighted work in new contexts. Journalists need to tread carefully, however, when borrowing what others have written or said.

Typically, in journalism the publisher of the newspaper or website, not the reporter, owns the copyright for published material. The work journalists do is known, most of the time, as work-for-hire. Thus, a sports reporter employed by a newspaper, broadcast station or website does not own the copyright on the work he or she does; their employer does. Securing written permission from the owner is the safe and fair way to use any copyright-protected work. Finding the current owner of a copyright, however, may not be easy. Copyrights are sometimes sold or the owner may have died, making it difficult to find the responsible party. Be aware that the process itself takes time.

ONLINE MEDIA ISSUES

Libel, copyright and commercial use laws that apply to print and broadcast media apply just the same to online media, whether a company website, a Facebook page or a personal email, according to Tidwell. Internet users are still exploring the frontiers of media and communication law. Online discussion groups, blogs and citizen journalist websites were an area of legal concern until the Supreme Court ruled that service providers are not responsible for messages posted by users. Thus, media websites that encourage public participation in blogs and instant messaging cannot be held responsible for the comments posted by their users.

Reporters who record interviews for rebroadcast at a later time, or broadcast telephone conversations live without the knowledge of the person speaking, open themselves to libel and invasion of privacy charges. Consent laws are at the heart of the matter. Some states are one-party consent territory, where a conversation may be recorded without the knowledge of both parties, while others are two-person consent states, where both parties must be aware that the conversation is being recorded.

A general rule of thumb is to document all calls by recording acknowledgment and permission from the person being called before beginning an interview or live broadcast. Call-in shows are an exception. Participants call with the intention of speaking live on the air and are personally responsible for what they say.

CODE OF ETHICS

Most newsrooms have ethics guidelines in their policies or stylebooks. The Associated Press Sports Editors (APSE), for example, has adopted guidelines specifically for sports. In principle, the APSE guidelines address the issues and situations that might compromise the integrity of reporters and editors and their ability to produce fair and unbiased sports news. If no such policies exist, media writers can also turn to the Society of Professional Journalists' (SPJ) Code of Ethics as a standard for their public communications. The SPJ Code sets forth four simple principles:

- Seek truth and report it. Journalists should be honest, fair and courageous in gathering, reporting and interpreting information.
- Minimize harm. Ethical journalists treat sources, subjects and colleagues as human beings deserving of respect.
- Act independently. Journalists should be free of obligation to any interest other than the public's right to know.
- Be accountable. Journalists are accountable to their readers, listeners, viewers and each other.

—Adapted from the Society of Professional Journalists' Code of Ethics

For a sports writer, these guidelines mean being extra diligent to represent both teams fairly in a story even if you're a homer at heart. It means

- Making just one more call after trying all day to reach a player and give her the chance to defend herself against an allegation before the story goes to press.
- Encouraging the public to express their opinions via email, tweet, blog or call.
- Treating sources, colleagues and the public with respect.
- Admitting to and correcting mistakes when you're wrong.

It also means not doing certain things:

- Accepting tickets, meals or gifts that might obligate you to provide a favor in return.
- Putting yourself in situations that might show support for one team over another.

UPON FURTHER REVIEW

1. Compare a story about your favorite sport in a newspaper or an online sports news site with the AP guidelines. Is the source consistent in its use of the guidelines? What exceptions, if any, did you find?
2. Ask for a copy of a local media style guide. Ask a reporter or news director to explain why the newsroom chose those specific guidelines. If your office or newsroom does not have a style guide, make a list of guidelines you would want to have included and ask others to contribute ideas. Draft a style guide and add to it as you find yourself questioning the way something should be written.
3. Study the headlines on five sports stories from several different media. What similarities do you notice? Differences? Rewrite some of the not-so-interesting headlines using higher-interest verbs. Count the number of headlines that begin with the name of a team, mascot, player or coach and calculate the percentage.
4. Should there be a separate code of ethics for sports journalists? Explain your rationale.

NOTES

1. Michael Sweeney, "The Guide to AP Style," Aug. 27, 2007, http://web.archive.org/web/20071024002142/www.usu.edu/journalism/faculty/sweeney/re.

2. Wilstein, "Associated Press Sports Writing Handbook," 182.

3. Sara Quinn, "EyeTrack07 ASNE Presentation Script," Poynter Institute, March 28, 2007.

4. Nora Paul, "Early Lessons from Poynter's EyeTrack07," *Online Journalism Review*, April 14, 2007, https://www.ojr.org/early-lessons-from-poynters-eyetrack07/.

5. Jayson Stark, "Whole New Ballgame: MLB's New Rules Changed Everything," *Athletic*, Nov. 17, 2023.

9

Making Numbers Count

Look at the beginning of a not-so-unusual sports story:

BLOOMINGTON, Ind. (AP): There was a tense second in the final minute of Iowa's one-point victory over No. 1 Indiana.

In a game full of thrilling emotions, this writer devoted the bulk of his lead to numbers: one second, the final minute, one point and number-one ranking. That sort of preoccupation is not unusual among sports writers. In fact, many of them, and fans for that matter, seem determined to quantify every aspect of their favorite game.

Baseball is perhaps the most notorious example of this obsession. You could probably find, for example, the statistical likelihood of a batter getting a hit in a Tuesday night game at home against a southpaw in July with the bases loaded. Who needs to watch? From the shelves of bookstores and on the airwaves, telecasts and websites, the number crunchers are out in force. We may be in the golden age of sports statistics. Two companies, the Elias Sports Bureau and the Sports Team Analysis and Tracking Systems (STATS), compile data for fans, professional teams, and print, broadcast and online media around the world. They can tell you worthwhile trivia (in 1971 the Dolphins and Chiefs played the longest game in NFL history at 82 minutes and 40 seconds) as well as esoteric non-information, such as which player hit the most foul balls. Consider this fun fact from one of baseball's greatest players:

> "During my 18 years I came to bat almost 10,000 times. I struck out about 1,700 times and walked maybe 1,800 times. You figure a ballplayer will average about 500 bats a season. That means I played seven years without ever hitting the ball."—Mickey Mantle[1]

DATA JOURNALISM

Data journalism has become a staple of reporting across beats and platforms. The ability to quantify information and present it in an engaging and accurate way is no longer only for a select few. Sports staffs, media relations crews and other organizations all speak the language of data and statistics. Journalists must become comfortable and confident in that language as well.

What do all these numbers add up to? In sum, they do three things for the intrepid sports writer: they provide new and interesting ways to understand and interpret the game, they provide lots of filler and fodder for radio and TV broadcasters, and they help us make smarter bets. Whoops, scratch that last one. Instead, let's say sports statistics help whether we're fans wanting to improve our chances in a fantasy league or players seeking to make a better arbitration case.

Understanding the Game

If historians were sports writers, we would probably know

- How long it took Washington to cross the Delaware, depending on whether the wind was blowing up or down the river.
- What size rock David used to beat Goliath, not to mention the brand of his slingshot.
- Why Gen. Custer, given his career record against the Lakota Sioux, should have thought better of engaging in the Battle of the Little Big Horn in 1876.

Few sports are as up close and personal as basketball for the reporter sitting on press row.
© Nebraska Wesleyan Sports Information.

It may seem odd to spend this passion for minutiae on a game, but here we are, in a new era of statistical curiosity. There is a statistic for virtually every situation, and a number of astute observers have figured out how to apply all this numerical data to gain a better understanding of their sport.

WHERE'S THE BIGGEST CLASSROOM?

Students may not get a letter grade for the hours they spend in the weight room and on the running track, but they often swear by the lessons they've learned through sports. The key is finding a good mix between papers and practices, between exams and games. Done well, an intercollegiate athletic program can enhance the lives of every student at the college, whether they suit up for a game or not.

"What's the biggest classroom at Carleton?" asked college president Robert Oden Jr. "People often guess one of our large classrooms, the concert hall, or Skinner Chapel," he said. "Almost nobody gets the answer I'm after: Laird Stadium where the football team plays. My point is that lots of teaching and learning happens in athletics."

Carleton competes in NCAA Division III, where 25 to 40 percent of the student body plays on varsity teams. Meanwhile, fewer than 2 percent of students at Division I schools are on athletic scholarships. What is it that students can learn from sports? Former athletic director Leon Lunder put it this way: "Some of the most important things you'll do in life will be done under pressure and in public. You'll have to make decisions without debating or taking time to consider. These are important skills, and you can learn them by participating in sports."

One former student athlete, Michael Armacost, president of the Brookings Institution, offered this view: "I learned the importance of subordinating individual aims to what was good for the team. I learned to hang in there when things got tough, to win with modesty and lose with grace, that luck often played a large role in the outcome of games, and that you can increase the odds of getting lucky by preparing more thoroughly and thoughtfully than your opponent."

Good advice for every student.

Covering a championship can be one of a reporter's most exciting experiences.
© Nebraska Wesleyan Sports Information.

Keeping Track

Let us consider how those numbers get compiled in the first place. Most of the time, sports writers try to keep "the book," that is, they keep their own statistics. At a basketball game, for example, they might keep track of points per player, rebounds and free throws. One of the best things about keeping your own stats is that the process forces you to pay close attention. You learn to focus on every play and every moment. Who can know, after all, when the game's turning point will come or what play will signal a shift that turns the game around?

Most of the time the home team provides an official scorekeeper, but in the case of high school games, that scorekeeper might be the coach's spouse, the town dentist or the bus driver. These people are probably reputable, but they may only keep track of made baskets and total points. The scorekeeper might leave the venue, too, before you have finished talking with the players and coaches. If the sports writer wants to look under the hood, so to speak, to see the hidden story of the game — the steals, assists and so on — she or he will need to keep track themselves.

In college games, the situation changes. The home sports information staff will usually provide a bevy of scorekeepers, each one responsible for a different statistic. One person, for instance, might record the time each point is made. These statisticians often work in pairs, one reporting the result out loud while the other records it. That way, the scorekeeper never needs to take his eyes off the game.

Competing Philosophies

Believe it or not, statistics play a role in two competing philosophies of sports coverage. On one hand, we have the sports writer who is intent on finding the story in the

WHEELCHAIR RACING

Cross-country is one of the few sports to be contested on a surface that hasn't been watered, mowed, weeded, pruned and cared for. Any bump, root or rut that might trip or impede a runner is just part of the challenge. And it's an especially big challenge for Abigail Harvey.

Abigail was born with spina bifida, a type of neural disability that in her case means she doesn't have any feeling from her knees down. As a seventh grader at Conestoga Junior High School in Nebraska, Abigail played a variety of wheelchair sports, including basketball, but at one point she became determined to join the cross-country team. "I really just wanted to be part of a team with my school because I had never really gotten to do that being a wheelchair athlete," she said.

Before Abigail, no one had ever competed in wheelchair cross-country in the state, according to the Nebraska Schools Activities Association. But in the fall of 2023, she participated alongside other runners in four races, each a little more than a mile long. Abigail said her teammates inspired her not to give up. "The girls have been amazing," she said. "They've helped me. They've encouraged me, they've made me stronger as a person and as an athlete."

Ryan Burns is the Conestoga Junior High cross-country coach. This season has been a first for him, too: coaching an athlete in a wheelchair. "We learned as we went, that's for sure," he said. "The arms were different for me. In the past we always trained our legs and our lungs, and this was very different."

For Abigail, it seems the training worked. She got faster throughout the season and already has a goal for next year: beating another runner in a cross-country race. "It was really hard at the beginning because I realized that my muscles were not strong enough at first, but then they got stronger throughout the season," she said. "And I got better."

Abigail uses a special wheelchair for cross-country practices and meets. Instead of pushing the wheel rims as she does in her standard wheelchair, she uses a hand crank in her racing wheelchair; she steers with her ankles. "It's a lot harder on grass than it is on the pavement, but usually I have a coach or a manager that runs along with me in case I get stuck in a rut," she said.

numbers. This writer would typically keep close track of several key statistics and then, as you might suspect, base the story mainly on those numbers.

Many fans appreciate this kind of writing, but there's a risk that the writer may rely too much on numbers. You may use a stat, for example, when you don't really need one, when a telling quote or sparkling description might work better. For example, notice all the numbers in the following description of a basketball game:

> For as cold as Southeast was in the first half, then again in the fourth quarter, it was as hot in the third period. Houser hit 3 three-pointers, Kastanek tallied six points, Katie Birkel chipped in four, and the Knights made good on 11 of 15 shots from the field while rolling up 26 points and streaking to a 41-26 lead after three periods.

That many numbers might make the reader's head spin. Why not just a quote from the coach: "I don't know how you can play good in one quarter and not good in three and still win."[2]

A sportswriter with a different philosophy, however, might spurn press row altogether and sit in the stands with a box of popcorn, hoping to catch the flavor of the game in a different way. This is the writer who notices what the kid on the end of the bench is doing or gauges the emotions of the fans on each sideline. For this writer, the story is more about people than numbers. Take, for example, this sentence from the writer Murray Kempton, describing a young Cassius Clay (later to become Muhammed Ali) about to enter the boxing ring against the champ, Sonny Liston:

> They met in the ring center with Clay looking over the head of that brooding presence; then Clay went back and put in his mouthpiece clumsily like an amateur and shadowboxed like a man before a mirror and turned around, still catatonic and the bell rang and Cassius Clay went forward to meet the toughest man alive.[3]

Neither approach is sufficient by itself. The best method is to blend some of each, discovering the key thread of the story through the players themselves and then supporting that concept with statistics. But don't worry if you feel a bit challenged by the numbers game. As we've indicated, other people are keeping track, too, and generally, they will provide the media with what is needed. At halftime of a basketball game, for example, you will get an update on who's scored how much and who's in foul trouble. And after the final buzzer, you've got a box score to examine.

BOX SCORE

A box score is a detailed summary of a game, usually in the form of a table listing the players and their individual performances. An abbreviated version called a line score basically duplicates the scoreboard on the field. Baseball box scores may look on the surface like a list of names and a jumble of numbers, but if you know how to read them, you can gather some genuine insights into how a game was played. Many fans check the box scores daily to see how their favorite players are doing or why their team stumbled in the ninth inning to lose a close game.

Henry Chadwick is credited with inventing the modern baseball box score when he adapted a score card he had used to cover cricket. His first box score, a grid with nine rows for players and nine columns for innings, appeared in the New York Clipper in 1859. To the great pleasure of anyone who has ever kept a scorebook, Chadwick created a way to keep track of the game's statistics as play proceeded. For example, each of the defensive players was given a number such as 1 for the pitcher and 2 for the catcher; letters of the alphabet corresponded to what a batter did — an "HR" stood for home run and "F" for fly ball. The somewhat puzzling use of "K" for strikeout was chosen for the last letter of "struck" as in "struck out."

This scoring system gave fans a shorthand way to keep track of what happened in a game. If baseball was to become America's national pastime, Chadwick believed, it was necessary "to obtain an accurate estimate of a player's skill, an analysis of both his play at bat and in the field." Chadwick also devised metrics such as batting averages for hitters and earned run averages for pitchers. Walks did not exist in cricket, and upon learning about them in baseball, Chadwick scored them as errors charged to the pitcher.

Use the box score on the following page to answer these questions.

1. What was the final score of the game?
2. In which inning did the winning team score the most runs?
3. Who were the winning and losing pitchers?
4. How many runners did Mudville leave on base?
5. Which batter had the most hits? Who did the most to raise his batting average?
6. Who were the pinch hitters?
7. How long did it take to play the game?
8. How many fans attended?
9. Who was the only batter to hit a triple?
10. Whose performance is most significant to use in writing a lead?

MUDVILLE	ab	r	h	bi	SPRINGFIELD	ab	r	h	bi
Orson, rf	4	0	1	0	Colbert, 1f	3	1	1	0
Lesco, ph	1	0	0	0	McHale, cf	4	0	2	2
Wylie, cf	4	1	0	0	Kerr, 2b	3	1	2	0
Madden, 3b	4	2	1	1	Carr, 1b	4	2	1	0
Thomas, 1b	3	1	2	0	Van Dyke, rf	3	1	0	0
Kane, 1f	3	0	1	1	Lathrop, rf	1	0	0	0
Panza, c	4	0	0	1	Peterson, 3b	4	0	1	2
Gomez, 2b	4	1	1	2	Polson, c	4	0	2	2
Davis, ss	4	0	2	1	Jones, ss	3	1	3	0
Roberts, p	1	0	0	0	Andre, p	2	0	0	0
Minello, p	1	0	1	0	Knight, p	1	0	0	0
Clayton, p	0	0	0	0	Quinn, p	0	0	0	0
Gray, ph	1	0	0	0	**Totals**	**32**	**6**	**12**	**6**
Totals	**34**	**5**	**9**	**6**					

Mudville	000	200	120 — 5
Springfield	011	003	10X - 6

E — Davis, Kerr. DP — Mudville 1, Springfield 2. LOB — Mudville 5, Springfield 6. 2B — Carr, Polson, Jones. 3B — Colbert. HR — Gomez (1). SB — Jones (14). HBP — by Andre (Roberts). T — 2:53. A — 30,649.

Mudville	IP	H	R	ER	BB	SO
Roberts(L)	5.3	8	5	3	3	3
Minello	1.6	3	1	1	2	1
Clayton	1	1	0	0	0	0
Springfield	IP	H	R	ER	BB	SO
Andre	(W)	6	5	2	2	1
Knight	2	5	3	2	2	0
Quinn	1	0	0	0	0	2

INTERPRETING THE GAME

Numbers tell stories about all kinds of things. Everything about America seems to be getting larger, for example, from the portions at fast food restaurants to the size of a chocolate chip cookie. And it's no different in the National Football League. Consider this: The average weight for pro players in 2022 was 245 pounds, 10 percent higher than in 1983. More remarkably, in 1976 just three NFL players tipped the scales at 300 pounds; in the 2019-20 season nearly one-quarter of the league's 1,700 players weighed that much.[4]

Do these numbers tell us anything beyond the fact that almost everything is getting bigger? They may, if we know how to interpret them, and interpreting numbers has been a lifetime obsession for Bill James. James is a baseball statistician who has written more than two dozen books analyzing how baseball could and should be played. The Boston Red Sox raised a few eyebrows when they hired James in 2002, hoping to somehow end a streak of 86 years without winning a World Series. Guess what? Since James came on board, the Red Sox have won baseball's championship twice.

Sometimes called the "professor of baseball" or the "sultan of stats," James began trying to work out baseball puzzles at his job as a night watchman in a pork-and-beans plant in Kansas. It was a good job, in the sense that he had a lot of time to keep to himself and think. Each day, he lugged his "Baseball Encyclopedia" and a stack of box scores to his boiler-room post and compiled evidence that began to challenge baseball's sacred cows. He concluded, for example, that starting pitchers have no effect on attendance and that ballplayers reach their peak in their late 20s.

By hiring James to be their senior baseball operations adviser, the Red Sox joined the ranks of several teams — such as the Oakland A's and the Toronto Blue Jays — now emphasizing mathematical data as an alternative to relying on weather-beaten scouts with radar guns and seat-of-the-pants hunches. James calls the effort "the search for objective knowledge about baseball."

In his first "Baseball Abstract," James wrote that he wanted to approach the subject of baseball "with the same kind of intellectual rigor and discipline that is routinely applied, by scientists great and poor, trying to unravel the mysteries of the universe, of society, of the human mind, or the price of burlap in Des Moines." He treated his readers to an egghead's theory of winning baseball, in which outs should be avoided at all costs and walks are really as good as hits. The result of this analysis indicates, James says, that sacrifice bunts are almost never worth the price, confounding a century of baseball's received wisdom.[5]

DO THE MATH

Remember that algebra you did in high school? Dust off those old formulas because sometimes you will have to plug some numbers into your calculator. Give these a try:

1. Julie Martinez, star shortstop for the Spitwads, has been at bat 77 times this season and gotten 24 hits. What's her batting average?
2. In 37 games, knuckleball pitcher Slim Pickens has thrown 186 innings and given up 47 earned runs. What is his earned-run average? (Hint: ERA is the number of earned runs given up per nine-inning game.)
3. Javon Wilson, North High's star tailback, has gained 812 yards rushing in the first six games of an 11-game season. If he continues at the same pace, in what game will he break the school record of 1,406 yards gained in a season?

Dollars and Cents

Although "Show me the money!" was just a catchphrase from a Tom Cruise film, it's now a common refrain among sports writers. You may find yourself writing about contracts, buyouts, lease arrangements and the cost of field turf, to mention just a few.

Take this example: College towns have become desirable places to live. People love the pageantry, tradition and idyllic settings of these towns and like to connect with the nostalgia they feel for their own happy college years. So you decide to write a feature about which college town has the most expensive houses and which has the cheapest. The answers, according to Coldwell Banker, are Stanford and Ball State. A modest four-bedroom home with a double garage in Palo Alto, California, home of the Stanford Cardinal, will set you back about $3.2 million. Meanwhile, a similar house in Muncie, Indiana, home of the Ball State Cardinals, would only cost $121,000.[6]

Arbitration Suits

Certainly, sports writers and fans love their stats, but it turns out, lots of players do, too. Awash in numbers, mesmerized by details such as pitch counts and runners in scoring position, some players have found their value escalating, depending on how the numbers play out. "We'll sometimes get involved in arbitration. Players want stats that make them look good while teams provide some stuff that make them look not so good," said Don Zminda, who writes the STATS Baseball Scoreboard.[7]

Players haven't always been the masters of their sums. Columnist George Will recalls the more innocent days of the past: "Honus Wagner, the greatest shortstop ever, rejected a salary offer from the Pirates of $2,000 by declaring: 'I won't play for a penny less than fifteen hundred dollars.'" An NFL running back got his own numbers confused not long ago when he said his goal was to gain 1,500 yards or 2,000 yards, "whichever comes first."[8]

Feeding the Fans

So who needs to know this stuff anyway? Basically, television and radio broadcasters need it to fill the dead air between pitches, plays and serves. According to statistician Gary Gillette, more than 500 stats were discussed by network announcers or displayed on the screen during just one World Series game.[9] Reading a stat sheet has become an occupational requirement. Besides a dictionary and a thesaurus, many sports writers now study an endless stream of numbers, charts, diagrams and box scores. Those box scores, by the way, have doubled in size as statisticians have added more and more items to measure.

So, while most sports fans may not know how to fix the plumbing or where their septic tank is, they can prove that a certain player's first pitch will be a strike more than 60 percent of the time. Some know their favorite baseball player's batting average to 1,000th of a point.

FOR THE RECORD

Compiling a sports record book at your school can create a tremendous resource for future reporters. Such a book includes team and individual records for each sport your school participates in over time. For example, suppose you wanted to know the fastest time anyone at your school had ever swum 50 meters or the highest anyone had ever vaulted or the farthest someone had thrown a discus. The record book should be able to provide the answers.

It's often fascinating to look back in history and discover that your tiny college once played Notre Dame in football (or perhaps the local high school and maybe in the same season). Remember, too, that records are made to be broken. Your sports record book will need to be updated each season as new marks are established.

UPON FURTHER REVIEW

1. How large a role should statistics play in how a reporter covers a story?
2. How can statistics be used to interpret or better understand a game?
3. List 10 different statistics you could compile for a sports event at your college.
4. Discuss which statistics seem most significant when analyzing a specific sport.

Answers to Do the Math

1. .312
2. 2.27
3. The last game (11th)

NOTES

1. This undated quote appears in QuoteFancy.com.

2. This game was reported in the *Lincoln Journal Star*.

3. This quote is reprinted in David Halberstam, ed., *The Best American Sports Writing of the Century* (Boston: Houghton Mifflin, 1999), 700. More on the Clay-Liston fight can be found in Kempton's article "The Champ and the Chump," *New Republic*, March 7 1964, also reprinted in *The Best American Sports Writing of the Century*.

4. More information about how everything is getting bigger in America, including the size of NFL players, can be found in Jess Blumberg, Katy June-Friesen, and David Zax, "Livin' Large," *Smithsonian*, Sept. 2007.

5. This quote appears in Ben McGrath, "The Professor of Baseball," *New Yorker*, July 14, 2003.

6. Coldwell Banker ranks the affordability of housing in major college football towns annu-ally. The study can be found at http://hpci.coldwellbanker.com.

7. Zminda writes for STATS, one of the world's leading sports information companies. Its work can be found at www.stats.com.

8. George Will, *Bunts* (New York: Scribner, 1998), 57.

9. Gary Gillette is coeditor of both *ESPN Baseball Encyclopedia* and *ESPN Pro Football Encyclopedia*.

Seeking Justice

Sports has long been an important battleground for human rights. Seven years before the U.S. Supreme Court banned segregation in public schools, major league baseball brought Jackie Robinson onto the playing field. That decision paved the way for countless other players of various ethnic backgrounds to get their chance to play, and that struggle for justice continues — in April 2018, for example, officials in Boston renamed a street next to Fenway Park. Instead of Yawkey Way, named for Tom Yawkey, who was the most resistant owner in baseball to signing Black players (he finally did in 1959), the street reverted to its original name, Jersey Street.[1] The world of sport, it seems, has often been in the vanguard of social change, whether it be the right to play or, as we will see, the right to play safely. To cover this additional dimension, reporters need a few more tools in their kit.

Those tools include at least a working understanding of tax law, criminal law and a variety of other legal disciplines that may have been on the periphery in years past. As one observer put it with an eye to future litigation, "When they add rules, even rock throwing becomes a sport." In this chapter we will explore a few of the rules that shape the contest — especially those that determine who will play and when and under what circumstances. In particular, we will focus on three key issues: should players be paid to play, should men and women have equal sporting opportunities and are some sports simply too violent?

IS AMATEURISM OUT OF DATE?

Modern college sports programs have evolved from 19th-century, student-run social and athletic clubs into powerful enterprises that generate billions of dollars in revenue each year. The scale of the revenue is what is new. The first intercollegiate athletic contest was actually a boat race — a rowing competition between Harvard and Yale on Aug. 3, 1852. The sponsor of the event offered both teams "lavish prizes" and "unlimited alcohol," an attractive reward, we can imagine, for undergraduates. Preparations and training were less rigorous than today; the Yale team spent the day fishing and "abstaining from pastry," while Harvard avoided practicing for fear of "blistering their hands."[2] Despite a broken oar, Harvard won by two lengths, or maybe four lengths; no one quite knows for sure. Remarkably, this annual race has been held 151 times since.

NCAA Supervision

College sports programs are supervised and coordinated by the National Collegiate Athletic Association, an organization that regulates the activities of some 400,000 athletes. One persistent point of contention, however, has been the very concept of a "student-athlete." The term was invented by the NCAA's former director, Walt Byers, in 1953, who thought athletes should be "patriots"; that is, they should play the game for the love of glory rather than out of greed as paid "mercenaries."[3] But years later, in his memoir, "Unsportsmanlike Conduct: Exploiting College Athletes," Byers said that he and the legal team had coined the term to prevent future generations of college athletes from looking for worker's compensation or pay for play. He acknowledged that "student-athlete" keeps college athletes in their place.

Over the past decade, the NCAA has been forced to loosen its once ironclad amateur rules. It removed restrictions on how much athletes could be fed after Shabazz Napier, a UConn basketball player, told reporters in 2014 that he went to bed hungry sometimes. And it had no choice but to allow education-related payments to players after a Supreme Court decision in the *Alston* case, which also opened the door to endorsement deals. Prior to *Alston*, businesses could sell T-shirts and any other kind of souvenir with an athlete's name, number or picture — and not a penny went to the athlete. The NCAA meanwhile resisted any "play for pay" plan. Officially, college was still an amateur sport, as it had been since 1869, but recently things have changed. Thanks to legal decisions and changes in NCAA policy, college athletes can now sign endorsement deals handled by booster-run collectives. In other words, players on the field are now permitted to legally put some money in their pockets.

These arrangements are typically referred to as "NIL," meaning name, image and likeness. In effect, players can sell the rights to their name, image and likeness and promote themselves through public appearances. This is potentially a huge windfall for the best-known athletes but also an untested arena more like the Wild West than any settled area of law.

When Did It Happen?

On July 1, 2021, nearly half a million college athletes suddenly became eligible to make money from sponsorships, endorsement deals and appearances, thanks to a

An elusive ball carrier may be as elusive as a game's key takeaway.
© Nebraska Wesleyan Sports Information.

unanimous Supreme Court ruling. In *NCAA v. Alston* the court ruled that the NCAA was not allowed to limit any education-related payments to students. From there, the NCAA deferred to states to create their own NIL rules. Where a state didn't pass a law, schools wrote their own rules.

NIL has exposed just how little control the NCAA presently exerts over college sports, or at least how much it wishes to exert. The NCAA is reaping what it has sown thanks to decades of defending a system based on the unpaid labor of its athletes — whittling its credibility to practically nothing over a long failure to be proactive about where college sports were headed. The NCAA had years to prepare for this day but chose not to, so now it's pinning its hopes on state and federal legislation to do the regulating.

Over 100 collectives now exist, with most having some relationship with a Power 5 school. Opendorse, a company that partners with schools to help track and monitor NIL deals, estimated nearly $1.2 billion would flow through the industry in 2023.

What Can You Do With NIL?

Athletes have been remarkably creative about how to take advantage of their new economic prowess. University of Florida gymnast Leah Clapper, for example, had always wanted to start her own business. Thanks to NIL, she created a gymnastics board game called "Balance Palace" and an e-commerce shop to sell it. Another innovative idea came from Kentucky linebacker Josh Paschal, who signed with Steckler Pediatric Dentistry. He stars in a commercial where he plays a dental ambassador for the company. He slaps sweets out of the hands of unsuspecting customers, gives pep talks on the importance of brushing and throws holiday parties.

A third example of NIL involved Ohio State's all-Big Ten defensive end J.T. Tuimoloau, who hosted a football camp for about 80 children backed by the Boys & Girls Club of Central Ohio and the Lindy Infante Foundation. "He talked to the kids, went to every station, signed autographs," said foundation president Stephanie Infante. "Non-profits struggle as it is to be able to interact and get involved with athletes — it's been such a great opportunity."

Some schools have tried to share the wealth with all the players on the team. Brigham Young University worked out a deal with Built Brands, a company that makes protein bars. In return for paying full tuition for the 36 walk-ons on BYU's roster, the team will wear Built Brands branded helmets in practice and participate in Built Brands events. They'll also include Built "fueling areas" in the two football locker rooms.

To help organize all these opportunities, "collectives" began forming in late 2021 to help players monetize their fame. Collectives are independent of universities; many of the deals they sign with athletes are worth six figures and some much more, especially for players whose value depends on their position, production or recruiting ranking. "1890," a typical collective, works to connect University of Nebraska athletes, particularly those in football and volleyball, to camps and clinics, community outreach, autograph signings, public appearances, social media promotions and other activities. "We operate independently from the university, independent of the athletic department," said Matt Davison, one of the 1890 founders. "At the same time, we want to be seen as another attractive piece that student athletes from across the country will be attracted to."

Is NIL Fair to Everyone?

The explosion of endorsement deals for college athletes has not been distributed evenly — women's sports have gotten a smaller share. Only 34 percent of collectives benefit women's sports, according to NIL marketplace Opendorse. Women's basketball, for example, accounted for just 12.6 percent of all deals, compared to football at 49.6 percent and men's basketball at 18.9 percent in 2022. Take Stanford women's basketball. The team won an NCAA title in 2021, made the Final Four in 2022 and has outdrawn men's basketball on campus by around 600 people per game. But that doesn't translate to higher NIL earnings.

MAKING THE UNIFORM FIT THE PLAYER

Basketball players haven't always worn long, baggy shorts. Back in the day, they wore tight, skinny shorts that barely covered their rear ends, the kind that kids wore in gym class. But one player and one team helped change the look of the sport.

First, Michael Jordan of the Chicago Bulls decided to wear extra big shorts so he could wear a good luck charm — his old North Carolina college shorts — underneath. Just as important, Michigan's Fab Five made a big wave with their distinctive look. In 1991 the University of Michigan recruited five freshmen who were destined to win a national championship. To create some solidarity, these five freshmen wore baggy shorts and black Nike socks with black Nike high-tops, the opposite of what everyone else was wearing; with their talent and joy for the game, they made basketball look effortlessly cool.

Uniforms are an important marker of change. A recent innovation in sports apparel, for example, represents an attempt to honor religious convictions. In 2018 Nike unveiled its Pro Hijab, a pull-on head covering made of light, stretchy fabric with tiny holes for breathability and an elongated back so it won't come untucked. Nike found a demand for its new hijab among American athletes, but it also wanted an opportunity to expand its market to the Middle East, where female athletes have begun to come into their own.

Helping Nike through the development of new products was a group of athletes that included Zahra Lari, the first competitive figure skater from the United Arab Emirates; Manal Rostom, a runner and triathlete currently living in Dubai; and Amna Al Haddad, an Olympic weightlifter from the United Arab Emirates. "There weren't any hijabi athletes to look up to when I was growing up, and I had to be my own pioneer," Rostom wrote over WhatsApp. "For young girls to see this revolutionary shift will change the face of sport for Muslim Arab girls, whether they wear hijab or not."

Playing sports and following religious strictures has been a challenge for Muslim women. "The one obstacle that's always there if you're a hijabi is, what to wear on your head?" Rostom wrote. Rostom said having Nike enter the picture was huge. "We came up with ideas and ways to be comfortable in what we wear, but to have the No. 1 sport and fitness brand in the world facilitate this process for us?" she wrote, "to provide something we can grab and wear in 10 seconds? It's going to change everything."[4]

"The schools can tell people to donate to collectives," said Kansas City-based college sports law attorney Mit Winter. "They can't direct people to give money to the collective for a specific sport or specific athletes. A coach can't say player X really needs some support, so please donate money to the collective for this specific athlete, or please donate money to support this specific sport or team. So that's kind of where that line is."

What Might the Future Look Like?

Many observers think college sports are on the cusp of unprecedented upheaval. Television money has caused schools to leap from conference to conference, hoping to find the best spot to land. Four West Coast schools, Oregon, Washington, UCLA and USC, have joined the Big Ten, previously a midwestern-based conference, and two other California schools, Stanford and Cal-Berkeley, have joined the Atlantic Coast Conference. As of this writing, the Big Ten has 18 teams, the ACC 17 teams, the SEC and the Big 12 each have 16 teams, and the Pac 12 has two. Go figure. Players are moving, too, thanks to new transfer rules.

The legal situation continues to evolve. Cases in federal court and before the National Labor Relations Board are testing whether athletes should be considered employees who are due wages and other benefits. Meanwhile, the Internal Revenue Service is raising questions about collectives that pass themselves off as charitable organizations. The NIL deals together with loosening transfer restrictions mean that athletes can now hopscotch from school to school based largely on where they will be paid the most endorsement money (in 2023, the three leading Heisman Trophy candidates were all transfer quarterbacks). "I would take less money for the players to have a share," said Jim Harbaugh, the Michigan coach who with incentives earned about $11 million in 2023. "I hope other coaches would use their voice to express the same thing."

"This is the highest level of distraction in the sport's history," said Michael LeRoy, who teaches sports labor law at the University of Illinois Urbana-Champaign. "It doesn't matter if you're an athlete, a coach, an athletic director or a university president, there's something to be distracted about."[5]

DO MEN AND WOMEN HAVE A LEVEL PLAYING FIELD?

Student athletic programs have also been one of the battlegrounds for the gender wars of the past 50 years. As recently as 1972, only 30,000 college women participated in athletics. Today, that number has increased roughly fivefold, to 150,000. Attendance, prize money and celebrity status have all grown for women's athletics, and sports writers are paying attention. Nebraska's Memorial Stadium, for example, is typically the home of the university's football team, but in August 2023, it hosted the school's

A forehand smash might provide the key point. Tennis is the only sport where one person (Renee Richards) has played in both the top men's and women's tournaments.
© Nebraska Wesleyan Sports Information.

volleyball team for a match that drew 92,003 spectators, breaking the world record for women's competition.

Title IX Turns 50

The year 2022 marked the 50th anniversary of the passage of Title IX, also called the Patsy Takemoto Mink Equal Opportunity in Education Act, which prohibits discrimination on the basis of sex. This simple-seeming law has had a seismic impact on women in sports — and beyond. By requiring that schools provide athletic opportunities for everyone, the law broke down barriers that had kept girls and women on the sidelines.

Along the way, Title IX shattered many myths, the biggest being that girls simply weren't interested in sports. Today, millions of girls grow up enjoying the benefits of running, jumping, kicking or throwing, gaining life skills that serve them long after their playing days are over. "There are a lot of big things that happened in the 20th Century — nuclear fission, civil rights and the computer," said former Nebraska volleyball coach Terry Pettit. "But the most impactful thing was the changing role of women that came about because of Title IX."

Before Title IX, as Kathryn Clarenbach, the first chairperson of the National Organization of Women, put it, women were expected to "stand decoratively on the sidelines of history and cheer on the men who make the decisions." But after Title IX, they could take their place alongside men on the athletic fields. Consider one example.

In 1884, Maud Watson won the first Ladies' Singles Tennis Title at Wimbledon. Her outfit consisted of a white corset and petticoat, and for her prize she received a silver flower basket. In 2018 Garbiñe Muguruza defeated Venus Williams to win a check for $3 million, and then got to wear a purple-and-gold badge signifying that she was a member of the All England Club, an honorary status accorded to tournament champions.[6]

When it was enacted on June 23, 1972, Title IX was just a 37-word passage that had been slipped into an education bill signed by President Richard Nixon: "No person in the United States shall, on the basis of sex, be excluded from participation in, be denied the benefits of, or be subjected to discrimination under any education program or activity receiving Federal financial assistance." Though there was little fanfare when it passed, the law meant that every school receiving federal funds had to provide fair and equal treatment for everyone in all areas, including athletics. In large measure the law worked: it transformed the United States into a bastion of female athletic talent. At the Olympics, American women now consistently claim enough medals on their own to top most nations. Fifty years ago, about 250,000 girls nationwide played high school sports; now more than 3.2 million do.[7]

Slowly the NCAA has expanded its marquee events so that the women's version more closely resembles the men's. The women's March Madness basketball tournament, for example, debuted a new format in 2022 with 68 teams, the same as for the men. The softball championship expanded its time frame to avoid the possibility of doubleheaders on consecutive days.

The law has also been life-changing for generations of American women off the sports field. One survey found that more than nine in 10 female business executives were athletes in school. In 1972, only 10 percent of medical students in the United States were women. Within just three years of Title IX's passage, the percentage of women in medical schools more than doubled. Today, more than half of all med school students are women. At the time of Title IX, women comprised only 43 percent of college students. Less than a decade after its passage, the percentage had risen to 52 percent. But athletics has become the biggest focus of Title IX — as well as its most controversial element.

For academic programs to be in compliance, they simply need to be open to anyone regardless of sex. But athletics are more complicated. Schools need to balance the sports they offer for men and women, and then to fund them in a way that creates gender parity and equity. That creates lots of legal gray area. As a result, Title IX implementation has been a contentious, decades-long process as it has played out across the country. The NCAA, at least initially, was more a roadblock than a slipstream. The male-dominated body that sanctioned college athletics sued to stop Title IX's implementation and refused to sponsor women's sports until 1982.

BARBIELAND COMES TO COLLEGE FOOTBALL

A distant outpost of Barbieland can be found deep in the bowels of the University of Iowa's Kinnick Stadium. Step into the visitor's locker room and you will find yourself awash in pink — everything is pink, the walls, the floor, the ceiling, the lockers, even the urinals.

But this is no wonderland for dolls. In 1982, football coach Hayden Fry had the visiting locker room painted pink, figuring that the color might lull opponents into less aggressive play. According to legend, Fry, who had earned a master's degree in psychology, thought that pink had a calming effect. "When I talk to an opposing coach before a game and he mentions the pink walls, I know I've got him," Fry wrote in his book, "A High Porch." "I can't recall a coach who has stirred up a fuss about the color and then beat us." During a 2005 update of the stadium, under a new coach, the university doubled down by painting the toilets, lockers and everything else a "dusky rose."

Some opposing coaches simply redecorate the area. In 2016, prior to their team's arrival at Kinnick, the Michigan equipment staff covered the walls with newspaper, blue tarps, and plenty of block "M" images — anything to cover up the pink. The school's fight song, "Hail to the Victors," played over the sound system.

But not all Iowans are on board with pink. Erin Buzuvis, a professor at Iowa's law school, complained that the locker room was misogynistic. "What you're really saying is you're weak like a girl. That belittles every female athlete out there." For her comments, Buzuvis received plenty of verbal abuse, including at least one death threat. Jill Gaulding, a colleague, came to her defense, telling a university compliance committee that the room "reinforces sexism."

But in 2023 pink became a symbol of empowerment thanks to the hit movie *Barbie*. There Barbie Land, dripping in pink, came across as a fun cotton-candy wonderland. One news report claimed that the production team bought so many cans of pink paint that it nearly depleted the world's supply. "For us it's really a symbol of empowerment," said Kim Culmone, Mattel's head of Barbie and fashion dolls design. "Barbie is the original girl empowerment brand." So perhaps pink gives the visiting teams a boost of energy after all.

Transgender Athletes

Sports groups, like society itself, have struggled to recognize the concerns and interests of the transgender population. "We had more and more schools saying, 'We have a student who is transitioning or transitions,'" explained Jamey Harrison, deputy director of the governing body of high school sports in Texas. "I think, without question, it has become much more of a common issue." Some athletic organizations, particularly the International Olympic Committee, have well-established policies including hormone testing to determine eligibility, but high school coaches and athletic directors are coping with small budgets and athletes who are almost all under age 18. Essentially, high school leaders are making up their own rules, state by state. The Nebraska School Activities Association, for example, relies on a Gender Identity Eligibility committee composed of a physician, a psychiatrist, a school administrator and an association staff member to make definitive decisions on an athlete's gender placement.[8]

The issue is especially challenging because some people argue that athletes who have transitioned from male to female might have a physical advantage over their peers, at least until their hormone therapy (which not every transgender person chooses to have) is complete. The generally accepted gap between elite women's and men's performance is 10-12 percent. The difference has a lot to do with testosterone, which is why hormone testing has emerged as the proverbial line in the sand when it comes to determining eligibility for competitions.[9]

Some schools choose to determine participation by the sex on a student's birth certificate, perhaps the most restrictive policy. Others allow participation as determined by the student's expressed gender. In such cases, the student must provide documentation, including proof of at least a year of hormone therapy. But hormone therapy can be expensive and inconvenient and thus not a choice for everyone. Perhaps the fairest test, according to Texas Children's Hospital endocrinologist David Paul, is a student's testosterone level. But even then, there are no simple answers. "The problem is," Paul says, "what testosterone level confers an advantage?"[10]

The issues have led to a conversation about "who counts as a woman," said Anne Lieberman, director of policy and programs at Athletic Ally, "and, how are we defining womanhood, either legally, or for sporting purposes."[11] Consider this comment from "Olivia," an athlete born male but now identifying as female: "Imagine you are practicing your favorite sport one day when somebody comes and tells you that you are not able to participate. Not only does this take away your right to play, but it takes away something that defines you."

South African runner Caster Semenya, a three-time world champion and two-time Olympic gold medalist in the 800 meters, caused international headlines in 2019 when she was sidelined by a Swiss court that banned athletes with "differences with sex development" unless they lowered their testosterone to a certain threshold.

Semenya refused to take further medication and has not competed in her event since. The trouble with using testosterone levels for testing is that it represents "a one-size-fits-all solution for an incredibly complex conversation about inclusion," Liberman said. "You're taking these things, and for what?" said Semenya. "They make you sick. They take the soul out of you. You're no longer living based on what you're supposed to be."

A Reluctant Pioneer

Discussions of when and where transgender athletes can compete continue to engage the world of sports. The opening salvo of that conversation took place nearly 50 years ago and involved a talented tennis player. Richard Raskind was a successful eye surgeon, husband and father who had been captain of the men's tennis team at Yale. At age 40, all seemed well, but Raskind felt unfulfilled. "I had this other side of me that kept emerging and that kept pushing back, until finally it just wasn't possible to submerge Renee anymore and Renee won out."[12]

Following gender reassignment surgery Renee Richards moved to California to start a new life ("Renee" is French for "reborn"). She matters to all of us because in 1977 she became the first transgender woman to play in a professional tennis tournament. The tournament was the U.S. Open, and it took place in Forest Hills, NY, just a short walk from Raskind's childhood home.

Controversy raged over whether Raskind should be allowed to compete. At 6 feet 2 inches tall and with a powerful left-hand serve, she was a daunting opponent. "I never had any intention of playing in the U.S. Open," Raskind said, "but when they said, 'You're not allowed to play,' that changed everything. I said, 'You can't tell me what I can or cannot do.'" When the USTA challenged Renee's right to play in court, they deployed a battery of witnesses who often relied on junk science and Cold War hysterics. The group's lawyer raised the specter of "worldwide experiments, especially in Iron Curtain countries, to produce athletic stars by means undreamed of a few years ago." Raskind's attorney had just one witness, but she was formidable: a world number one player and a tennis icon — Billie Jean King.

"My lawyer had an affidavit from Billie Jean King that said she had met me," explained Raskind, "that I was a woman, that I was entitled to play, and that I couldn't be denied. And that was it. We won."[13] King has never wavered from her advocacy for equality in sports. "She's continued to live by what she believes: that sport is for social change," said Stacey Allaster, the United States Tennis Association's chief executive. "It's not what you get, but what you give."[14]

To this day, Richards is the only player in history to reach the top level in both men's and women's competitions. She was a reluctant pioneer. "The whole world seemed to be looking for me to be their Joan of Arc," she said. Despite never having been an activist, Renee is now hailed for her courage. But her perspective is different: "I am first and last an individual."[15]

Taking the Lead

Having passed the 50th anniversary of Title IX, the struggle to find an equitable answer to the question of gender fairness continues. The tenacity of those who stood in gymnasium doorways to block female athletes from entering is sobering. Yet thanks to the efforts of individuals such as Renee Richards and many other brave athletes, progress has been made. It is worth remembering that in 1971, just before Title IX took effect, women athletes were almost invisible. At Brown University, for example, the women's athletic program was funded by a bake sale.

CAN SPORTS BE TOO VIOLENT?

Many consider violence in sports a natural part of the game. But for almost everyone, there comes a moment when things cross a line. "I've been coaching football for a long time," an older man said, "but I have never seen such a dangerous play. If that's allowed, it's not a sport."[16] The play the man was describing would not seem out of the ordinary to most American fans. It involved a quarterback who rolled to his right and threw an incomplete pass. As his momentum carried him toward the sideline, a defensive player charged across the field, lowered his head and hit the quarterback in the small of his back. The player's head snapped back, and he soon left the game. The offending player was penalized for unnecessary roughness but allowed to keep playing.

What makes this play so remarkable is that it took place just outside Tokyo and matched two Japanese college teams, Nihon and Kwansei Gakuin. What is even more unusual is that the play created a viral sensation and precipitated a national conversation about the inherent dangers of the game and its place in Japanese society.

Perhaps we can use a Japanese lens for just a moment to consider violence in sport, a frequent topic of discussion in the American media ever since the discovery of chronic traumatic encephalopathy (CTE), a degenerative brain disorder associated with repetitive head trauma. Several studies have linked CTE to suicidal behavior, dementia and memory loss. Although professional athletes may be at highest risk for CTE, up to 3.8 million sports-related concussions occur in the United States each year at all levels; younger players are not immune.[17]

The loss of a young son is deeply tragic, but for Michael Locksley, head football coach at Maryland, it was also a mystery. His 25-year-old son Meiko was a standout football player who drifted from college to college as his mind and life dipped into darkness. Meiko was shot and killed in 2017. After his death, his father asked for an autopsy and in 2023 announced publicly that his son had CTE. No one knows the precise role that CTE played in Meiko's decline because researchers cannot make direct links yet. Were Meiko's symptoms and mental-health issues caused by, exacerbated by or unaffected by CTE?

The brain of Meiko Locksley, along with those of 152 other student-athletes, belongs to the Unite Brain Bank at Boston University. In a paper published in 2023 in *JAMA Neurology*, researchers reported that 63 of the athletes, or 41.4 percent, had CTE. Most were football players who never played past college, sometimes not past high school. That does not mean, however, that nearly half of young football players will get CTE; the brain donations were made by families desperate to find answers, most often after a suicide. But the trend is frightening. "This study clearly shows that the pathology of CTE starts early," said Dr. Ann McKee, a neuropathologist and director of Boston University's CTE Center.

Meanwhile, Coach Locksley needed to design a safer practice plan for his team. "I want to be able to teach it and present it as safe as possible while still allowing this great game to give the rewards that it's given to so many families," he said. "My goal is to walk that thin line very truthfully."[18]

Football in Japan

That football incident in Japan has shaken a country with a solemn commitment to "fair play" in sports and prompted coaches, university officials and politicians to question whether existing rules are adequate to quell the growing violence. The father of the injured quarterback, for example, filed a complaint with the police. The Japanese football association suspended the defensive player indefinitely and issued a warning to his coach. Other teams canceled their games with Nihon, turning the school into something of a pariah. The defensive player later said, "I don't think I have a right to continue playing football, and I have no intention to do so."

Teddy Roosevelt's Summit

Would something like this ever happen in the United States? Remarkably, it did, more than a century ago. The year was 1905 and although football was popular, it was becoming too brutal — 18 young men died that year playing football, many from internal injuries, broken necks and concussions. The Washington Post reported that "nearly every death may be traced to 'unnecessary roughness.' When the victim was picked up, unconscious, from beneath a mass of other players, he was usually found to have been kicked in the head or stomach so as to cause internal injuries or concussion, which, sooner or later, ended life."[19]

President Teddy Roosevelt decided something needed to be done to save the game, a game he loved because it promoted the "strenuous life," a form of manliness he thought would help prepare the nation for tough times. Roosevelt was no stranger to a rough lifestyle. A veteran of the Spanish-American War and a former commissioner of the New York Police Department, his own personal life led him to believe that Americans should be scrappy fighters — and football was just the game to teach them how to do it. "I believe in rough games and in rough, manly sports," Roosevelt explained. "I do not feel any particular sympathy for the person who gets battered about a good deal so long as it is not fatal."[20]

At the time, however, football fatalities were indeed caused by a style of play and set of rules that permitted an extremely rough kind of game. A first down, for example, required just five yards, not 10, and the forward pass was illegal, so the game's basic strategy was to use a mass formation to creep forward just a few feet each play. As Nate Jackson, former NFL player and author, put it, "Not much misdirection and no downfield action. Every play was shot from a cannon."[21]

To calm the public, Roosevelt called a football summit at the White House and invited representatives from the powerhouses of college football: Harvard, Princeton and Yale. He asked those at the meeting to "reduce the element of brutality in play." Fortunately for the future of football, the summit members created several rule changes that transformed the game. The new rules spread action across the field and dramatically reduced the likelihood of fatalities. First, the forward pass was legalized. Second, a neutral zone was established between offense and defense. Third, the members doubled the first-down distance from five yards to 10. Officials were instructed to stop the game when a player fell on the ball to avoid heaps of men piling on top of each other, and players could now kick the ball down the field. Some observers were critical (one cartoonist drew football players in tutus), but the changes worked. In 1906, the year after the summit, the number of players killed during play was reduced by nearly half.

These rule changes led to a safer game, but they also made for a more exciting and popular one. In 1913 Notre Dame became famous for its use of the forward pass, and 1920 saw the formation of the new National Football League. But people sometimes drag their feet when it comes to changing a game they love. The most important safety feature — the helmet — would not be mandated until much later, in 1939.

When sports organizations are not open to changing the rules, other remedies must be sought. In the case of hockey, for example, fighting is part of the game that fans have come to expect, even celebrate. As one humorist said, "A puck is a hard rubber disc that hockey players strike when they can't hit one another." But even fighting behavior in hockey can go too far.

A shockingly brutal fight during the 1969 season caused Boston Bruins hockey coach Milt Schmidt to buy two dozen helmets and pass them out to his players. When he showed up for practice the next day, however, no one was wearing one. He ordered the team to put on their helmets or get off the ice, but when the team's star and one

FOOTBALL PRACTICE IS CHANGING, AND NOT A MOMENT TOO SOON

Football is a tough, physical game, but recently coaches have discovered that hitting and more hitting are not necessarily the best preparation for weekly games. Jeffrey Vlk, for example, coach at Buffalo Grove High School outside Chicago, has eliminated full-contact practices to help protect players from injury. When Vlk played football in the 1990s, he took and delivered countless hits during practice. Hitting was a given, as were injuries, including concussions. Later Vlk became a coach and by 2019 he was thoroughly discouraged by losing players to injury. He eliminated the heavy hitting. Now players wear shoulders pads just once a week, on Wednesday, when they can wrap up teammates but not throw them to the ground. The result: Vlk said no starting player has been injured in practice over the past four years. His approach to limiting contact in practice has been slowly spreading throughout the football world.

Recent research shows that a player's chances of developing CTE aren't related to a single, brutal hit. Instead, chances of injury are determined by how many hits the player absorbs and the cumulative impact of those hits. In other words, it's not just about how hard you get hit but how often. "We're now getting a better understanding of what causes CTE pathology," said Dr. Daniel Daneshvar, assistant professor at Harvard Medical School. "The latest data seems to support the idea that, yes all these hits matter, they all add up," said Dr. Eric Nauman of the University of Cincinnati.

Other sobering research indicates that men aren't the only ones at risk for CTE. In July 2023, Heather Anderson, an Australian rules football player, became the first female professional athlete to be diagnosed with the degenerative brain disease. As the number of women in professional contact sports is growing, cited the report, "it seems likely that more CTE cases will be identified in female athletes." Anderson competed in the top women's league for the Adelaide Crows. She had one confirmed concussion in her career and as many as four more suspected by her family but not formally diagnosed. She died by suicide at age 28.[22]

of hockey's all-time greats, Bobby Orr, slowly skated to the edge of the rink, the coach knew his plan was in trouble.

What caused Coach Schmidt to ask players to wear helmets in the first place was a battle between Boston's Ted Green and rookie Wayne Maki from the St. Louis Blues in an exhibition game played in Ottawa, Canada. During the exchange, Green happened to turn away just when Maki swung his stick, catching Green on his unprotected head. Green collapsed and was rushed to the hospital where five hours of surgery were required to stop his brain from hemorrhaging and save his life. The event was not much worse than most hockey fights, but it was enough for the media to pressure Canadian authorities to act. The Ottawa police investigated the case and two months later filed criminal charges against both players for "assault occasioning bodily harm." Both were eventually acquitted of charges, and each returned to the ice. Surprisingly, nothing in hockey changed. Bob Gainey, the general manager of the Montreal Canadiens, said that adding rules to stop fighting would diminish the "robust physical play that attracts all of us to the game." This early attempt to make hockey safer through the court system had failed.[23]

Change Is Hard

The Maki-Green confrontation marked the first time in professional sports that police became involved with player conduct during a game. But the fact that Maki and Green were each acquitted may have slowed the progress of reform. It took until March 2010 for the NHL to finally ban blind-side hits to the head. In the early days of sports, leagues worked to ensure that any conflicts were resolved in-house. But as sports have evolved in terms of fan scrutiny and sophistication, we have learned that the law, through its instrument — the courts — can play a role in stemming unnecessary violence.

UPON FURTHER REVIEW

1. Imagine that you have been appointed a federal judge to determine whether college athletes should receive a regular salary as part of a revenue-sharing plan. What would your ruling be?

2. Should athletes be subject to testosterone or other hormone-level tests to determine whether they can participate in sports events? What alternatives might be better?

3. If football were invented today, would the rules be different? What, if any, rules in football or hockey would you change to protect the health of the players?

NOTES

1. Katherine Q. Seelye and Daniel Victor, "Yawkey Way, Where Red Sox Fans Converge, Will Be Renamed Over Racism Concerns," *New York Times*, April 26, 2018.

2. James Wellman and Walter B. Peet, *The Story of the Harvard-Yale Race 1852-1912* (New York: Harper and Brothers, 1962), 15.

3. Roger I. Abrams, *Sports Justice: The Law & the Business of Sports* (Hanover, NH: University Press of New England, 2010), 69.

4. Valeriya Safronova, "Nike Reveals the 'Pro Hijab' for Muslim Athletes," *New York Times*, March 8, 2017.

5. Billy Witz, "Conferences Are Changing. The Sport Is Too," *New York Times*, Sept. 1, 2023.

6. Adrian Kajumba, "Winning the Wimbledon Women's Final Really Is Garbine Muguza's Cup of Tea," *Mirror*, July 16, 2017, https://www.mirror.co.uk/sport/tennis/muguruza-surprise-extra-wimbledon-prize-10810177.

7. Katie Barnes, *Fair Play* (New York: St. Martin's Press, 2023), 42.

8. Nebraska School Activities Association, "Gender Participation Policy," https://nsaahome.org/about/gppolicy.pdf.

9. Malika Andrews, "How Should High Schools Define Sexes for Transgender Athletes?," *New York Times*, Nov. 8, 2017.

10. Andrews, "How Should High Schools Define."

11. Barnes, *Fair Play*, 71

12. Steve Tignor, "40 Years Later, Renee Richards' Breakthrough Is as Important as Ever," Tennis.com, Sept. 20 2017, https://www.tennis.com/news/articles/decades-later-renee-richards-breakthrough-is-as-important-as-ever, and Jon Wertheim, "She's a Transgender Pioneer, but Renée Richards Prefers to Stay Out of the Spotlight," *Sports Illustrated*, June 28, 2019.

13. Tignor, "40 Years Later."

14. Liz Robbins, "Fifty Years Ago, Bill Jean King Won Equal Pay—but She's Not Done Yet," *New York Times*, July 25, 2023.

15. Tignor, "40 Years Later."

16. Ken Belson, "The Football Hit Felt All Over Japan," *New York Times*, May 22, 2018.

17. Ann McKee et al., "Chronic Traumatic Encephalopathy in Athletes: Progressive Tauopathy Following Repetitive Head Injury," *Journal of Neuropathology & Experimental Neurology* 68, no. 7 (July 2009): 709–35.

18. Material comes from Ken Belson and Benjamin Mueller, "Collective Force of Head Hits, Not Just the Number of Them, Increases Odds of C.T.E.," *New York Times*, June 20, 2023, and Victor Mather, "C.T.E. Found for First Time in Female Pro Athlete," *New York Times*, July 4, 2023.

19. Katie Zezima, "How Teddy Roosevelt Helped Save Football," *Washington Post*, May 29, 2014.

20. Christopher Klein, "How Teddy Roosevelt Saved Football," History.com, Sept. 6, 2012, https://www.history.com/news/how-teddy-roosevelt-saved-football.

21. Nate Jackson, "What If Football Were Reinvented Today?," in *Upon Further Review*, ed. Mike Pesca (New York: Grand Central, 2018), 105.

22. McKee et al., "Chronic Traumatic Encephalopathy."

23. Brian McFarlane, "A Dreadful Incident: Green Versus Maki," ithappenedinhockey.com, 2011.

11

Broadcast

As technology continues to evolve, so does the sports journalism industry. And the ever-growing list of responsibilities has changed with the times for sports journalists. Thirty years ago, sports writers were merely that: writers. There'd be the occasional radio "hit" — industry speak for "appearance" — on a sports talk show or a guest appearance on a TV special, but for the most part, writers stuck to their craft. These days, the lines are more blurred than ever.

As a sports reporter for the Lincoln Journal Star, Amie Just says, "These are my responsibilities: writing the columns and features I set out to do each week, two weekly podcasts — both of which have video versions — and weekly radio appearances on various stations within Nebraska and the nation."

DIVE INTO PODCASTS

Podcasts. They're an almost unavoidable part of life these days. Every person has their favorite listen — whether it's work-related or about something they're interested in or simply entertainment. Podcasts have become so ingrained in today's culture that it's easy to forget that they didn't exist 25 years ago. Even the term "podcast" itself is a portmanteau with dated origins — coming from the combination of iPod and broadcast, first used by a British journalist Ben Hammersley in 2004. "Who has an actual iPod anymore?" Just asks. "And no, the green fourth-generation iPod nano collecting dust in my childhood bedroom doesn't count."

Just describes her job as an eclectic grab-bag of responsibilities. "Even though I'm a sports writer, I've lost count of the number of traditional 'broadcast' things I've done as a part of my job. There's no telling how many short videos I've taken, radio hits and podcast appearances I've made and TV specials I've been on. I've had on-air appearances with the BBC, NPR, Sirius XM, ESPN Radio and a host of local radio and TV stations. And yet, that's not what I studied in college or set out to do with my career. But it's a major part of it now, whether we like it or not."

Even lining up a putt takes the sort of intense concentration that helps make sports exciting.
© Nebraska Wesleyan Sports Information.

The diversity of platforms makes sense. People consume their news in different ways. Some people like to read. Others prefer to listen. Many people retain information better by watching videos or looking at still images. Why would news consumption be any different? And now there are relatively affordable tools for newspaper folks to dip their toes into the broadcasting arena and vice versa.

But what if broadcasting makes you nervous? Welcome to the club.

Get Comfortable With Broadcasting

It's a common feeling for people to be uncomfortable with hearing their own voice after recording something or seeing themselves on camera. Even some of the most veteran broadcast journalists began their careers with nerves. Take KOLN-TV sports director Kevin Sjuts, for example. Sjuts, a 2003 graduate of the University of Illinois, said it took him "a few years" to get comfortable on camera.

"At first it's very nerve-wracking," Sjuts said. "There are different forms of being on camera. There's in-studio. There are live shots, out in the field on camera where there's no teleprompter, and that's a whole other set of nerves initially. And then there's also stuff you do on tape where you can do it as many times as you want. But two to three years from when you start, you start to just forge ahead and just do it."

OK, so nerves are common. How do you alleviate them? For starters, act like you would writing any story — be prepared. Know what you're going to talk about, get your facts in order. Being prepared is always the first step toward success.

If you're recording a podcast, write out an agenda. It doesn't need to be a verbatim script but more of an outline. Include bullet points of what you intend to talk about, so you avoid the potential for getting off track. In the outline, include the facts and stats so you don't have to look things up while you're on the fly. If you're talking about an athlete with a tricky-to-pronounce name, write the phonetic pronunciation in your notes. If you're recording a short stand-up video, write down what you want to talk about. Typically, these videos are no more than two to three minutes long, so keep it brief.

If you have enough time, write out your script. It might help alleviate some nerves or at least make you feel better prepared. If you're recording immediately after the final whistle, position yourself if possible so you can see the scoreboard with the stats while you're recording; that way you don't need to rely on a piece of paper during your video.

Your broadcast work doesn't need to be perfect. Getting started is the first step. That's part of what college is for, trying and learning new things. There are plenty of opportunities within journalism schools across the country to get early experience, like on-campus TV stations or immersive experience labs.

Reporters Amie Just and Luke Mullen of the Lincoln Journal Star discuss the results of a Nebraska football game as the crowd clears out.
© Lincoln Journal Star.

BEISBOL IN SPANGLISH? ONLY IN PHILADELPHIA

Is it "La Serie Mundial" or the "World Series"? A "cuadrangular," a "jon-ron" or a "home run"? The answer probably depends on who you're listening to for your baseball broadcasts. Bill Kulik, a Spanish-language radio broadcaster for the Philadelphia Phillies, mixes English and Spanglish, to the delight of some listeners but the irritation of others. Nicknamed "El Gringo Malo" (The Bad Gringo) Kulik is a pioneer of Spanish sports broadcasting, even though his critics find his mangled syntax distracting and his on-air persona a bit annoying.

As of 2023, 16 of 30 major league baseball teams had some form of Spanish-language broadcast, and a share of that credit goes to Kulik, who is in his 19th season with the Phillies. His particular style, however, has raised questions about language and culture in a country with roughly 62 million Latinos. He deliberately uses Spanglish, he said, to better connect with the many Puerto Ricans in the Philadelphia area. "There is no way we are going to appease everybody," Kulik, 61, said. "Oscar is going to give you more of the old school and the Gringo Malo is going to bring you the new school." Kulik's radio partner, Oscar Budejen, is a native Spanish speaker who provides some ballast to the broadcasts. "And hopefully in between you're going to like our broadcast because we're going to be different."

Kulik has been in the business for decades. After years in Boston working in marketing and producing a local baseball show, he put Red Sox games on a Spanish-language radio broadcast to appeal to the city's growing Latino community. In 2001 he established the Spanish Beisbol Network, planning at first to be a producer but eventually transitioning into an on-air host. Two years later, Kulik moved to Philadelphia, where he now calls the games in his own peculiar blend of Spanish and English.[1]

Broadcast classes can help you hone your craft even if you don't intend to be a full-time broadcaster. "It doesn't hurt to learn a new skill," Sjuts said. "It just makes you more marketable. Especially with the trends of everything in the industry. Like it or not, print people are being asked to do video. It would be wise to learn that and experiment with it."

Sjuts still carries the lessons he learned in his early broadcast classes with him — even now crediting one of his professors with one of the most helpful pieces of advice. "Find your three things," Sjuts said. "He would have all the students identify three things that we need to do before we go on camera to help us be successful, and it's different for each person. I identified mine in college as R-C-S — relax, have confidence and smile. I do it maybe once a month, even now. It's stuck with me, almost 20 years later."

CROSS-OVER SUCCESS

Even if you're set on being a print reporter, you never know what the future will hold as the industry changes. Sports writers across the country have found success in the broadcasting industry. On the big stage, look at ESPN's "Around the Horn." Many of the panelists featured on that show began their careers as writers or remain writers, like Woody Paige, Bob Ryan, J.A. Adande and Bill Plaschke. Stephen A. Smith, long before he became a talking head, worked in the newspaper industry. His career began at the Winston-Salem Journal and took a winding road along the East Coast before he worked at the Philadelphia Inquirer. Same goes for Tony Kornheiser and Michael Wilbon. ESPN's "Pardon the Interruption" was born out of the two arguing about the day's sports news while in the newsroom at the Washington Post.

Nicole Auerbach — who began her career at USA Today after a host of internships at the Boston Globe, the Detroit Free Press and the Cape Cod Times — wears a lot of hats as a national college sports reporter. She writes for the Athletic while also hosting a radio show on Sirius XM and doing contract on-camera work for the Big Ten Network.

It's not only the biggest names in the industry having success with their broadcast ventures. The list is lengthy. Courtney Cronin and Michael Rothstein, for example, are both beat reporters for ESPN's "NFL Nation" and host shows on ESPN Radio. Graham Couch, the sports columnist for the Lansing State Journal, hosts a live podcast three times a week. Sean Callahan, who covers Nebraska for On3, does football analysis for KETV and KAFB Radio, and also does a weekly TV show during football season.

Moral of the story: being amenable to adapting serves people in the industry well.

What College Students Can Do

The options are endless for college students to broaden their sports broadcasting horizons. If you work for the student newspaper, look for ways to augment your coverage. Start a podcast. There are plenty of free, or affordable, tools to help you edit. Work with the student radio station to see if there's any airtime for a new show, even if it's only an hour. Maybe a professional radio station has something available. See if the on-campus TV station wants to collaborate for an analysis segment. Do a stand-up video after the game (or meet or event) you're covering concludes. Record video of the press conference or postgame availability. Post those to the student newspaper's website and embed them in or at the top of your story.

FUTURE PRESIDENT HAS A BROADCAST MOMENT

One of the longest at-bats in baseball history took place in the mind of a future president, Ronald Reagan. In the 1930s Reagan was the baseball announcer for WHO radio, doing play-by-play for the Chicago Cubs. The fans heard what Reagan's imagination and Western Union (the telegraph service) allowed them to hear. In the gloom of the Depression, his melodious voice reached thousands of listeners on the strength of a 50,000-watt radio station, telling them that there were still heroes in America.

Reagan had an enviable power to create illusions on air: he typically reconstructed baseball games from sketchy wire reports, enhanced by studio gimmicks. His older brother, Neil, said, "When we were still in school at Eureka College, he'd sit in a corner of the frat house driving everyone out of their minds broadcasting an imaginary football game between two imaginary teams. That's how he got his job at WHO." There was never any dead air with Reagan in the booth. "He could always think of something to say," recalled WHO program director Myrtle Williams Moon. He looked like a sportscaster, too. "Usually, he wore his letterman's sweater. It was maroon, with a gold letter, and a big 'E' woven on the left," college teammate William Burghardt said.

As a baseball announcer, Reagan had the barest minimum to work with. "The Western Union operator sat on one side of the glass booth and would pass the wire through a slot," said Neil Reagan. "It was just balls or strikes, safe or out. He put in the rest. He had a mitt on the table with a ball. While he was talking, he'd slam the ball in the glove. For the sound of the bat hitting the ball, they had a little thing with a cantilevered arm and a small ball attached. He'd hit it with a length of broomstick. You couldn't tell it wasn't a real ball."

Reagan's stickiest moment came the day the wire went dead. It happened to him with the Cubs' Augie Galan at bat. Reagan already had the pitch on the way when Curly, his telegraph operator, slipped him a note saying he had lost contact with the ballpark. "So I had Augie foul this pitch down the left-field foul line," Reagan wrote in his autobiography.[2] I looked expectantly at Curly. He just shrugged, so I had Augie foul another one, and still another; then he fouled one back into the box seats. I described in detail the red-headed kid who scrambled to grab the souvenir ball. Then the batter fouled one into the upper deck that just missed being a home run. He fouled for six minutes and 45 seconds until I lost count.

"I began to be frightened that maybe I was establishing a new world record for a fellow staying at bat hitting fouls, and this could betray me. Yet I was into it so far, I didn't dare reveal that the wire had gone dead. My voice was rising in pitch and threatening to crack — and then, bless him, Curly started typing. I clutched at the slip. It said: 'Galan popped out on the first ball pitched.' Not in my game he didn't — he popped out after practically making a career of foul balls."[3]

If you're looking to expand your skill set, apply to work for the athletics department at your university, either on their creative team or for the video production department. Apply to be an intern at any of the local media companies, whether that be newspaper, TV, radio or digital media. "There are so many different avenues collegiately," Sjuts said. "My number one piece of advice would be to get involved early."

The more you practice, the better you get. The more comfortable you get, the more creative you get with your storytelling formats. The more you stand out, the easier it will be for you to get a job in your preferred field. What are you waiting for? Get out there and try your best.

BROADCAST STYLE

Unlike print journalism, where readers can return again and again to check facts or review a message, broadcasters have a small and fleeting window of opportunity. The fact that broadcast news is here one second and gone the next has a great deal to do with why broadcast news takes the form it does.

How Broadcast Sports Differs From Print Sports

The great strength of broadcast is, of course, its immediacy — its power to give a viewer or listener the feeling that "I'm there" as news is happening. Television gives viewers the sights and motions of an event. Radio gives listeners sounds: the crack of the bat at a baseball game or the chants of the crowd.

Broadcast news segments are limited by time, not space. Many stories must be told in 30 seconds or less. That's not very long to cover a story in any detail. In fact, if you took all the words spoken during a 30-minute television news show and printed them in a newspaper, they wouldn't even cover the front page. Print journalism may provide greater substance in its reporting, but broadcast journalism often lends itself better to our fast-paced lives and short attention spans.

BROADCAST FIRSTS

Not many would associate the annual Army-Navy football game with technological innovation, but the fact remains, covering that contest in new ways has significantly changed the way people watch sports. The first instant replay, for example, happened during the 1963 game when viewers saw Army quarterback Rollie Stichweh score a touchdown from a yard away. And then they watched it happen again. Calls flooded the CBS switchboard as fans sought to clarify their confusion even though announcer Lindsay Nelson warned, "This is not live. Ladies and gentlemen, Army did not score again."

What viewers were seeing was the brainchild of CBS Sports Director Tony Verna, who used equipment he described as "the size of two refrigerators." Verna actually wanted to capture a replay of Navy quarterback Roger Staubach, that year's Heisman Trophy winner, but the equipment was unpredictable. "You needed time to run back the tape," Stichweh said, "so there weren't many opportunities that game. Scoring that touchdown was one of them."

In fact, an urban legend has it that CBS sent a staffer on the field acting like a drunk fan to delay the game long enough for Verna to queue up the replay. One of his biggest worries was that CBS was taping over an old tape of "I Love Lucy"; the slightest mistake might have had viewers watching a different show entirely.

Less-than-instant replay had been used in sports broadcasting for a few years already via videotape, but the system had never been attempted during a live broadcast. Instant replay, however, soon changed the viewing experience and eventually allowed officials to change calls on the field, the diamond, the ice and the court. Verna knew just what he had done when he titled his book "Instant Replay: The Day That Changed Sports Forever." By the way, the Army-Navy game was also instrumental in pioneering the SkyCam (1984), the virtual first-down line (1998) and network broadcasting in HD (1999).

Writing to Pictures and Sounds

In television, reporters write their stories to fit the pictures, a process that generally involves "underwriting." In other words, reporters don't try to describe what viewers can see for themselves but instead provide brief snippets of supplementary information. Typically, the pictures carry the story, and the words serve mainly to complement what the viewers see. "One always writes with a picture in mind," explained longtime CBS correspondent Charles Kuralt.

Radio broadcasts, like television, consist of more than just words. In radio stories, reporters use natural sound, or "nat sound" for short, to present a story with the noises and voices that provide background context.

Making Broadcasts Dramatic

Broadcast news generally requires a little tension, a little drama, a little something extra to pull listeners or viewers in. Broadcast writers try to sustain interest by creating a feeling of drama or suspense. Those who write for broadcast make an effort to find an especially dynamic verb, to avoid dense collections of facts and to round off numbers so they are more listener friendly.

In broadcast news, reporters try to hold a listener's interest throughout the story. That's why clever writers introduce new thoughts as the story moves along. One technique some reporters use is called a reveal. This technique requires the writer to hold back a key piece of information and then reveal it as the story develops. For example, a reporter might begin a broadcast segment this way: "Maven Johnson is an airline pilot. He's been flying from Los Angeles to New York and back several days a week for the past twenty years." So far, so good, but nothing very interesting has been said. Now comes the revealing part of the story: "Johnson is blind." A typical newspaper reporter might write the same story this way: "A blind pilot has been flying the friendly skies for twenty years." That story, however, does not approach having the kind of impact or listener appeal that the broadcast version does.

A story also ends quite differently in broadcast. "I give equal attention to the end of a story," noted Kuralt. "The way a story ends gives the thought or feeling a viewer will take away." Frequently, broadcast reporters save their most poignant piece of information for the end. No editor could afford to cut from the bottom in television or radio reporting.

Conversational Style

Andy Rooney of CBS's "60 Minutes" said that broadcast news aims for a middle ground between how people talk and how they write. "When we talk," Rooney says, "we repeat ourselves and beat around the bush." Those flaws can be avoided in broadcast news writing, but the sound should still be conversational. After all, on both television and radio, the announcer is still "saying" the news to an audience.

Broadcast stories must above all be clear. The viewer or listener has only one chance to grasp the meaning of a story. A newspaper reader can take five, 10 or 20 minutes to study a story, but a television or radio listener must grasp a story in as little as 30 seconds. This requires a certain simplicity in language and presentation. Consider this lead from the Baltimore Sun regarding an unusual Chinese cultural custom. "Under pressure from international animal-rights groups, the Chinese government has drafted regulations to prohibit the feeding of large mammals — such as live cows, pigs and sheep — to tigers and lions as a form of public entertainment."

That lead is more than a mouthful, especially from a broadcast perspective. The sentence is far too long and clogged with dependent clauses and participial phrases. Much of the vocabulary, too, is inappropriate for the conversational style of broadcast reporting. Words such as "drafted regulations" and "prohibited," for example, are within most adults' reading vocabularies but rather hard to follow in spoken conversation. A broadcast version of that story might start like this: "Lions and tigers and bears will have to settle for pet food instead of snacking on cows and pigs if new laws in China take effect."

An observant sports writer can see communication happening between players and thus be ready for the action ahead.
© Nebraska Wesleyan Sports Information.

Clear and direct language is at the heart of effective broadcast writing. "Whenever I see 'which's,'" explains Joyce Davis of NPR, "I take them out." Davis says that besides simplifying language and shortening sentences, she tries to find a lead "as grabby as possible." You've got to hook the reader after the first five or 10 seconds of the story, she says.

UPON FURTHER REVIEW

1. Compare the coverage of a recent game on television and in print. What differences can you detect? If possible, compare a radio version of the same story.
2. TV broadcaster Kevin Sjuts advises young journalists to "find your three things," three things you need to do to be comfortable on camera. Choose three things for your approach.
3. What opportunities are available in your community or at your college to gain broadcast experience?

NOTES

1. Story based on James Wagner, "He Announces Baseball Games in Spanish. It Is Not His First Language," *New York Times*, Oct. 2, 2023.

2. Ronald Reagan, *Where's the Rest of Me?* (New York: Duell, Sloan & Pierce, 1965).

3. Material drawn from Jane Leavy, "Midwest Fans Tuned in to 'Dutch,'" *Washington Post*, Sept. 30, 1980, and Chris Landers, "How Spring Training Put Ronald Reagan on the Path to Stardom—and the Presidency," MLB.com, Feb. 20, 2019, https://www.mlb.com/cut4/how -spring-training-made-ronald-reagan-president-c304102714.

Highlighting the Greats

Not long ago, a high school reporter in California was assigned to write a story on the lacrosse team. Grant Damon, the reporter, had a brainstorm. What better way to get the inside scoop on the team than by joining it? His personal experience would give him a microscopic look at what really happens during practice and games.

Lacrosse, Damon learned, is "the only sport that combines football's 'we've-got -pads-and-helmets-for-a-reason' toughness with basketball's speed and agility, soccer's 'run-till-you-puke' endurance, hockey's vicious body checks, and baseball's fascination with balls and sticks." Playing lacrosse meant learning to throw a ball with a stick, catching passes left-handed, spinning and switching hands. It also meant learning a new vocabulary — "coast to coast," "grandma goal" and "walk the dog."[1]

Damon eventually filed an interesting and informative story, but he probably didn't realize he was walking, or running, in the footsteps of another noted sports writer, one who took the idea of participatory journalism to the highest level.

PARTICIPATORY JOURNALISM

The ability to see the game from the inside has long been a hallmark of sports journalism. Readers expect to be taken inside the huddle, the meeting at the pitcher's mound and even the locker room to gain insights into coaches' strategies and learn the personalities of their favorite players. In 1963 George Plimpton pulled off something the rest of us can only dream about. Plimpton (at age 36) pretended to be a rookie quarterback in the Detroit Lions' training camp, turning his experience into the best-selling book "Paper Lion." In the process, Plimpton helped fans imagine what it would be like to suit up with their gridiron heroes.

Plimpton was able to capture the inside story of a professional football team, from the drudgery of classroom sessions to the hijinks of men playing a boys' game. He also

Lacrosse is the oldest organized sport in North America and is based on a game played by Indigenous people.
©Tempura / Getty Images.

learned something about the society of athletes, something you could only find in the huddle. Plimpton called himself the "last-string quarterback" and, appropriately, wore the number zero. "There are people who would call me a dilettante," he said, "because it looks as though I'm having too much fun. I have never been convinced there's anything inherently wrong in having fun."[2]

It seems unlikely that Plimpton's feat will be repeated in today's multi-billion-dollar, win-at-all-cost NFL. Fortunately, Plimpton was a gifted storyteller. His engaging and thought-provoking style made his adventures all the more enjoyable. For example, here is a sample of what he wrote about calling a play: "Everything fine about being a quarterback — the embodiment of his power — was encompassed in those dozen seconds or so: giving the instructions to ten attentive men, breaking out of the huddle, walking to the line, and then pausing behind the center, dawdling amidst men poised and waiting under the trigger of his voice."

Playing for the Lions was only one of Plimpton's many insider stories. In 1960, he pitched against the top American and National League hitters in a postseason exhibition game. Later, he sparred for three rounds with boxing greats Archie Moore and Sugar Ray Robinson, and he trained as a hockey goalie with the Boston Bruins. Plimpton's classic "The Bogey Man" recalls his attempt to play professional golf on the

PGA Tour. Among other challenges for Sports Illustrated, he also attempted to play top-level bridge and spent some time as a high-wire circus performer.

As a "participatory journalist," Plimpton believed that it was not enough for writers to simply observe; they needed to immerse themselves in whatever they were covering. He believed, for example, that football huddles and conversations on the bench constituted a "secret world, and if you're a voyeur, you want to be down there, getting it firsthand."

GIANTS OF THE PAST

Plimpton is one of the figures who helped transform sports writing. Let's take a trip back in time to find out what sports writing looked like a century ago. One of America's first notable sports writers was Grantland Rice, famous for a poetic couplet that forever established the code of sports: "When the one Great Scorer comes to write against your name, He marks — not that you won or lost — but how you played the Game."[3]

Grantland Rice

Rice joined the Nashville News as a sports reporter for $5 a week and then worked in Atlanta and Cleveland before finally reaching New York, where he became the country's best-paid, best-known sports writer, earning as much per year as Babe Ruth. But the style of those days strikes us now as hopelessly extravagant. Consider, for example, this account of a baseball game between Detroit and Washington in 1907. Notice the long sentences, extended descriptions and florid prose. Note, too, some early signs of greatness from a certain "Tyrus Cobb":

> Detroit's pennant aspirations were placed in jeopardy this afternoon when the Washingtons got an early lead on their opponents and looked to be almost certain winners of a battle that deeply interested the whole baseball world.
>
> Detroit responded with superb gameness and Tyrus Cobb, a new star among baseball men, took up his mighty cudgel and opened the way to victory. His liner to safe territory inspired others, and before the last man in the sixth inning was declared out, the Tigers had saved the day for themselves.

That "mighty cudgel" hints at the mountain of sports jargon to come, and the whole scene smacks of Homeric hyperbole. Indeed, in the early days of sports writing, games were reviewed as if they were performances covered by theater critics. But things would change. By 1910, almost every daily newspaper had a sports section, and by 1920 sports stories were appearing regularly in general interest magazines. Here is Heywood Broun's 1921 description of a Babe Ruth home run:

In the fourth inning Ruth drove the ball completely out of the premises. The ball started climbing from the moment it left the plate. It was a pop fly with a brand new gland and, though it flew high, it also flew far.

When last seen the ball was crossing the roof of the stand in deep right field at an altitude of 315 feet. We wonder whether new baseballs conversing in the original package ever remark: "Join Ruth and see the world."[4]

As the most widely read sportswriter of the 1920s, Rice became as famous as the sports stars that he covered. He was the leader of what became known as the "Gee-Whiz" school of writing, an approach that basically praised and glorified athletes. "When a sports writer stops making heroes out of athletes," he said, "it's time to get out of the business." Or, as one of his colleagues said, "If he couldn't say anything nice about an athlete, he was likely to write about another athlete."

On Oct. 18, 1924, in about 30 minutes in a noisy press box, Rice took this theme to its most magnificent heights. On the following morning, about 10 million people (subscribers to newspapers across the country) awoke to read this about the Army-Notre Dame football game.

Outlined against a blue-gray October sky, the Four Horsemen rode again. In dramatic lore they are known as Famine, Pestilence, Destruction and Death. These are only aliases. Their real names are Stuhldreher, Miller, Crowley and Layden. They formed the crest of the South Bend cyclone before which another fighting Army football team was swept over the precipice at the Polo Grounds yesterday as 55,000 spectators peered down on the bewildering panorama spread on the green plain below.

That apocalyptic prose elevated sports writing to epic grandeur. Rice, who came to be known as the "Dean of American Sportswriters," was born in 1880 and grew up in Nashville, where, on his first Christmas he got a football, a baseball and a bat. He recalled these later as "the sounding instruments that directed my life." After playing semi-pro baseball for about a month, Rice returned to Nashville to work in a dry goods store but, not liking the job, decided to become a reporter. "My dad figured that inasmuch as I hadn't gone in for engineering, law or medicine at college — but had done creditably well in the arts — I might try my hand at journalism."

Rice moved to New York in 1912, where he wrote sports for the next 42 years. During the 1920s, when he was making $100,000 a year and had his column, "The Sportlight," syndicated in more than 250 newspapers, he freelanced for other magazines, edited the American Golfer magazine and wrote the first movie script about a baseball player (Ty Cobb in "Somewhere in Georgia").

Rice steadfastly wrote about "good news." "If anything, I give the other guy a break," he said. "That's because I've been an athlete and made mistakes, too. In a 2-0 baseball game, for instance, I tend to give the pitcher credit for pitching a good game, instead of belaboring the other team for poor hitting." But Rice was not above the prejudices of his day. Racism was still unfortunately obvious in what he wrote about Jesse Owens and other Black athletes at the 1936 Olympics. Rice was unwilling or unable to avoid the common stereotypes of his day.[5]

At his funeral, longtime friend Bruce Barton summed up Rice's philosophy:

> He was the evangelist of fun, the bringer of good news about games. He was forever seeking out young men of athletic talent, lending them a hand and building them up, and sharing them with the rest of us as our heroes. He made the playing fields respectable. Never by preaching or propaganda, but by the sheer contagion of his joy in living, he made us want to play. This was his gift to his country; few have made a greater [one].

OTHER SPORTS WRITING PIONEERS

What can we learn from the great sports writers of the past? Certainly, we all stand on the shoulders of those who went before us. Knowing some of the great writers of the past, and a few contemporary masters, will help you step up your own game.

Henry Chadwick

Sometimes a chance event changes everything, and that was true for 32-year-old Henry Chadwick, who happened upon a baseball game outside New York City. Previously he had found the sport "juvenile and uninspiring," but suddenly he became fascinated by the game's speed and ruggedness. He decided that baseball was ideally "suited to the American temperament." Chadwick's enthusiasm for baseball led to his becoming the country's first full-time sportswriter, a perch that helped him take sports journalism into a new era.[6]

On that memorable fall afternoon in 1856, Chadwick, then a New York Times reporter, was leaving a cricket match when he noticed two teams playing baseball nearby. Impressed by their skill, he found himself watching with more and more interest. Twelve years later he recalled the moment as an epiphany: "It was not long before I was struck with the idea that baseball was just the game for a national sport, and it occurred to me, on my return home, that from this our people could be lifted into a position of more devotion to physical exercise and healthful outdoor recreation.

"Americans do not care to dawdle over a sleep-inspiring game all through the heat of a June or July day," he proclaimed. "In baseball, all is lightning; every action is swift as a seabird's flight." His success with promoting baseball was aided by a growing national interest in sports. To capture the trend, the New York Clipper hired Chadwick in 1857, and by 1860 he was spreading news about baseball far beyond New York through his magazine, Beadle's Dime Base-Ball Player.

Chadwick became even more than someone who simply wrote about the game. He helped shape the rules. As a member of the rules committee of the newly formed National Association of Base Ball Players, he helped standardize many aspects of play. He preferred, for example, the "fly catch" where a fielder would catch a ball in the air over the "bound catch" where a batter was out if a fielder caught a ball on the first bounce, and his argument won the day. He helped promote the overhand pitch and established the distance between the pitcher's mound and home plate.

BASEBALL'S OLDEST FIELD GETS A NEW LOOK

One of the numbers sports fans love to think about is simply the date something happened. Nearly every fan looks back fondly at something or other that took place many years ago. No one has a more finely tuned sense of history than the committed baseball fan.

Those fans were no doubt thrilled when they learned that Major League Baseball decided to play an official game in the oldest professional field in the country, one older even than Boston's Fenway Park or Chicago's Wrigley Field. Rickwood Field in Birmingham, Alabama, which played a pivotal role in the career of Willie Mays, hosted a game between the San Francisco Giants and the St. Louis Cardinals in 2024. Some of the famous figures in baseball lore who played there include Satchel Paige, Pie Traynor and Bo Jackson. Another was Michael Jordan, who spent the 1994 season in Birmingham attempting to transition from professional basketball.

Rickwood Field opened in 1920 and has been home to several teams over the years including the Birmingham Black Barons of the Negro American League. Mays, who grew up only a short distance away, played for the Barons as a 17-year-old before reaching the big leagues. The MLB game there coincided with Juneteenth to highlight the history of the Negro leagues. "I can't believe it," Mays said. "We can't forget what got us here, and that was the Negro leagues for many of us."

In 1861 Chadwick created a way to keep track of a game's statistics. He gave each defensive player a number (i.e., 1 for the pitcher and 2 for the catcher) and assigned letters for what a batter did (K, HR and F for strikeout, home run and fly ball, respectively). This scoring system gave fans a shorthand way to keep track. If baseball was to become America's national pastime, Chadwick believed, it was necessary "to obtain an accurate estimate of a player's skill, an analysis, both of his play at bat and in the field." He created some of the other statistics at the heart of the game, including a pitcher's earned run average and a hitter's batting average.

Midy Morgan

Maria "Midy" Morgan, the first American female sports writer, was born on an Irish estate in 1828, where she grew up riding horses. She became extremely knowledgeable about animal husbandry, a skill that would serve her well in the United States, where she emigrated in 1869. That's when she arrived at the office of Horace Greeley, editor of the New York Daily Tribune. At 6 feet 2, Morgan was probably not the new female reporter Greeley expected to see. She didn't get that job, but she did get one for the New York Times covering horse races at the Saratoga Racetrack.[7]

Over the next 23 years Morgan became one of the country's experts on horse breeding and horse racing. "Few could match her," said historian Ishbel Ross. "Midy sat on fences with the experts and brought her trained eye to bear on the animals parading past. At first the breeders looked with amazement at the huge awkward girl who went about chewing straws, but after watching her work they doffed their hats to her."

During her career Morgan became one of the nation's first women journalists of any kind, covering horse racing, the stockyards and the transportation of livestock. Perpetually facing hostile men who felt threatened by her competence and knowledge, she won them over with her wit and honesty. Morgan became friends with Commodore Cornelius Vanderbilt and former presidents U.S. Grant and Chester Arthur. In 1873 the New York State Legislature invited Morgan to speak about the need for skilled agricultural workers; her answer showed her unique perspective: "Better to own stock on the boundless prairies, to own flocks and herds, than to own stocks in Wall Street," she said.

HARLEM GLOBETROTTERS COMPILE WINNING STREAK

The world's longest winning streak is on the line each time the Harlem Globetrotters take the court. By one count, the Trotters have won 16,000 games in a row (their last loss coming to the Washington Generals in 1971), but then winning games really isn't the point. Keeping fans laughing and happy is.

Two decades before the NBA would appear, a team of African American basketball players from Chicago (not New York), began touring the Midwest playing local teams in Illinois, Iowa and Wisconsin. At first, they were out to win — they would usually beat the top amateur or semipro teams around. The first group of Trotters took the name "Harlem" because they wanted their opponents to know that they were African Americans (Harlem by then had become identified with the Black community). In 1948 the Globetrotters beat what the mainstream press considered the world's best basketball team, the Minneapolis Lakers, reigning NBA champs. Not once but twice. The Globetrotters later played doubleheaders with pro teams to help the NBA draw crowds.

So, if the Globetrotters were so good, how did they become funny? Legend has it that during a game in Canada in 1939, as the Trotters were beating a local team, fans became unruly and the atmosphere grew tense. A few of the players decided to do their fancy dribbling exhibitions, dazzling the crowd and releasing some of the tension. Many of the Globetrotters' comedy routines were drawn from the minstrel tradition and baseball antics. Their first real "clown" was Goose Tatum, who joined the team in 1946.

The rise of Globetrotters hijinks came at the same time that the NBA became integrated and top Black players like Elgin Baylor, Wilt Chamberlain and Oscar Robertson became stars in the league. These days the Globetrotters play real basketball about 40 percent of the time and devote the rest of the game to their scripted routines such as pulling their pants down, pulling off intricate passing displays or having dunking contests. The fans wouldn't want it any other way.

Wendell Smith

"A baseball box score, after all, is a democratic thing," wrote Wendell Smith, the first Black sports writer to be inducted into baseball's Hall of Fame. "It doesn't say how big you are or what religion you follow. It does not know how you voted or the color of your skin. It simply states what kind of ballplayer you were on any particular day."

The ballplayer Smith was writing about on a spring day in 1947 was Jackie Robinson, baseball's first Black major leaguer. Smith wrote for the Pittsburgh Courier, the nation's largest Black newspaper, but he was also working for Branch Rickey, general manager of the Brooklyn Dodgers. Smith made $50 a week for each job, but no one seemed concerned about conflicting loyalties, especially because the Dodgers gave Smith a front row seat for what it called "the Jackie Robinson beat."

Smith also served as Robinson's companion on the road, finding places where he could stay and eat, alerting Rickey to other players in the Negro leagues who had the potential to play in the majors and handling public relations. As Robinson's press agent, Smith ghostwrote 25 columns called "Jackie Robinson Says" that ran during the 1947 season. Smith never doubted the importance of this "grand experiment." For almost a decade prior, he had led a group of Black sportswriters in a campaign to desegregate the majors.

Smith said the national pastime didn't need to see a million Black ballplayers, it just needed to see one — the right one. He convinced Rickey that a ballplayer with a "me first" attitude (Satchel Paige, for example) would hurt the effort, so he recommended that the Dodgers sign Robinson, an Army veteran with a college education. "When I said, 'Jackie Robinson,' Mr. Rickey raised his bushy eyebrows and said, 'I knew he was an All-American football player and an All-American basketball player, but I didn't know he was a baseball player.'"

"He's quite a baseball player," Smith said, in one of history's great understatements. On April 15, 1947, a crowd of 26,000 fans came to Ebbets Field to see the Dodgers open the season and to watch Robinson. In a ho-hum game, Robinson went hitless in three at bats, but he kept his cool. "If Jackie Robinson felt his nerves jumping or was even conscious that he was about to take part in a momentous baseball event, he kept his feeling remarkably well concealed," wrote Gayle Talbot of the Associated Press.

As the season progressed, Robinson's skill and Smith's diligence proved themselves. "Everywhere we went, Wendell Smith was there," said Brooklyn pitcher Don Newcombe, a former Negro leaguer who followed Robinson to the bigs in 1949. "He was instrumental in so many things that happened."

Smith continued to write commentary until his death in 1972. He was the right journalist at the right time, the optimist who could see what perhaps nobody else could: a change in American attitudes. He saw how Robinson's teammates warmed to the rookie. In his May 31 column, he interviewed Brooklyn coach Clyde Sukeforth, who said he sensed a new attitude. "The guys on the team are all for him," Sukeforth said. "Yes, sir, Mr. Jackie Robinson's going to be all right."[8]

Roone Arledge

Without Roone Arledge, there would be no "thrill of victory or agony of defeat." We have Arledge to thank for that famous catchphrase, which he invented for a groundbreaking television show called "Wide World of Sports." His creativity, technological innovation and leadership made him a major force in the development of television sports.

When Arledge was named the producer for ABC's coverage of college football in 1960, he said, "We are going to add show business to sports!" and he wasn't kidding. Arledge used cranes, blimps and helicopters to provide something new. He equipped technicians with handheld cameras for close-up shots of cheerleaders, band members and crazy spectators, and with rifle-type microphones to pick up the thud of a punt or the crunch of a hard tackle. At the time, sports television consisted of little more than a fixed camera recording events from a great distance. Arledge had something else in mind: "We set out to get the audience involved emotionally," he said. "If they didn't give a damn about the game, they might still enjoy the program."[9]

During the first half of his career, Arledge led sports programming from its small weekend window into prime time in 1970 thanks to ABC's "Monday Night Football." MNF paved the way for sports events of all kinds to move to the main stage. The year after "Monday Night Football" became a success, baseball moved one game of the World Series into the evening. Within a few years, all the World Series games were played at night as networks sought more viewers and advertising revenue.

Two of Arledge's signature touches came thanks to his college English courses: the importance of narrative and the role of the hero. The announcers at ABC Sports were taught to emphasize the storyline of whatever game they were covering and to focus on a star with a compelling personal story. The "up close and personal" biography of an athlete, which ABC's Olympic coverage developed to introduce obscure foreign athletes, became the template for personalizing stars in every sport.

Under Arledge, ABC dominated television sports for two decades. He pushed for more technical innovations: instant replays, slow motion, cameras in race cars and on skiers' helmets. ABC Sports acquired a swagger that came from Arledge's larger-than-life personality. Instead of suits, he wore safari jackets, aviator glasses and big jewelry. He also let his bright orange hair go long. "He was always seeing just beyond the horizon," news anchor Diane Sawyer said. "You always felt if you could just follow his gaze, you could stay ahead of everyone."

Claire Smith

Claire Smith, one of the first female baseball beat writers, became a fan as a third grader after watching a movie about Jackie Robinson. Her attraction to baseball sprang from its power to break down social barriers. She described Robinson and other African American players as "heroes and role models" and said, "Their story is intertwined with everyone who grew up in Black America."[10]

In 2017 Smith became the first woman and fourth African American voted into the writers' wing of the Baseball Hall of Fame. She spent 32 years in the newspaper industry before becoming an editor at ESPN in 2007. "I was from the generation of journalists where it was not acceptable to write 'I' or 'me.' You never wanted to be the story." One of Smith's admirers was Bart Giamatti, Major League Baseball commissioner, who considered her the best baseball writer in the country. Giamatti's successor, Fay Vincent, said he recommended Smith to the New York Times.

During her career in New York, it wasn't unusual for Smith to have multiple bylines in the Sunday sports section. As the national baseball writer for the Times, she became skilled at packing for long road trips with the team — often a two-week, six-city excursion. One of those trips took her to Chicago in 1984 for game one of the National League Championship Series. The visiting San Diego Padres refused to let Smith in the clubhouse after the game for interviews, citing vague "religious reasons." Coming to her aid, however, was Padres first baseman Steve Garvey, who became "a million-dollar stringer" for Smith, racing in and out of the clubhouse with quotes from his teammates. The next day the baseball commissioner made it league policy that all clubhouses would be open to credentialed writers.

A MORE MUSCULAR PROSE

Smith belonged to a generation of sports writers inspired by Ernest Hemingway. Another of those was William Bryson, who covered every World Series for the Des Moines Register beginning in 1945 and ending 40 years later with his retirement. One of his favorite moments came in 1960 when Bill Mazeroski of Pittsburgh hit a ninth-inning home run to beat the Yankees. Most of the papers in the country reported the news in the usual sober fashion, but people in Iowa got to read something different:

> The most hallowed piece of property in Pittsburgh baseball history left Forbes Field late Thursday afternoon under a dirty gray sports jacket and with a police escort. That, of course, was home plate, where Bill Mazeroski completed his electrifying home run while Umpire Bill Jackowski, broad back braced and arms spread, held off the mob long enough for Bill to make it legal.
>
> Pittsburgh's steel mills couldn't have made more noise than the crowd in this ancient park did when Mazeroski smashed Yankee Ralph Terry's second pitch of the ninth inning. By the time the ball sailed over the ivy-covered brick wall, the

rush from the stands had begun and these sudden madmen threatened to keep
Maz from touching the plate with the run that beat the lordly Yankees, 10 to 9,
for the title.[11]

The attention to physical detail — the dirty gray sports jacket, the steel mills and ivy-
covered brick walls — are all echoes of Hemingway, as is Bryson's description of the
umpire. He sounds almost like a matador, "broad back braced and arms spread," as he
holds off the crowd. Bryson's story gave a hint of an important future trend in sports
writing. He turned his attention away from the spotlight to find those fascinating side-
shows that have delighted sports fans ever since. As Bill Heinz, another of the era's
top sports writers put it, "I eventually discovered that there was a lot more dandruff
to that world than stardust," speaking of the glamorous world of professional sports.[12]

The athletes of that day were exceptionally accessible to the enterprising reporter
and often unguarded in their comments. Who could forget, for example, these memorable quotes from Yankee catcher Yogi Berra:

- "You can observe a lot just by watching."
- "It ain't over 'til it's over."
- "Half the lies they tell me aren't true."
- "If people don't want to come out to the ballpark, nobody's going to stop them."
- "Pitching always beats batting — and vice-versa."[13]

Modern Masters

An important change in the modern era is the rise of women's sports, thanks
largely to the passage of Title IX, federal legislation that guaranteed women an equal
chance to participate in varsity sports. And as women's sports have grown, so, too, has
the presence of women sports writers.

Women Enter the Locker Room

In the mid-90s there were about 10,000 sports reporters, but just 250 of those were
women. By 2005, that number had doubled, and "today female sportswriters are all
over the place," says Vince Doria, vice president and director of news at ESPN. "No
one gives it a second thought."[14]

ESPN was the first network to hire women as sports anchors and to make them part
of reporting teams for high-profile events. Doria believes that in some cases women
have an edge over men. He notes that men have been bombarded by sports clichés
from an early age and often look for the conventional angle. Women might be more
likely to offer a fresh view.

One thing that male sports writers could once offer their readers was an exclusive look at an all-male domain: the locker room. Stepping into that sacrosanct area sometimes gives a reporter the most immediate impression after a game. Here, for example, is a San Francisco player grieving after a close Super Bowl loss:

> LAS VEGAS — Christian McCaffrey barely moved as he sat in his cubicle in the visiting locker room of Allegiant Stadium. Paralyzed by the pain. His eyes widened, locked straight ahead, as his mind processed the agony. His shoulders slumped as reality wrenched his gut in real-time. Visceral enough to be visible.[15]

Until 1990 that cubicle was off-limits to female reporters, but then Lisa Olson of the Boston Herald arrived on the scene. Her story began innocently enough when she covered the New England Patriots for the first time and asked defensive back Maurice Hurst to meet her in the media room for an interview. "The player, however, insisted I come to him," wrote Olson, "saying he was icing his knee or ankle. I did, and, as we sat on the bench in front of his locker, the prank began."

Christian McCaffrey breaks free against the Kansas City Chiefs in the 2024 Super Bowl.
© UPI / Alamy

The camaraderie between players and coaches is a hallmark of college sports.
© Lincoln Journal Star.

Other players began to approach Olson, flashing themselves at her while other players egged them on. Afterward, Olson was attacked by fans of the team — trash was thrown at her during Patriots games, and one day she came home to find "Leave Boston or die," written in red spray paint on her living room walls. Things got so bad that Olson requested a transfer and took one to the farthest place from Boston — Sydney, Australia. Eventually, she settled a civil harassment suit against the Patriots, and after six years of exile returned to the United States to work for New York's Daily News.[16]

The locker room culture, however, had changed. If a male reporter is allowed access, female reporters must be given the same access. More often, reporters provide the names of players they would like to speak with, and the players report to an interview room.

SPORTS WRITING BECOMES RESPECTABLE

Gender diversity isn't the only major change to touch sports writing in the last generation or so. Thomas Boswell, Washington Post sports columnist, began his career with "little status, less respectability, and $90 a week." Back then, Boswell notes, nobody called sports writing a profession. It was just a job: "Get the facts straight. Work hard when hard work is needed. Don't blow deadlines. Nobody thought sports writing was a stepping stone toward a TV career, a six-figure talk radio gig or a big book contract. If you were in a rush, you were in the wrong racket."

Then sometime between the late-60s and the mid-70s, it all changed, thanks largely to the astronomical growth of sports on TV. The whole country watched the same games and then wanted to read and talk about them the next day. Many of the top athletes became entertainers and sports commentators. So, as Boswell continues, "We became respectable. More and more the new generation of sports writers resemble dentists or stockbrokers. They tend to have brains, ambition, organization, dedication, degrees from good colleges, straightforward writing styles, and upright private lives."[17]

Sports departments have become so respectable, in fact, that Boswell says he sometimes doesn't feel at home there anymore. It's easy to see why: "The ballpark is the place you go to play hooky," he writes. "When you get there, you scream, yell insults at millionaires, knock people aside chasing foul balls and eat nachos until your stomach is so full that you have to switch to ice cream sandwiches."

As a professional reporter, Boswell serves up journalism's daily slice of life. But he is under no illusions about the artistic grandeur of his work. Boswell promises his reader that he will never scrub the sport behind the ears or make it appear more upstanding or respectable. With the advent of internet journalism, print people have had to become dramatists, not just journalists; they must be storytellers. Now their major task is to explain what happened and why and what these athletes are really like.

McPhee and Reilly

We shouldn't leave the topic of great modern sports writers without mentioning two more, John McPhee and Rick Reilly. McPhee is widely considered one of the pioneers of creative nonfiction. Along with Tom Wolfe and Hunter Thompson, he helped kick-start the "new journalism," which revolutionized nonfiction writing.

McPhee has written on a marvelous variety of topics, including hiking, canoeing and fishing. But it was his fascination with the Princeton basketball star Bill Bradley (a future presidential candidate) that helped launch his career. One day, McPhee took Bradley over to a local high school gym to study his shot-making ability. Much to McPhee's surprise, Bradley missed shot after shot. Finally, in frustration, Bradley told McPhee that he was struggling because the rim was half an inch too low. Stunned, McPhee found a ladder and a tape measure to check Bradley's assertion. Sure enough, he was right.

McPhee's attention to detail means that sometimes the story away from the action *is* the story. Here is his description of Tiger Woods, for example, being distracted by a nearby train:

I am inside the ropes and close beside a back-nine tee, watching Tiger Woods making arcs in the air as he prepares his next shot in the U.S. Open. A couple of yards toward the back of the tee box, Woods stands motionless, feet together, his gaze leveled on the fairway, his posture as perpendicular as military attention. He steps forward and addresses the ball. About to hit he hears the long whistle of a locomotive, on a track quite nearby. Approaching a grade crossing, the train completes its trombone chords: long, long, short, long. Woods backs off, waits. Now he re-addresses the ball. But another grade crossing is close to the first one. The engineer, at his console, again depresses his mushroom plunger. Woods again backs off, idly swings his club, resumes his pre-shot routine. Now, reorganized, he is over the ball, but once again the engineer depresses the plunger. Backing off, Woods looks up at the sky.

We never find out how well Tiger hit that drive, but we do have an insight into the man's patience, deliberation and intense competitiveness.

Like George Plimpton, Rick Reilly also had his share of participatory journalism. He flew upside down in an F-14, drove a stock car, competed for a spot in the WNBA, did three innings of play-by-play for the Colorado Rockies and staggered through 108 holes of golf in a single day. What gives Reilly his enduring appeal, however, is his ability to celebrate everyday heroes. In the following story, "Worth the Wait," he uses a litany of questions to ponder why fans are so excited by the slowest runner in cross-country history:

> Why do they come? Why do they hang around to watch a guy at the back of the pack? Why do they want to see a kid finish the 3.1 miles in 51 minutes when the winner did it in 16?
>
> Why do they cry? Why do they nearly break their wrists applauding a junior who falls flat on his face almost every race? Why do they hug a teenager who could be beaten by any other kid running backward? Why?
>
> Because Ben Comen never quits.

The answer, as the reader soon discovers, is that Ben has cerebral palsy. The disease doesn't affect his mind, but it seizes his muscles and contorts his body, giving him the balance, as Reilly puts it, "of a Times Square drunk." Yet he competes, week after week. Why, Reilly asks?

"Because I feel like I've been put here to set an example," says Ben, 16. "Anybody can find something they can do — and do it well. I like to show people that you can either stop trying or you can pick yourself up and keep going. It's just more fun to keep going."

THE INTERNET CLAIMS ANOTHER VICTIM

Diehard Sports Illustrated fans were willing to set aside their weekly dose of feature stories and photos from their beloved magazine each February for one exotic anomaly — the annual swimsuit issue. Just what sport that issue was supposed to cover is hard to say, but then nothing much was covered anyway.

For decades, Sports Illustrated was a weekly must-read for sports fans. It once had over three million subscribers, and its writing, reporting and photography were considered the pinnacle of the craft. Landing on the cover, the most coveted real estate in sports journalism, was the best endorsement an athlete could receive, even well into the television and internet eras.

"I think it is one of the best magazines to ever exist, with some of the best photographers, writers and editors that have ever been in one building," said Rick Reilly, who for years wrote the magazine's popular back page. Nate Gordon, a former picture editor at SI, said, "You would get that cover and you'd be like: 'Man, that's so cool.'" Famous athletes like Muhammad Ali, Michael Jordan and Tiger Woods landed on the cover dozens of times, but making an appearance there was a mixed blessing. Some were spooked by the so-called Sports Illustrated cover jinx, which was said to inflict injuries or poor play on those who made the cover.

Isiah Wilkins of the University of Virginia, for example, was on the cover in March 2018, previewing the Final Four. Soon after, his Cavaliers became the first No. 1 seed to lose to a No. 16 seed. Carolina Panthers quarterback Cam Newton made an appearance in February 2016, just prior to the Super Bowl, a game the Panthers promptly lost. And baseball's Albert Pujols, described on a March 2012 cover as the "game's greatest slugger," did not hit a home run for the next two months.

But a combination of factors like the growth of sports cable channels doomed the magazine. The vast migration of advertising from print to online media caused a slow decline for SI, first from a weekly to a monthly, and then in 2024 it nearly abandoned a print edition altogether. Yet it is hard to overstate the power it once had.

The magazine was first published in 1954, the brainchild of Time's patriarch Henry Luce. Early critics called it "Muscle," "Jockstrap" and "Sweat

Socks," doubting that an all-sports magazine could survive. By 1965, however, the staff was providing crisp, bright images and the "illustrated" part of the title took off. The magazine also helped launch the careers of writers such as Frank Deford and Rick Reilly.[18]

UPON FURTHER REVIEW

1. One of George Plimpton's stunts was trying to catch a grape dropped from the top of a New York City skyscraper. Think of three activities you could try as a way of developing an insider, participatory story.
2. How has Title IX changed the way a sports department covers the news? Should coverage be evenly balanced between men's and women's sports?
3. Discuss five offbeat sports stories you could cover on your campus. Consider, for example, profiles of trainers, statisticians, groundskeepers, volunteer coaches or injured players.

NOTES

1. The lacrosse story appeared in the *Bark*, Larkspur, Calif.'s high school paper, on May 13, 2005.

2. Terry McDonell, "The Natural," *Sports Illustrated*, Oct. 6, 2003.

3. The Grantland Rice couplet appears in a review of *Sportswriter: The Life and Times of Grantland Rice* by Charles Fountain published in the *American Journalism Review* in April 1994.

4. Broun's description of Babe Ruth can be found in "Ruth Comes Into His Own with Two Homers," *New York World*, Oct. 12, 1923.

5. Joe Rexrode, "How He Played the Game: Assessing the Complicated Legacy of Grantland Rice," *Athletic*, June 18, 2020.

6. "Henry Chadwick, Class of 1938," National Baseball Hall of Fame website, Nov. 24, 2023.

7. "Dark Horse? The Tale of Midy Morgan," *Through the Hourglass*, March 11, 2020, https://www.throughthehourglass.com/2020/03/dark-horse-tale-of-midy-morgan.html.

8. "The Wendell Smith Papers," Baseball Hall of Fame, https://baseballhall.org/discover-more/stories/wendell-smith/373.

9. Bill Carter, "Roone Arledge, 71, a Force in TV Sports and News, Dies," *New York Times*, Dec. 6, 2002.

10. Lauren Amour, "The Pioneering Claire Smith, First Black Female Sports Reporter," Sports Illustrated, March 24, 2022, https://www.si.com/mlb/phillies/news/exclusive-interview-phila-delphia-phillies-claire-smith-first-black-female-mlb-reporter.

11. The stories appeared in the New York Times and the Des Moines Register on Oct. 14, 1960. This description is presented in Bill Bryson's book *The Life and Times of the Thunderbolt Kid* (New York: Random House, 2006).

12. Heinz is quoted in Bryson, *Life and Times of the Thunderbolt Kid.*

13. Many of the malapropisms attributed to Yogi Berra were stories originally told by Joe Garagiola, Berra's childhood friend. Many of these can be found at Wikiquote, https://en.wikiquote.org/wiki/Yogi_Berra.

14. Doria's comments and a discussion of the battle for equality can be found in Sherry Ricchiardi, "Offensive Interference," *American Journalism Review*, Dec./Jan. 2005.

15. Marcus Thompson II, "For Christian McCaffrey, This Wasn't How His 49ers Super Bowl Debut Was Supposed to Go," *New York Times*, Feb. 12, 2024.

16. Olson's saga is recounted in Ricchiardi, "Offensive Interference."

17. Boswell's description of the sports writing profession can be found in his introduction to *The Best American Sports Writing 1994* (New York: Houghton Mifflin Harcourt, 1994).

18. Nicole Kraft, "Mass Layoff Appears to Be the End of Sports Illustrated," *Forbes*, Jan. 21, 2024.

Appendix
The Society of Professional Journalists' Code of Ethics*

PREAMBLE

Members of the Society of Professional Journalists believe that public enlightenment is the forerunner of justice and the foundation of democracy. Ethical journalism strives to ensure the free exchange of information that is accurate, fair and thorough. An ethical journalist acts with integrity. The Society declares these four principles as the foundation of ethical journalism and encourages their use in its practice by all people in all media.

SEEK TRUTH AND REPORT IT

Ethical journalism should be accurate and fair. Journalists should be honest and courageous in gathering, reporting and interpreting information.

Journalists should:

- Take responsibility for the accuracy of their work. Verify information before releasing it. Use original sources whenever possible.
- Remember that neither speed nor format excuses inaccuracy.
- Provide context. Take special care not to misrepresent or oversimplify in promoting, previewing or summarizing a story.
- Gather, update and correct information throughout the life of a news story.
- Be cautious when making promises, but keep the promises they make.
- Identify sources clearly. The public is entitled to as much information as possible to judge the reliability and motivations of sources.

---

* Reprinted by permission of the Society of Professional Journalists © 2014. www.spj.org.

- Consider sources' motives before promising anonymity. Reserve anonymity for sources who may face danger, retribution or other harm, and have information that cannot be obtained elsewhere. Explain why anonymity was granted.
- Diligently seek subjects of news coverage to allow them to respond to criticism or allegations of wrongdoing.
- Avoid undercover or other surreptitious methods of gathering information unless traditional, open methods will not yield information vital to the public.
- Be vigilant and courageous about holding those with power accountable. Give voice to the voiceless.
- Support the open and civil exchange of views, even views they find repugnant.
- Recognize a special obligation to serve as watchdogs over public affairs and government. Seek to ensure that the public's business is conducted in the open, and that public records are open to all.
- Provide access to source material when it is relevant and appropriate.
- Boldly tell the story of the diversity and magnitude of the human experience. Seek sources whose voices we seldom hear.
- Avoid stereotyping. Journalists should examine the ways their values and experiences may shape their reporting.
- Label advocacy and commentary.
- Never deliberately distort facts or context, including visual information. Clearly label illustrations and re-enactments.
- Never plagiarize. Always attribute.

MINIMIZE HARM

Ethical journalism treats sources, subjects, colleagues and members of the public as human beings deserving of respect.

Journalists should:

- Balance the public's need for information against potential harm or discomfort.
- Pursuit of the news is not a license for arrogance or undue intrusiveness.
- Show compassion for those who may be affected by news coverage. Use heightened sensitivity when dealing with juveniles, victims of sex crimes, and sources or subjects who are inexperienced or unable to give consent. Consider cultural differences in approach and treatment.
- Recognize that legal access to information differs from an ethical justification to publish or broadcast.
- Realize that private people have a greater right to control information about themselves than public figures and others who seek power, influence or attention. Weigh the consequences of publishing or broadcasting personal information.
- Avoid pandering to lurid curiosity, even if others do.

- Balance a suspect's right to a fair trial with the public's right to know. Consider the implications of identifying criminal suspects before they face legal charges.
- Consider the long-term implications of the extended reach and permanence of publication. Provide updated and more complete information as appropriate.

ACT INDEPENDENTLY

The highest and primary obligation of ethical journalism is to serve the public. Journalists should:

- Avoid conflicts of interest, real or perceived. Disclose unavoidable conflicts.
- Refuse gifts, favors, fees, free travel and special treatment, and avoid political and other outside activities that may compromise integrity or impartiality, or may damage credibility.
- Be wary of sources offering information for favors or money; do not pay for access to news. Identify content provided by outside sources, whether paid or not.
- Deny favored treatment to advertisers, donors or any other special interests, and resist internal and external pressure to influence coverage.
- Distinguish news from advertising and shun hybrids that blur the lines between the two. Prominently label sponsored content.

BE ACCOUNTABLE AND TRANSPARENT

Ethical journalism means taking responsibility for one's work and explaining one's decisions to the public.

Journalists should:

- Explain ethical choices and processes to audiences. Encourage a civil dialogue with the public about journalistic practices, coverage and news content.
- Respond quickly to questions about accuracy, clarity and fairness.
- Acknowledge mistakes and correct them promptly and prominently. Explain corrections and clarifications carefully and clearly.
- Expose unethical conduct in journalism, including within their organizations.
- Abide by the same high standards they expect of others.

The SPJ Code of Ethics is a statement of abiding principles supported by additional explanations and position papers [at spj.org] that address changing journalistic practices. It is not a set of rules, rather a guide that encourages all who engage in journalism to take responsibility for the information they provide, regardless of medium. The code should be read as a whole; individual principles should not be taken out of context. It is not, nor can it be under the First Amendment, legally enforceable.

Glossary

access: The ability and permission to approach and speak with players, coaches or other members of a sports organization.

acronym: A special type of abbreviation that forms a possibly pronounceable word from the first letters of a phrase or name. BOGO, for example, for "buy one, get one [free]."

action verb: A dynamic word that expresses an activity someone can do, such as "jump," "run" or "leap."

advance: A story about an upcoming game that compares teams and players, discusses team records and gives lineups.

ageism: Discrimination based on someone's age.

AI: Artificial intelligence is the science of making machines that can think like humans.

allusion: A reference to a well-known person, place or event, often literary or historical, in relation to a current person or topic.

anecdote: A short, self-contained story that usually highlights some aspect of a person's character.

angle: The perspective or lens a writer uses to frame a story. This strategy often leads to a fresh approach; imagine, for example, what the story of the three little pigs might look like from the wolf's point of view.

anonymous sources: Unnamed sources, known only to reporters and their supervisors, who become primary sources, usually in a breaking news story.

"Associated Press Stylebook": Style guide published by the Associated Press; regarded as the standard for print and online writing.

attribution: Crediting a quotation or information to a source.

backgrounder: A story that contains information about the sport, team, coaches, events and issues that could potentially be covered in future stories.

beat reporter: A reporter who covers the same team or the same sport on a regular basis.

behind-the-scenes sources: People who provide pertinent information or ideas for stories but aren't used as primary or secondary sources.

blog: An online journal maintained by a person or entity to engage a community in conversation; often themed, blogs invite web users' participation.

blurb: A summary sentence, inserted between the headline and the text of an online news story, that gives readers concise information in a few words.

box score: A statistical tabulation of a game giving the names and positions of the players and a record of their individual performances.

branding: A digital marketing strategy in which people or businesses distribute content on social media platforms to increase their brand recognition and build connections with their target audience.

B-roll: Video or visuals without audio; generic footage of place or event used to give background visuals for a story.

byline: Name of reporter, usually at the top of a print story or beginning and end of broadcast story on location.

caption: Words describing the action and identifying the people in a photo; usually written by photographer; also called "cutline."

chronic traumatic encephalopathy (CTE): A progressive and fatal brain disease associated with multiple traumatic brain injuries, including concussions.

circular story structure: Typical of broadcast media, circular stories follow a "round" pattern where they begin and end the same way. Rather than providing a clear conclusion, the story returns to the point where it began.

cliché: Overused phrase that betrays the lack of an original thought.

clips: Examples of a reporter's work; the term evokes the images of clipping an article out of a newspaper but now includes any sort of work, print, audio or video

code of ethics: Written statement of expectations or conduct in the pursuit of a profession or within a workplace. In this book, we refer to the Society of Professional Journalists' Code of Ethics, reproduced in the appendix.

collective nouns: These are words for a single group of people or things, such as sports teams.

collectives: Booster funds that create opportunities for donor money to go back to the athletes themselves.

column: Regular opinion feature by one author.

commercial use: Use of copyrighted material in a way that will make a profit for a person or business; illegal without written permission; applies to team logos or mascots.

conflict: A news value where the opposition of people or forces results in drama.

conflict of interest: A situation where someone's personal interests could compromise their judgment—imagine a sports writer covering a game where his son is one of the players.

consent laws: These laws govern whether the media can record telephone calls—in some states, for example, a conversation may be recorded without the knowledge of both parties; in other states both parties must be aware that the conversation is being recorded.

copyright: Legal protection of the right to ownership of an original work produced in a tangible form (writing, photos, art, etc.); protects works from use by others without permission.

cutline: Traditional term for words describing the action and identifying the people in a photo; usually written by photographer; also called "caption."

data journalism: A system of reporting based on the filtering and analysis of large data sets for the purpose of creating or enhancing a story.

dateline: Appears at beginning of a story or news release; indicates where story originated; historically, dateline also includes the date the story was written.

deadline: The last time or date by which a story must be completed.

delayed lead: Story lead in which the focus is not known for several paragraphs; also called an indirect lead.

direct lead: Story lead that tells most of the 5 Ws and an H in the first one or two paragraphs.

direct quotation: An exact, word-for-word account of what a person said, enclosed in quotation marks and attributed to the source.

down style: Headline with only the first word and proper nouns capitalized; also called "sentence style."

electronic interview: Any interview conducted through electronic means, such as telephone, video teleconference or Zoom meeting.

electronic wristband: An electronic device similar to a watch or Fitbit that conveys information from one person (usually a coach) to another (usually a player).

embargo: A request by source that media not publish the story until a specified date.

esports: Video games that are played in a highly organized competitive environment.

euphemism: A word or phrase used in place of another to make the topic sound less harsh; dressing up plain language.

fair comment: Legal protection for journalists who offer opinion or commentary on the performance of anyone in the public eye.

fair use: The fair use doctrine enables reporters to briefly quote books, movies, songs and other works to report on them.

feature story: Story that focuses on people, places, issues or the human side of a story; less timely, can run anytime and be equally newsworthy.

flash interview: An unusually quick and informal interview when a reporter and athlete or coach speak just outside the locker room or off the field.

follow-up question: Question asked to clarify or expand on an original question.

gamer: Full story, usually with quotations, about a game or competition.

gender-biased language: Language that favors one gender over another; for example, avoid use of language that assumes all sports fans are 20-something males.

gender parity: This is one of the goals of Title IX legislation, namely, to use budgets, roster and other measures to achieve gender equality on the playing field.

ground rules: An informal code of conduct that helps reporters and sports personnel know how to work with each other fairly and effectively.

hard copy: Story in print or a script for news or sportscaster.

hashtags: Words or phrases preceded by the pound symbol (#), used to categorize content and make it easier to find on social media.

headline: Summarizes the story; usually written by copy editors and appears in larger type above the story it describes.

high profile: Someone who attracts lots of attention from the public or the sports world.

homer: Reporter who shows bias for the team he or she primarily covers.

hot take: A strong opinion likely written for the purpose of provoking a reaction.

human interest: One of the news values, this investigates people's problems, concerns or achievements.

hyperlink: A digital reference to data that the user can follow. For example, you could quickly move from a team's home page to a player's biography.

idiom: A term or phrase that, when taken as a whole, has a meaning you wouldn't be able to deduce from the meanings of the individual words, e.g., "out of your league" for an opponent who is too difficult.

impact: This news value analyzes which stories have the greatest consequence for readers and viewers in your area.

impromptu questions: These questions pop up without being planned or rehearsed, but they reflect the reporter's experience and judgment.

inclusive storytelling: This kind of reporting and writing gives voice and visibility to all people, especially those who have been previously missed or misrepresented.

interview: A conversation or discussion between a reporter and a source designed to bring information and views to the public.

inverted pyramid: Most common structure for news stories; information is organized in most important to least important order.

-isms: Short for words that end in -ism, such as "ageism," "racism," "sexism"; a practice likely to offend large segments of audience.

jargon: The technical terminology or characteristic idiom of a special activity or group.

lead: Beginning of a story that tells most of the 5 Ws and an H in the first one or two paragraphs.

leading question: Question that tries to lead the source to respond in a certain matter.

legwork: Routine work that usually takes the reporter out of the office and into the wide world in a search for information.

liaison: A person who facilitates a smooth working relationship between a reporter and a sports organization.

libel: A false published statement that damages a person's character and causes that person to be ridiculed or jeopardizes his or her occupational credibility.

line score: A summary of a game's events displayed in the form of a horizontal table; for example, in baseball as an inning-by-inning record of the runs scored followed by the total of each team's runs, hits and errors.

link: A connection between pages within a website and other pages or sites; a shortcut to reach supplementary material.

live tweeting: Engaging on X during a sports event by sending a series of tweets on various aspects of the event as it unfolds.

material sources: Physical items such as record books, media guides or other stories that can provide information for a reporter.

media credentials: Passes assigned to reporters or news organizations that provide access to games, news conferences, practices or other game-related activities.

media guide: A sports-related press kit, distributed and published by sports organizations before the start of a season. It features information relating to players, history, statistical records and other similar items.

message boards: A website or web page where users can post comments about an issue and reply to other users' postings. They promote online discussions.

minutiae: Precise details or small, trifling matters, depending on your point of view.

mobile journalist: Mobile journalists use portable equipment such as cameras, microphones and laptops to report on events, record interviews and produce news stories in real time. Their flexibility allows them to work remotely, covering events and stories from all corners of the world.

mug shot: Head-and-shoulders photo; close-up photo of a person's face.

mulligan: A do-over, or second chance, especially in golf when a golfer hits a tee shot he would rather forget. The term is also applied to other sports and life situations.

name, image and likeness (NIL): This term is what the NCAA uses to describe the identifiable factors that make a player unique. Thanks to several court rulings, players are now allowed to use NIL to earn money in addition to tuition and other educational benefits.

National Collegiate Athletic Association: The NCAA was founded in 1906 to provide support for college athletes. Membership now includes over 1,000 colleges and universities that represent almost a half million athletes.

natural sound: The noise and voices that provide background context for a radio broadcast.

networking: Interacting with others to exchange information and develop professional or social contacts.

new journalism: A style of news writing that uses literary techniques.

news conference: A formal interview setting designed for sources to share information simultaneously with members of the media and, usually, for the media to ask questions. Also called "press conference."

news cycle, 24/7: This term indicates that demand for digital news and information is ongoing—the audience wants a refresher virtually every minute.

news release: Publicity tool; information sent to media with the intention of attracting interest that will result in a story.

news tip: Reader tips are a key source of information for reporters. The best tips are specific and include documentation. Problems that potentially affect many people are most likely to catch the media's attention.

news values: The elements of story that journalists have used for decades to quickly assess and determine whether an idea or event is newsworthy.

nonverbal signs: Indications of what people are thinking and feeling conveyed through body language and tone of voice.

novelty: Stories that are odd, unusual or surprising represent one of the news values. An example would be a story about an athlete who is especially skilled at running backward.

nut graf: Paragraph or two that tells the reader or listener exactly what the story is about; may occur several paragraphs into the story.

off the record: One of the ground rules of an interview, this statement means that a source will continue to talk to the interviewer so long as their comments will not be recorded or repeated.

open-ended questions: Questions that ask for an opinion or interpretation from a source.

original content: Information or other material a reporter generates that is different from what any other reporter has.

paraphrase: A summary in the reporter's words of what a source said, attributed to that source; does not require quotation marks.

participatory journalism: When a reporter becomes a participant in the story he or she is covering; in another sense, this also happens when citizens contribute their own blogs, photos or videos to a mainstream journalism outlet.

perspective: A point of view a writer or reporter can offer that helps to explain complex matters.

platform: Social media platforms allow their users to generate content and engage in peer-to-peer conversations.

podcast: An audio program that combines the concepts of an iPod and broadcast.

post: To upload information or a story to a website.

postgame analysis: An attempt to break down the various successes and failures of a team during a recent game.

press box: A group of seats at an athletic event that usually provide a good view of the entire field, reserved and equipped for members of the media.

press conference: The more inclusive term "news conference" is preferred.

press pass: A privileged form of ID that allows qualified journalists special access to people, places and events.

press row: A row of seats at an athletic event that are reserved for the press, sometimes at courtside.

primary sources: Sources with information or opinions vital to a story.

private figures: In law, a person unintentionally exposed to public view who suffers mental distress as a result of the publicity.

privilege: A defense against libel; a journalist's right to report what government officials say and do in the conduct of their official duties without fear of being sued for libel.

prominence: This news value refers to well-known people, places and events, all likely to attract more readers than usual.

pronouncer: Phonetic spelling inserted in parentheses (pah-REN-tha-sees) for unfamiliar names and words in a broadcast script.

proofreading: Carefully checking a text for errors before it is printed or broadcast.

proximity: A news value that equates to "nearness." Audiences are more likely to pay attention to stories that take place in their local community.

public figure: A person who voluntarily seeks the role of prominence in society or who gains persuasive power and influence through that role or who intentionally inserts himself or herself into public controversies.

quotation: Citation and attribution of the exact words of a source.

quote sheet: A written transcript of a news conference.

radio hits: Appearances on a radio program by an ordinarily print reporter.

recap: A brief summary of the outcome of a game or competition.

redundant phrase: Using two or more words that mean the same thing. For example, "The Department of Redundancy Department."

reveal: A technique where the writer holds back a key fact until later in the story.

rule of five: A rule of thumb that suggests that the largest number of people you need to identify in a photo caption is about five.

scoop: Reporting a story before any of your competition does.

scorekeeper: Someone who keeps score during a game and is responsible for compiling the official results.

scrum: A small to medium-sized group of reporters, normally in a hallway or locker room, surrounding one source for media interviews.

secondary headline: Sentence or phrases inserted between the main headline and the story; adds information and entices reader into the story; also called subhead or deck.

secondary sources: Sources that aren't essential to the outcome of a story but add information that makes a story more complete.

sentence style: Headline with only the first word and proper nouns capitalized; also called "down style."

sexism: Discrimination based on a person's gender. Sports journalists are expected to avoid the use of "girls," for example, when referring to the members of a women's college volleyball team.

shooting percentage: A measure of a basketball player's accuracy determined by dividing the number of made shots by the number of attempts.

shoutcasting: What traditional broadcasting is called in esports.

sidebars: Short, related stories run in conjunction with a larger news story.

slander: Spoken defamation of character; libelous scripted words read during a broadcast.

social media: Forms of electronic communication (such as websites for social networking) through which users create online communities to share information, ideas and personal messages.

sound bite: Prerecorded excerpt inserted in audio or video programming.

source: People or reference material from which information is gathered for news stories.

Spanglish: A language variety that results from conversationally combining Spanish and English.

sports feature: Story that entertains more than informs, perhaps a player profile, a seasonal story about training camp or bowl selections or one on sports medicine or nutrition.

sports information director: Also known as media relations director, the person responsible for managing communications between teams and media; job includes preparing news releases, arranging news conferences and interviews, publishing a media guide and providing statistics and data to media during games.

sports media relations department: People who work in sports media relations focus on developing and maintaining relationships with media sources, such as sports news reporters, bloggers and writers.

sports record book: Similar to an almanac, this compilation of sports performances over time can be a valuable resource for writers; entries often include career leaders, longest plays and individual and team records; the book is typically updated at the end of each season.

standard readability: The average American is considered to have a readability level equivalent to a seventh or eighth grader (12 to 14 years old). This level is often used as a benchmark for written guidelines in the media.

statement questions: These interview comments aren't questions but statements that the reporter expects the subject to respond to, such as "Your team had a poor fourth quarter."

statistics: The collection, classification, analysis and interpretation of numerical facts that help sports writers analyze a game; commonly known as stats.

story pitch: A brief description, usually no longer than 500 words or two paragraphs, intended to convince an editor, agent or publisher to commission the piece.

streaming: Sending compressed audio or video in a continuous stream over the internet; programming from radio or television distributed via the internet.

subject-verb-object: The basic pattern of sentences in the English language—a subject followed by a verb followed by an object. An example would be "She spiked the ball."

Substack: An all-encompassing publication that accommodates text, video and audio. Anyone can start a Substack and publish posts directly to subscribers' inboxes—in email and in the Substack app.

sunshine laws: Regulations requiring transparency and disclosure in government or business. Sunshine laws make meetings, records, votes, deliberations and other official actions available to the public and the press.

talk-about question: Similar to the statement question, the reporter asks the subject to simply talk about a subject without the useful prompt of a question.

timeliness: One of the news values, this one prioritizes the most recent news over news that happened in the past, even a day or two ago.

Title IX: Also known as the Patsy Mink Equal Opportunity in Education Act (1972), this law essentially banned discrimination on the basis of sex; although the law itself doesn't mention sports, its passage led to the establishment of varsity athletic teams for women at the high school and collegiate levels.

toss: When an anchor or reporter turns over a portion of the show to another anchor or reporter.

trademark: Name or logo registered by a college or a business; users must have permission, and sometimes pay a fee, to reproduce a trademark in any context.

transcription: An exact written record of spoken words.

transfer portal: A process managed by the NCAA that permits student athletes to place their names in an online database declaring their desire to transfer.

trolls: Social media users who send negative tweets to garner a reaction from the original person who tweeted.

Twitter feed: Your list of updates from users you are following. It is also where your tweets appear to your followers. Note that Twitter is now called X.

Twitter followers: People who receive your tweets. You can have a private conversation with them. Note that Twitter is now called X.

update: The newest information that people connected to a central computer system can see, when the information changes regularly.

verify: Confirm or corroborate factual information reported by a media representative.

visual narrative: A visual narrative, or visual storytelling, can help make complex stories easier to understand and, as a result, deliver a more impactful message thanks to use of images such as photographs, drawings and diagrams.

weasel words: Words that are intentionally misleading or needlessly ambiguous.

wire services: Organizations that gather news from around the world and distribute it to local members; the way most local media outlets receive national and international news.

work-for-hire: Work created for an employer, such as stories a reporter writes for a newspaper or website; such work is usually the property of the employer, not the creator.

wrap: A broadcast story that begins and ends with the reporter's voice.

Index